# THE
# YORK
# BOOK
## OF
# DAYS

# ROBERT WOODHOUSE

I am indebted to my wife Sally for her research and unstinting support, and to Liz Taylorson for her administrative skills. My gratitude goes to: John Woodhouse; Bob Eastwood; John Oxley; staff at York, Northallerton and Middlesbrough libraries; York Tourist Information Centre; Katy Porter of York City Publicity Department; and Melody Wright (York Museum Service).

The Julian calendar was in use until Wednesday, 2 September 1752. The following day, the Gregorian calendar was adopted, making the date Thursday, 14 September 1752. The dates in this book before and after this shift correspond to the respective calendars.

References for extracts appear in brackets at the end of each entry.

*Robert Woodhouse, 2011*

First published 2011

The History Press
The Mill, Brimscombe Port
Stroud, Gloucestershire, GL5 2QG
www.thehistorypress.co.uk

British Library Cataloguing in Publication Data.
A catalogue record for this book is available from the British Library.

ISBN 978 0 7524 6045 1

Typesetting and origination by The History Press
Printed in India
Manufacturing managed by Jellyfish Print Solutions Ltd

# January 1st

**1881:** On this day, pedestrians were allowed to cross the newly-completed Skeldergate Bridge for the first time. This splendid Victorian structure was the third modern road-bridge to span the River Ouse in York (following the Ouse Bridge, possibly dating from the ninth century, and Lendal Bridge 1861–3). A survey by the Corporation of York during 1873 indicated that in excess of 800 people were using the Skeldergate ferry each day, and in 1875 the York (Skeldergate Bridge) Improvement Act was passed. The original architect was Thomas Page, who had also designed York's Lendal Bridge and Westminster Bridge in London, but he died during the early phase of the development and was succeeded by his son, George Page. In some respects Skeldergate is similar to Lendal Bridge. Both are built from iron and have a wealth of Gothic detail. In the case of Skeldergate, there is a parapet with ornate ironwork. (www.historyofyork.org.uk)

———◆———

**1967:** The Eastern and North Eastern regions of British Rail were amalgamated and the headquarters of the expanded Eastern region was moved from London to York. Large-scale new office blocks were built in the yard of the old station to supplement offices in the former North Eastern region headquarters and in the old station buildings. (Hoole, K., *A Regional History of the Railways of Great Britain, The North East*, Vol. 4)

# January 2nd

**1790:** *The York Herald and County Advertiser* was first published on this day. At the end of July 1833, it passed into the ownership of the Hargrove family, who remained in charge for many years. William Hargrove (1788–1862) was closely involved in the campaign to preserve York's city walls, as well as setting up the Parliament Street market and the cattle market. In 1818, he published a highly informative *History of York*. During January 1856, William Wallace Hargrove and Alfred Hargrove became partners in the business. When Alfred retired in 1873, W.W. Hargrove was left as sole proprietor. The newspaper was published in Coney Street in the former office of *The York Courant*, which had been bought by William Hargrove in 1815. *The York Herald* became a four-page penny daily on 1 January 1882, and in 1882 W.W. Hargrove founded the *Yorkshire Evening Press*, the first edition appearing on 2 October. During the centenary year of *The Herald*, the title of the daily was changed to *The Yorkshire Herald*. The daily newspaper was published for the last time on 31 December 1936, and from 2 January 1937 the weekly paper was known as *The Yorkshire Herald*. (Pocock, M., *Old Towns and Cities – York*)

# January 3rd

**1843:** George Baines, landlord of the Durham Ox in North Street, appeared in court charged with refusing to entertain and provide for William Cockerill and John Saddler, two privates in the Buckinghamshire Regiment of Foot. In his statement to the court, Baines explained that when the men had arrived he already had one soldier billeted at the inn and family members occupying other beds. His impression was that the men had been sent to him by mistake, but the court fined him the sum of £2. In May 1854 there was a similar case, when Francis Redfern of the Elephant and Castle in Skeldergate was accused of failing to provide accommodation for a recruit – only to have the case dismissed by the Lord Mayor. (*York Herald*)

———◆———

**1765:** On this day, Joseph Baker opened a new theatre with room for about 550 patrons. On 8 January, it was described in the *York Courant* as 'by far the most spacious in Great Britain, Drury Lane and Covent Garden excepted, and for Convenience and Elegance it is thought to be equal, if not superior to either of them'. The new theatre had an additional tier, and playbills state that there were now boxes at a charge of 2*s* 6*d*. Prices for other areas were 2*s* for the pit, 1*s* 6*d* for the first gallery and 1*s* for the upper gallery. ('Theatre Royal York', *York History Journal*, No. 4)

# January 4th

**1841:** A new railway station and offices was opened for the Yorkshire and North Midland Railway. It replaced a temporary terminus built outside the city walls. The architect was George Townsend Andrews (1804–55). Company meetings were held in the new offices and Robert Stephenson was present on the first occasion, 29 January, when his father, George Stephenson, who had served as an engineer, was elected a director. Access to the new station via Toft Green, Barker Lane and North Street was difficult. Most passengers and goods traffic used North Street, but this narrow thoroughfare often became badly congested and the company prepared plans for a new bridge over the Ouse at Lendal, as well as a roadway to link the station with Micklegate. York City Commissioners agreed at the meeting in November 1843 to pay £1,000 towards construction of the road link to Micklegate. The completed route was named Hudson Street, after the chairman of the railway company (George Hudson). Deliberations about a bridge at Lendal were more protracted and building work, which got underway in 1860, eventually totalled a sum of £35,000. (Benson A.R.I.B.A., G., *An Account of the County and City of York*)

# January 5th

**1990:** This day saw a record attendance for a rugby league match in York, with 4,997 spectators watching the Ryedale-York team against Halifax in a Division 2 fixture at the Huntingdon Stadium. Starting in 1868, the club had little cash and no permanent ground. Goal posts for matches were moved from pitch to pitch on a cart, until Robert Christison formed York Amateurs and secured a permanent pitch on Knavesmire, opposite the grandstand. During the 1870s results improved and in 1877, York lost to Halifax in the final of the Rugby Union Challenge Cup. But there was a major development in April 1898, when northern teams broke away from the Rugby Football Union. York's first match under Northern Union rules was a defeat (28–2) against Hull Kingston Rovers. After the First World War, they were known as The Dreadnoughts. York's best moment came in 1931, when they reached the Challenge Cup Final for the first time (where they were defeated 22–8 by Halifax). In recent years, the club moved to the Huntingdon Stadium (1989). It was known as York Wasps (1996–2002) but currently is called York City Knights. On 26 September 2010, they won the Cooperative Championship League 1 Play-Off Grand Final to gain promotion to the Championship. (Official York City Knights website)

# January 6th

**1959:** On this day, York City Council agreed to pay 600 guineas for a painting by the impressionist artist, Loiseau. The purchase of this oil on canvas, entitled *Port de Goulphar Belle Ile En Mer*, provoked heated debate. Councillor R.A. Cattle described the picture as 'like Flamborough Head on a foggy night'. He said that 600 guineas would have been far better spent on providing more light for the city during winter but, after further discussion, the council approved the recommendation of the Finance Committee to purchase the painting. Following the previous evening's meeting (5 January), the painting was already on view in the York City Art Gallery and the press report ended with the statement, 'The York Gallery is one of the foremost galleries in the country and this reputation has been obtained for little expenditure.' The painting was completed between 1897 and 1903 and is still on display in the Burton Gallery of York Art Gallery. (*York Evening Press* and material supplied by York Art Gallery)

# January 7th

**1839:** During the night of 6/7 January, a 'great gale' swept across northern areas of the British Isles, leaving widespread destruction in its wake. Between 250 and 300 people were killed in Ireland as hurricane-force winds left thousands of homes uninhabitable. In the York area, a simple stone pillar (with considerable significance) was blown down during the tumult. Sandburn Cross was given Grade II listed status on 29 January 1953. Located about 100 metres north of the Tanglewood Inn, beside the A64 at Stockton on Forest, it is set in a socketed base and stands about 1½ metres tall. It marked the boundary of Monk Ward Stray under the heading 'EBOR'. Faces of the cross bear the names of Pasture Masters and the statement, 'This Cross Repaired in the Year 1782'. Following the gale damage in 1839, the cross was replaced by the Duchess of Sutherland during the following year. In 1912, the Sandburn estate was sold at auction to Mr John Hetherton and he carried out restoration work on the cross. When he died, aged seventy-four, on 14 February 1937, his ashes were scattered around the stone base. (Benson A.R.I.B.A., G., *An Account of the County and City of York*; www.britishlistedbuildings.co.uk)

# January 8th

**1863:** The opening of Lendal Bridge provided the second of York's modern road crossings (in addition to the Ouse Bridge) and replaced a ferry service that ran from Barker Tower, on the south-west bank, to Lendal Tower. York's growing importance as a railway centre during the first half of the nineteenth century caused severe congestion for passengers making use of the ferry to travel to and from the original station in Tanner Row. Replacing Lendal ferry service with a bridge was proposed in 1838, but the Corporation of York and railway companies failed to agree on who was responsible for construction work. An Improvement Act was passed in 1860 and, with William Dredge in charge of design work, foundations were laid for the bridge later in the same year. Tragically, this structure collapsed during 1861 and five men were fatally injured. New designs were prepared by Thomas Page, who also worked on York's Skeldergate Bridge and Westminster Bridge in London. Lendal Bridge opened in 1863. Until 1894, tolls were charged at a rate of half a penny for foot passengers, a penny for animals and two pence for horse-drawn vehicles. The ferryman who had been put out of business by the bridge was granted compensation of £15 and a horse and cart. (www.historyofyork.org.uk)

# January 9th

**1959:** A serious blaze at the Railway Street premises of York Cooperative Society almost completely gutted the ballroom. Five fire appliances directed three jets of water on the upper floors of the building in an attempt to curb the spread of the flames, but it was some time before the fire was brought under control. It was the most destructive fire in York for many years and the damage was considerable, though no one was injured. On the building's lower floor, firemen struggled to protect goods from water. A Cooperative spokesman reported that the prompt efforts of the firemen had saved a large amount of stock. The ballroom was festooned with Christmas decorations at the time of the fire and, during the blaze, parts of the ceiling in the ballroom collapsed and the rostrum for bands at dances was completely destroyed. A passing taxi driver had raised the alarm after seeing 'a flash of flame' from the Cooperative Society building, 'which lit up the sky'. In the aftermath, members of staff were struggling to 'dry off' and sort out goods. The store was open to customers the next day and business was carried out as normally as possible. (*Yorkshire Evening Press*, 9 January 1959)

# January 10th

1715: John White, a printer, died in Stonegate at the age of eighty, a year after being installed as a City Chamberlain, and was buried in St Michael le Belfry Churchyard. He left his second wife, Grace, half of his business, and the other half went to Charles Bourne, a grandson from his first marriage (to Hannah Broad). Grace continued the business to her death in 1721 and gained a place in York's printing history by becoming the first woman to set up a newspaper, *The York Mercury*. The first issue arrived from her press in Coffee Yard, Stonegate on 23 February 1718, and was published in conjunction with Thomas Hammond, Quaker bookseller and publisher. (William, K. & Sessions, E.M., *Printing in York*)

---

1952: The unique headquarters of York Arts Society was opened in the newly restored Marygate Tower by the Lord Mayor Alderman J.H. Kaye. After refurbishment as a studio and library, it was the first permanent headquarters of the society in its thirty-one years' existence. History was repeating itself, as until 1644 it was used as a repository for records relating to all former religious houses north of the Trent, under the custody of the King's Council in the North. (Newspaper cuttings)

# January 11th

**1919:** Advertisements in the local newspapers make most interesting reading. In terms of cinema and theatre-going in York, there was plenty of choice between the City Picture Palace, the Theatre Royal, The Opera House and Empire, the Electric, the Picture House and Café, the Victoria Hall and the Grand Picture House. Admission prices were not always given, but in January 1919 tickets at the Empire varied from 5s in the front row of the dress circle, to 1s in the pit. Advertising columns also included a range of remedies for just about every known ailment, but prices were perhaps surprisingly high. Beecham's Pills were 'sold everywhere in boxes, labelled 1s 3d and 3s 0d ', and other well-known brands that were on offer on 11 January were Dr J. Collis Browne's Chlorodyne, Phosferine and Dinneford's Magnesia. Support for Phosferine was supplied by Pt Meise, a member of the Mediterranean Expeditionary Force (it cost 1s 3d for a small amount), while Dinnefords claimed there had been no increase in their prices of 1s and 2s 6d per bottle (but did not give a date). They also made the claim that it was 'the safest aperient for Delicate Constitutions of Ladies, Children and Infants', and then somewhat demolished this statement by adding a health warning that advised sufferers to take the potion in a 'solid' form and then watch out. (*York Herald* and *Yorkshire Evening Press*)

# January 12th

**1797:** Among over 1,000 messages of love on Valentine's cards at York's Castle Museum is one that was sent on 12 January 1797 by Catherine Mossday to a Mr Brown, who lived in Dover Place, Kent Road, London. The delicate card is pierced in the corners to produce a lace effect and is decorated with cupids, doves and flowers, which were probably hand-coloured after printing. It was published on 12 January 1797 by John Fairburn of 146 Minories, London and includes the following verse printed around the edge:

> Since on this ever happy day,
> All Nature's full of love and play
> Yet harmless still if my design
> 'Tis but to be your Valentine.

A handwritten message inside reads:

> As I have repeatedly requested you to come I think you must have some reason for not complying with my request, but as I have something particular to say to you I could wish you make it all agreeable to come on Sunday next without fail and in doing you will oblige your well wisher.
> Catherine Mossday

(www.yorkcastlemuseum.org.uk)

# January 13th

**1645:** The city council followed an order from parliament to remove and disenfranchise six aldermen, including three knights named Cowper, Belt and Jaques. This was on account of their loyalty to the King. At the same time, the city walls were ordered to be repaired. (Benson A.R.I.B.A., G., *An Account of the County and City of York*)

---

**1856:** This day was the birth of Henrietta Eliza Vaughan Stannard, daughter of Reverend H.V. Palmer, Rector of St Margaret's. In 1884 she married Arthur Stannard, a civil engineer, and pursued a career in writing. Her earliest published work, under the name 'Violet Whyte', appeared in the *Family Herald* and she followed this with a collection of regimental tales, including *Cavalry Life* in 1881 and *Bootles Baby* in 1885, which established her reputation with over two million copies sold in the first ten years. In total, she published about 100 novels and ten other books, as well as articles for *The Cornhill* and *Temple Bar*. Between 1891 and 1895, she published her own weekly magazine and wrote *Confessions of a Publisher* in 1892, which mocked patronising male publishers of the time. She was the first president of the Society of Women Journalists and became a Fellow of the Royal Society of Literature. (www.ampltd.co.uk/digital_guides)

# January 14th

**1719:** Sir John Vanbrugh, architect of Blenheim and Castle Howard, married Henrietta Maria Yarburgh of Heslington Hall at St Lawrence's Church on Lawrence Street, York. The present building dates from 1883 and is the largest parish church in the city – a reason for it often being referred to as 'the Minster without the walls'. It contains three interesting stained-glass windows and the fourteenth-century font came from the previous church on the site, which was largely destroyed during bitter fighting in the Civil War. Henrietta Maria was aged twenty-six when they married; her husband was fifty-five. In spite of the age difference, it seems to have been a happy marriage, during which they had two sons. Most of their married life was spent at Greenwich in the property on Maze Hill, which is now known as Vanbrugh Castle – a miniature Scottish Towerhouse designed by Vanbrugh in the earliest stages of his career. (*Encyclopaedia Britannica online*; *Dictionary of National Biography*)

———— • ◆ • ————

**1906:** A crowd of 10,000 gathered outside the De Grey Rooms to hear the result of the poll in the General Election. The Liberal candidate, Hamar Greenwood, gained most votes. (Peacock , A.J., *York 1900–1914*)

# January 15th

**1195:** Hugh of Lincoln visited York during his time as Bishop of Lincoln (1186–1200). Born in 1140 at Avalon Castle in Burgundy, he became a Carthusian in 1160 while visiting Grand Chartreuse. In 1175, he was invited by King Henry II to found the first English Charterhouse of the Order at Witham in Somerset (as part of the King's penance for the murder of Thomas Becket). In 1181, he was appointed sixth Bishop of Lincoln and soon afterwards began the planning and building of the choir and other eastern parts of Lincoln Cathedral. He died at Lincoln on 16 November 1200 and at the funeral his bier was carried by notable figures, including the Kings of England and Scotland. Canonised in 1220 by Pope Honorius III, he became the first Carthusian saint and his tomb became a popular pilgrim site until it was despoiled on orders from King Henry VIII in the sixteenth century. (*The Catholic Encyclopaedia*)

———◆———

**1829:** The last reference to active waits (small groups of musicians who performed in their locality, most notably at Christmas) is minuted in the city records of 15 January 1829, around six years before they were abolished by the Municipal Corporation Act of 1835. It reads '…Daniel Hardman of York, musician, appte one of the City Waits with the usual salary.' (Merryweather, J., *York Music: The Story of a City's Music from 1304–1896*)

# January 16th

**1959:** Two 'tramps' stole the show, and at the same time almost wrecked it, when the York Old Priory Choir gave a concert to raise funds for the New Earswick Operatic and Dramatic Society at the Folk Hall. Just before the interval, two 'tramps' forced their way into the hall, despite the efforts of the attendants, and demanded that they be allowed to sing. They were quickly thrown out after a short tussle. A few minutes later, however, back they came and this time they 'overpowered' the attendants. With their clothes tattered and their faces dirty, they advanced up the aisle and said they did not want to cause any trouble, but as they had brought some music they wanted to give their audience a turn, after which they would leave. After discussing the situation with the choir conductor, Mr J.L. Huntington, the 'tramps' sang the well known 'Two Beggars' and the audience, still mystified, gave them tremendous applause, demanded an encore and showered coins on to the stage. They then disappeared. It was not until the end of the show that choir members were let into the secret that the two vagrants were in fact two of their own members, Henry Rennison (tenor) and Digby Graham (bass). Later, the two 'tramps' came back on stage in normal dress to join the choir and sing solos. (*Yorkshire Evening Press*)

# January 17th

**1858:** Making the long journey by railway from Ramsgate, a sailor, William Fox, arrived in York during the evening of 17 January and made his way to an inn on King's Staith, where he met Mary Ann White. He enquired about lodgings and she invited him to her home, but before leaving they got through liberal amounts of brandy, beer, oranges and oysters. On the way back they bought meat for supper along with a quart of ale – at Fox's expense – and before going to bed in the early hours of the morning, they got through three or four half pints of gin. When her guest seemed to have fallen asleep, Mary Ann crept into his bedroom and began to search his clothing, but William Fox soon wakened, accused her of robbing him and chased her downstairs. A court case was held the next day, where Mary Ann denied the charge and claimed they were drunk together. However, she had faced similar charges before and the Lord Mayor gave both of them well-chosen words of advice before they left the Guildhall. (*Yorkshire Herald*)

# January 18th

**1777:** The press gang arrived in York on 18th January as reported in the *York Courant* (on 21st January): 'On Saturday evening a lieutenant, with several sailors in a pinnace and two yawls arriv'd in this city on the Impress Service and to beat up for volunteers. They pick'd up five hands in their passage hither. The Lord Mayor and Aldermen have backed their warrant, and last night they impressed several men.' Such an event was more common on the Thames, with the fear of being suddenly seized by licensed press gangs for the navy or by unlicensed kidnappers of labour for plantations. At this time the English fleet was manned partly by the press gang, some of whom were criminals, and partly by inducements to able-bodied seamen of bonuses ranging from 30*s* to 100*s*. Naval service offered only considerable hardship and poor reward: pay was 19*s* to 24*s* a month, and not payable until the Fleet returned to England, at which point it was liable to deductions by agents, the navy pay department or even their own officers. (*York Courant*, 21 January 1777)

# January 19th

**1778:** Pawnbrokers seem to have originated during the reign of William I, with the practice of lending money on items deposited as security. It was not only confined to the poorer members of society either. In 1338, King Edward III pawned his jewels to the Lombards in order to raise money for his wars with France. Henry V embarked on a similar exercise in 1415. On the local front, Alexander Lenox Esquire of Saint Saviourgate seems to have visited his local pawnshop only twice. On the first occasion, on 19 January 1778, he pledged his gold watch and his stone ring – each one for the curious amount of £6 2s 2d. He called the next day to redeem both items. Lenox was probably the sort of customer the pawnbroker hoped to attract because he accepted a large cash sum (promoting good interest rates), redeemed the pledge swiftly and pawned saleable items in case they remained unclaimed (keeping storage space free). (Blackhouse, A.A., *The Worm-Eaten Waistcoat*)

---

**1909:** Early in 1909, 'New Street Palace of Varieties' opened in a former chapel. On 19 January of that year, shows featured film footage of the recent earthquake at Messina and the world heavyweight title fight between Tommy Burns and Jack Johnson. (*Yorkshire Evening Press*)

# January 20th

**1927:** The siting and design features of public conveniences always seem to provoke an amount of controversy. On this day, a group of local tradesmen, led by William Dove, presented a petition against a proposed lavatory on Pavement. Mr Dove's ironmonger's shop on the corner of Pavement would overlook the planned ladies' convenience and his petition was signed by most of the adjacent Parliament Street shopkeepers. He argued that the proposed building, with measurements of 37ft length, 20ft width and 19ft to the ridge, would be a disfigurement and inconvenience to such a busy thoroughfare. The height of the building, he claimed, would totally cover shop names and fascia signs from the opposite side of the roadway, and such a building, at a location where five roads converged, would seriously endanger pedestrians by blocking lines of vision. A week later, it was decided that the petition should be ignored, but an amount of behind-the-scenes lobbying led to a rethink by the council. An alternative site in Parliament Street had to be rejected because of problems with existing sewers and it was with great relief that a site in St Sampson's Square was finalised in June 1927. (Murray, H., *Where to Go in York: The History of Public Conveniences in York*)

# January 21st

**1959:** On this day, the *York Herald* reported on the York City Baths Club annual meeting. Four members had swum for England in the last year, but members were also saying a sad farewell to their coach of thirty years. Mr A.C. 'Lonz' Webster was widely regarded as the man who had made the club great and was known among swimmers at home and abroad. He was retiring as superintendent of St George's Baths in York and ending most of his active swimming work, but was to continue as president of the club. Speeches were made highlighting Mr Webster's overwhelming enthusiasm and he was presented with a cheque for £100 by Alderman A. Franks, chairman of the City Parks and Baths Committee, which he was going to use to buy a writing bureau and studio coach. Membership of the club was down by 131 on the previous year's total of 669, but this was mainly due to the age limit on learner members because of congestion on Monday nights. The treasurer reported balances and assets of £424, with a few small losses during the year. Presentation of trophies was accompanied by the wealth of talent among junior men and, although talent among girls was apparently not so abundant, it was still good. (*York Herald*)

# January 22nd

**1909:** On this day, Mrs Edith Beatrice Bateman, wife of Dr Hinton Bateman of 48 Micklegate, won the Joicey West of Scotland Challenge Cup offered by the British Sea Angling Association (BSAA), for the heaviest catch of fish by an angler in the West of Scotland on any given day in the year. She was a recent recruit, as the previous year was only her fourth season 'with the rod at sea but during her visit to Gairloch last September she gave a fine display of her skill.' One day, fishing in a boat four miles from the coast, she had landed 89lbs of fish, consisting principally of pollock, skate and whiting. It is for this performance that Mrs Bateman was awarded the Joicey Cup. In conversation with the *Daily Mail*, Dr Bateman said the rod used by his wife weighed only 12oz. The fish were taken within six hours and during the whole time that Mrs Bateman was fishing, the weather was wet and squally. He had also won two silver medals of the BSAA for sea fishing but his wife had 'gone one better in winning the open challenge cup'. (*York Herald*)

———— ◆ ————

**1999:** A gang of gunmen stole a total of twenty paintings from the City of York Art Gallery, with an overall value of £1.7 million. These included works by Turner, Sickert and Bartolommeo, but they were recovered on 17 May 1999. Gang members were caught and convicted during the year 2000, with convictions, in some cases, of fifteen years' imprisonment. (www.news.bbc.co.uk)

# January 23rd

**1991:** Full Sutton Prison near York was ready to receive Britain's Iraqi detainees, if the need arose, during the Gulf War conflict. According to the prison governor, there was no certainty that prison accommodation would be needed for the seventy or so Iraqis who were regarded as security risks and the Home Office were not making a comment, but staff at Full Sutton had spent five days preparing facilities. Staff in the E Wing of the prison had dusted rooms, washed floors and moved furniture in readiness for the possible arrival of detainees, but so far there were no exact details on rules for such prisoners, who would be expected to have more rights than other inmates. Members of staff were intending to treat them as remand prisoners, separate from other categories of prisoners, and were adding to their knowledge of religious practices from Muslims within Full Sutton. Pentonville Prison, a Victorian building, was already holding Iraqis in a very different setting to Full Sutton, which opened in 1987. Two new wings at Full Sutton added 192 cells to the original 440, and more than 100 extra officers were being recruited. (*Yorkshire Evening Press*)

# January 24th

**1328:** Edward III married Philippa of Hainault in a ceremony held at York Minster, during a period of great pageantry and flourishing heraldic art. During his reign, Edward gained a reputation for extravagance and self-indulgence, as well as for displaying a passion for fighting. After an unsuccessful attempt to subjugate Scotland, he turned to a more profitable prey in the form of France and, in 1337, the Hundred Years War began. It was King Edward III who first gave the Dukedom of York to his favourite son, Prince Edmund of Langley (1341–1402) and it is claimed that the title was created because he had a particular liking for the city. During 1348–9, the Black Death swept through Europe from the east and England's population was reduced from about four million to little more than two. Inevitably this brought a whole series of disastrous social and economic consequences. Edward III died on 21 June 1377 at Shene Place in Surrey and was interred in Westminster Abbey. (Halliday, F.E., *A Concise History of England*)

# January 25th

**1914:** It was announced that the York School Attendance Officer, Mr William Thorpe, was to retire after thirty-three years' service. Born on 10 April 1840, he had walked 100,000 miles up and down the town to fulfil his duties as Attendance Officer and according to the press report, '...it seems a fair good amount of walking, even if you take it as extending over thirty-three years. Allowing for Sundays and holidays this works out as twelve miles per day for thirty-three years.' His service did not come under the superannuation scheme, but it was recommended that he should receive an honorarium of a year's salary. In his early working life he was apprenticed to a courier and then worked in a clothier's business for eight or nine years. After moving away from York for a short time, he returned as Attendance Officer from 1880. Eighteen months before his retirement, he was made responsible for children who were just of school age (five years). This entailed a very considerable amount of walking as families were continually moving. (*York Herald*)

———◆———

**1924:** The Lord Mayor of York (Alderman W. Dobbie) and the Sheriff of York (Councillor W.H. Shaw) were bidding farewell to William Woodhouse, the Yorkshire roller-skater, who began his long skating journey to London bearing a message from the Lord Mayor of York to the Lord Mayor of London. Mr George Bell, who recently rode his horse 'Yorkshire Boy' from York to London and back, wished Woodhouse good luck. (*York Herald*)

# January 26th

**1777:** The activities of the press gang, as reported on 18 January 1777, aroused a considerable amount of anger and hostility and on 26 January 1777, the Lord Mayor of York received a letter containing threats to burn down the Mansion House if the gang was not sent away from the city. It read:

> My Lord
> You may take this for a warning that if you do not send the press gang out of York before next Tuesday you may expect your own house set on fire and the Manchon House too. There is 273 Young Men set there hands to put the A. Bove into execution [*sic*].

Alarmed by this threat, the Corporation ordered that 'a Reward of 100 guineas be paid out of the Common Chamber… to any person or persons discovering the person who wrote the letter to the Lord Mayor, such reward to be paid on the Conviction of the offender.' Twelve men were also appointed to patrol the streets and protect the Mansion House. An account dated 14 February gives details of the cost of their watch: £8 9s 1½ *d*, including ale and rolls of bread. The press gang finally left York on 14 February, 'having picked up a great Number of Hands for His Majesty's Service'. (*York Courant*)

# January 27th

**1699:** On this day, Clifford's Tower was sold by Lady Suzanna Thompson to Richard Sowray, who had already bought the adjacent property in 1671. He now owned the mount, with ruin on the summit to provide an appropriately decorative setting for his nearby home. During the early fourteenth century, York often served as the seat of government while monarchs did battle with the Scots. Documents, packed in barrels, were transported by the wagonload from London. The keep was usually referred to in official documents as the King's Tower, but from 1596 the current name of Clifford's Tower appears. Cracks in Clifford's Tower were reported in 1358, possibly as a result of severe flooding in 1315–16, and although expensive repairs were carried out, it was still in a dangerous state in 1377. Gold and silver coins were minted in the castle between 1353 and 1546, but it remained in a state of disrepair. In 1614 it was sold and, after being garrisoned during and after the Civil War, Clifford's Tower was burnt out during 1684, in what was probably an arson attack. At this point, its only use was as a garden feature, until it was incorporated into prison extensions during 1825. (Knight, C.B., *A History of the City of York*; Clifford's Tower HMSO Publication)

# January 28th

**1869:** John Wood, a former serving soldier with limited mobility, had resorted to begging on the streets of York, but between 9 p.m. and 10 p.m. on Thursday 28 January he made his way into the Old Turk's Head at the top of the Shambles and requested a penny or two from the landlord, Robert Dutton. When the landlord refused his request, Wood smashed two squares of glass in the window. He appeared in court the next day and in spite of his infirmity he was detained for fourteen days in the House of Correction. (*York Herald*)

———◆———

**2010:** The Yorkshire Air Museum was voted Top Attraction 2010/11 by the national attraction and tourism publication *Going Places*. It is the largest independent air museum in Britain and also the location for the Allied Air Forces Memorial. Set in 20 acres of parkland, on the former Second World War Bomber Command Station at Elvington, it represents the largest and most original Second World War station open to the public. Attractions include many different types of military vehicles and fifty historic aircraft. (www.yorkshireairmuseum.org)

# January 29th

**2011:** One of the leading figures in contemporary stained-glass design, Harry Harvey, died aged eighty-eight. Born on 22 November 1922 in Birmingham, he served as a signalman with the Royal Navy during the Second World War, before moving to York in 1947 as assistant to Harry Stammers at the York School of Glass Painting. During 1956, Harvey opened his own studio in York and continued to work in the area until his retirement in 1987. In total he completed more than 220 windows. Probably his best-known composition is the large and colourful window in York's restored Guildhall. Reopened in 1960, this fine building is an ideal setting for the window, which depicts some of the city's best-known buildings and most memorable events. Harvey's work is represented in over seventy churches in Yorkshire and he also decorated the Astronomical Clock in York Minster. Further afield, his skills are displayed in churches from Carlisle Cathedral to Shooters Hill in London, and from Builth Wells in Brecon to Great Thurlow Parish Church in Suffolk. Elected a Fellow of the British Society of Master Glass Painters in 1962, Harry Harvey also had a great fondness for cricket. He played club cricket and coached in the York area for many years. (*Yorkshire Post*; *Daily Telegraph* obituaries)

# January 30th

**2011:** On this day, one of the most successful of all film composers, John Barry, died aged seventy-seven. With a classical pianist mother and a father who owned a chain of cinemas across the north of England, the young John Barry Prendergast closely observed films and helped to run the films from the projection box. He began to study the piano at the age of nine and the trumpet at sixteen, as well as taking lessons in composition from Francis Jackson, organist of York Minster. After spending his schooldays at the Bar Convent, St Olave's and St Peter's, John Barry completed his National Service before starting a rock 'n' roll band, the 'John Barry Seven', in London during 1958. After orchestrating the theme for the Bond movie *Dr No*, Barry completed more than ninety films plus work for television over a fifty-year period. In addition to Bond themes, he wrote scores for films including *The Ipcress File*, *Zulu* and *Midnight Cowboy*. Awards included five Oscars, an OBE and a BAFTA fellowship in 2005. Although he lived in Oyster Bay, New York for many years, his close friend, Don Black, recalled, 'There was no trace of America about him – he brought York to New York.' (Press cuttings including *Daily Telegraph* and *Yorkshire Post*)

# January 31st

**1887:** York City Council agreed to celebrate the jubilee of Queen Victoria's reign by adopting the Public Libraries Act. It appointed a sub-committee to confer with committees of the York Institute and the Fine Art Institution, in order to determine whether one of these buildings could be made available as a public library. Costings were made, but the proposal met opposition from within the council chamber and elsewhere. A poll was held on 2 September 1887 to determine the views of York citizens. The result was that 2,832 voted against and 2,015 voted for the scheme, so the library proposals were dropped. A third poll of citizens was held in October 1891, and by this time the York Institute and Fine Art Institution building had been acquired. Frequent discussions meant the public were much better informed and a majority of 2,961 voted in favour of a library. (Knight, C.B., *History of the City of York*)

**1953:** The last train to take the York to Pickering line ran on the night of a savage storm that resulted in widespread flooding along England's eastern coastline. In spite of atrocious weather, many people braved the conditions on this day to pay their last respects. (Hoole, K., *A Regional History of the Railways of Great Britain, The North East*, Vol. 4)

# February 1st

**1945:** On this day, airman J.E. McDonald engraved his name on a mirror in Betty's Tearooms in York, along with hundreds of other names of young airmen fighting in the Second World War. Betty's Tearooms are renowned far and wide for fine food and drink in a luxurious setting. The first tearoom was opened on Cambridge Crescent in Harrogate by Frederick Belmont, in July 1919, and others followed in Ilkley, Northallerton and York. During the Second World War, Betty's Bar, or 'The Dive' as it was affectionately known, became a popular meeting place for hundreds of airmen who were based in the Vale of York. From 1943, many of the regular customers were Canadians who made up Number 6 Bomber Group, based around York, and this splendid wood-panelled downstairs space also became known as 'The Briefing Room'. Airmen claimed that they could discover all they needed to know about their next mission over a drink. Pride of place in 'The Dive' belongs to a huge picture mirror on which are engraved the names of some 600 young airmen – many of whom died on operational missions. One engraving reads 'J.E. McDonald 1-2-45'. Jim Rogers, who borrowed a barmaid's diamond ring to add his name to the mirror, revisited the place in 2007 during an emotional return to Linton-on-Ouse. (Wild, J., *Hearts, Tarts and Rascals*; www.bettys.co.uk)

# February 2nd

**1829:** There was calamity on this day at the Cathedral and Metropolitical Church of St Peter in York, or York Minster as it is better known. This is the largest Gothic cathedral in Europe north of the Alps, and its history has been far from uneventful. After service on 1 February 1829, Jonathan Martin hid in the Minster until the doors were locked and then crept into the bell tower. Cutting rope attached to the prayer bell, he fashioned it into a rope ladder before heading down the nave and on into the choir area, where he placed prayer and hymn books in two separate piles and then set them on fire. Before leaving he took a Bible, 'on the Lord's orders', and then made his escape along the nave and into the transept, where he climbed through a small window next to the Five Sisters. During the early hours of 2 February, flames were seen and noises heard from the Minster, but nothing was reported to the authorities. At about 7 a.m., a young boy slipped on ice and looked skywards to see smoke billowing from one of the towers. As Minster staff and passers-by salvaged items, the Minster engine and York City appliance tackled the fire and they were soon joined by a dozen more fire engines. Despite their efforts, the organ was destroyed and the full length of the 130ft-long choir roof collapsed. (Naismith, J.S., *Tales from the Scaffold*)

# February 3rd

**1910:** The extent of skating fever in York during the Edwardian period is illustrated by the fact that Miss Edith Rawdon, daughter of Canon Rawdon of Stockton on Forest, dressed her four bridesmaids in 'skating costume' on this day for her wedding. The York Roller Skating Rink Co. opened the city's first rink on the Sycamore estate in July 1909 and this was followed by another, which was initially housed within a large tent behind Fishergate School. Measuring 180ft by 90ft, it was opened in May 1910 by Mrs Preston of Middlethorpe Manor. Midsummer saw work underway on a third venue – the City Roller Skating Palace – located on land between the glassworks and Blue Bridge Lane. The skating area covered 25,000sq.ft and, with a projected opening date in mid-October, the prospectus for the new rink said that skating, 'has taken a keen and firm hold on the public fancy… and is a favourite form of recreation with all classes… and has become delicious… by reason of the use of ball-bearing skates on maple floors.' A hockey club was established, speed competitions held and 'historical pageants' staged as the skating craze took hold. (*Yorkshire Evening Press*)

# February 4th

**211:** On this day, Emperor Septimus Severus died in York after a reign covering eighteen years (with the last three years spent in the northern city). It is said that his reforms altered the character of Roman government by creating a larger and more expensive army and increasing the power of lawyers in administration. His success at imposing order through force of arms and force of law throughout the Roman Empire did not transfer to family matters, and in an attempt to moderate the behaviour of squabbling sons he moved his family to Britain in AD 208. Caracalla was involved in directing the army's campaigns while Geta held civilian authority. Tribes in Scotland were attacked but never totally subdued, so Hadrian's Wall was strengthened and Septimus Severus left his mark on his homeland city of Leptis Magna (now in Libya) by adding significant buildings. The Septizodium in Rome dates from his reign. Septimus Severus became known as the 'African Emperor' and his death in York was marked by a huge ceremony which culminated in his body being carried through the city before being burned on a funeral pyre. Eighteen hundred years later, a month-long series of events, including a Roman-based fashion exhibition and film and theatre productions, marked the anniversary of his death in York. (Meckler, M.L., *Roman Emperors*; www. information-britain.co.uk)

# February 5th

**1733:** On this day it was agreed that a sign for the Star Inn would be erected. This establishment on Stonegate is probably the city's best-known hostelry and this is largely due to the sign that stretches across the roadway. The inn itself is set within its own courtyard and behind a house on Stonegate, with its entrance down a side passage. It now has a Grade II listing and was known to be an inn during the English Civil War period (1642–51), when the cellar, which is believed to date from the tenth century, was used as an operating theatre for injured soldiers. A yard adjacent to the inn had a well, which at one time was the only source of pure water in the area. In 1792, the Star Inn was again put up for sale and because it was attached to another property, a fee of 25s had to be paid annually. Several ghosts are said to haunt the inn and these include two cats that have been 'bricked up' in a pillar between the door and bar. Their presence is said to account for strange noises and the odd behaviour of dogs. Ghostly screams of pain have apparently been heard from injured soldiers treated here in the Civil War. (www.york-united-kingdom.co.uk; *The history of the Olde Star Inn*)

# February 6th

**2011:** Officers, staff and 750 cadets aged thirteen to twenty paraded from Clifford's Tower through the streets of York to take part in a service at the Minster, to mark the 70th anniversary of the formation of the Air Training Corps (ATC) on 5 February 1941. It was the biggest procession of cadets to have been staged in the area, with squadrons drawn from towns such as Scarborough, Stockton-on-Tees, Darlington and Knaresborough, as well as York. They comprised the Central and East Yorkshire Wing and lined up in three formations, with each one led by an air cadet band. The salute was taken at the Mansion House by Lord Crathorne, Lord Lieutenant of North Yorkshire, and the Lord Mayor of York, Councillor Susan Galloway. The Air Defence Cadet Corps (ADCC) was set up in 1938 to train young men in various aviation skills. On 5 February 1941, the government established a new organisation – the Air Training Corps – with King George VI as Commodore-in-Chief. He issued a Royal Warrant setting out aims of the Corps. The motto 'Venture Adventure' was adopted by the ATC and incorporated into their badge. Women were admitted to ATC from the 1980s and it is made up of six wings nationally, with an ATC squadron in most large UK towns. (www.yorkpress.co.uk; http://en.wikipedia.org/wiki/Air_training_corps)

# February 7th

**1328:** On this day, King Edward III held parliament in York following his marriage to Philippa of Hainault at York Minster on 24 January 1328. During this early period of his reign (following his coronation on 1 February 1327), Edward and his queen were frequently in York and from 1328–37, parliament met seven times in the city. During 1328, when the Dowager Queen Isabella and Earl Mortimer were governing on behalf of the underage Edward III, letters patent were issued by parliament at York, setting out an agreement for peace with the Scots. On 17 March, negotiations ended and a formal treaty was signed in the King's Chamber of the Abbey of Holyrood, Edinburgh. (www.englishmonarchs.co.uk)

———— ◆ ————

**1987:** Margaret Thatcher, the Prime Minister, placed in position the 12,000th overhead line mast at York station, to mark the start of railway electrification in the York area. The first mast was erected at Peterborough on 7 February 1985. (Appleby, K., *Britain's Rail Super Centres: York*)

# February 8th

**1836:** An Act of Parliament ended a number of aspects of civic life, including musicians who were responsible to their mayors for civic entertainment and ceremony – the City Waits. An entry from the council minutes from 8 February 1836 gives details of their demise:

> The number of City Waits was formerly five, but is now reduced to two, the vacancies occasioned by death not having been supplied. Mr Christopher Brown and Mr Daniel Hardman are the survivors. Their salaries are £4 per annum each, with Livery Coats and Hats found once in six years, the expense whereof has averaged £1 1s od per annum each.
>
> Your committee are of the opinion that the waits and the Tipstaves may be dispensed with, and they recommend those offices to be abolished.

(Merryweather, J., *York Music*)

———— •✦• ————

**2011:** Work begun on the £2 million revamp of York's Barbican Centre, with a scheduled re-opening in May – six years after it closed its doors. Redevelopment of the 5½ acre site will enable as many as 250 events, including the Festival of Remembrance and city carol concerts, to be staged each year. (*Yorkshire Post*)

# February 9th

1904: The Labour Representation Committee, forerunner of the Labour Party, was established during 1903 and on 9 February 1904, local press outlets reported the setting up of the first ward association (Micklegate) in York. Unemployment was still a major problem in the city and early Labour leaders such as George Harold Stuart, adopted as York's first parliamentary Labour candidate in November 1903, emphasised this aspect in their campaigns. (*Yorkshire Evening Press*)

———◆———

2011: Rare textiles and embroidery dating back to the fifteenth century were saved from decay by staff at York Minster. An embroidery, 'The Virgin and Child', which dates from the period 1490–1520, was bought by York Minster in 1955 and is one of a number of pieces that have undergone careful restoration. A routine inspection of the Cathedral's textile store uncovered mould, which could have seriously damaged the historic artefacts. The piece depicts the Virgin Mary as Queen of Heaven, surrounded by female saints including Mary Magdalene. The specialist work to restore affected pieces was carried out by Clare Cumming, the vestment keeper, under the supervision of Caroline Rendell, textile conservator. (www.yorkpress.co.uk/news)

# February 10th

**1934:** On this day York's rugby team enjoyed a record attendance to a cup match. Following the establishment of the Rugby Football League in 1901, the Lancashire and Yorkshire leagues combined in 1902/03 to form a second division, and York was one of the new teams to join this lower tier. After the First World War, they became known as The Dreadnoughts and the inter-war years brought an amount of success. In 1931, they reached the Challenge Cup Final for the first time, but lost 22–8 to Halifax. On 10 February 1934, York's record attendance was set, when 14,689 spectators watched a Challenge Cup match against Swindon, which ended scoreless. At the end of the same season, York beat Hull Kingston Rovers 10–4 in the Yorkshire Cup Final. (www.yorkcityknights.co.uk)

———— ◆ ————

**2011:** The Roman Catholic Bishop of Middlesbrough, Terence Patrick Drainey, laid and blessed the foundation stone at the site of Our Lady Queen of Martyrs Primary School in York. Construction work had been due to start in December last year, but bad weather delayed the project, which is to replace Our Lady's in Acomb and English Martyrs in Hamilton Drive. The buildings will accommodate 420 primary school children and fifty-two nursery children, and some fixtures from the existing schools will be incorporated into the new building. (*Yorkshire Post*)

# February 11th

2011: Details were released about the recent York Residents' Festival (held from 29 to 31 January) when nearly 30,000 visits were made to venues around the city. The annual festival began in 1996 and is organised by Visit York, the city's official tourism organisation, as a way of showing gratitude to local residents for the welcome they offer to 7 million annual visitors. As well as offering free admission to well-known locations such as York Minster, Barley Hall, York Castle Museum and the National Railway Museum, the festival saw local churches staging exhibitions and guided tours. These included the Unitarian Chapel in St Saviourgate, which hosted a display about the life and work of Elizabeth Gaskell, the famous Victorian novelist. New additions to the 2011 festival included Penn House, Castle Howard, York's Roman Fortress tour and behind the scenes tours of York Minster. Among the most popular destinations were Castle Howard, with 1,750 visitors, and York Minster, which hosted 4,236 visitors for a range of activities including trips up the tower and bookmaking workshops. The total number of visitors for this year's festival represented a 48 per cent increase compared with numbers for 2010 and Visit York's chief executive, Gillian Cruddas, commented 'We were delighted with the turnout this year.' (*Yorkshire Post*; www.visityork.org)

# February 12th

**1687:** The shock of an earthquake was felt in the Feasegate area of York with an even more serious tremor at Gate Fulford, where a noise in the ground sounded like cannonfire. There was also alarm among people living at Naburn. (Hargrove, W., *History and Description of the Ancient City of York*)

———◆———

**1877:** Fire swept through the interior of the Church of St Oswald, Fulford, causing damage worth £4,000 according, to the estimation. However, the tower remained intact and the clock was undamaged. Repairs soon got underway and the Archbishop of York preached the inaugural sermon on 28 February 1878, when it reopened with a number of improvements and enlargements. (Knight C.B., *History of York*)

———◆———

**2011:** An 'Art in Yorkshire' programme was launched on 12 February with the unveiling of David Hockney's largest work to date, 'Bigger Trees Near Warter'. This massive work of art is made up of fifty smaller canvasses portraying an East Yorkshire landscape and was painted 'en plein air' (in the open air) – a method used by French impressionists and their followers. 'Bigger Trees Near Warter' was first exhibited at the Royal Academy in 2007, and was presented to the Tate Gallery by David Hockney. It is at the centre of a year-long celebration of visual arts in nineteen galleries throughout Yorkshire. (*Yorkshire Post*; *Northern Echo*)

# February 13th

**1992:** On this day police were hunting a masked gunman who robbed a York petrol station earlier in the day. Investigating officers were linking the 5 a.m. raid at London Bridge service station in Tadcaster Road, Dringhouses with a later car fire at Hob Moor. A video recording of the incident at the twenty-four-hour garage showed a man holding what appeared to be a handgun, demanding cash from a terrified cashier through the security window. The sales assistant, a man in his fifties, was seen to hand a small amount of cash to the robber, whose face was partly covered by a red and white patterned scarf. The robber left the scene in a dark car and, minutes later, a red Vauxhall Nova, stolen earlier that day in Bishophill, was found ablaze about a mile away. This latest incident was the second robbery at the garage in less than two years (following a raid on 30 March 1990, when two men on a motorcycle used a sawn-off shot gun to force a female cashier to hand over money) and it was the latest in a series of raids in the York area. (*Yorkshire Evening Press*)

# February 14th

**1777:** The press gang finally departed from York on 14 February, to the great relief of the local population. Rumour-mongers and impersonators had added to bad feeling and distress in recent times. One local resident, Thomas Waite, accused other citizens of '…raising a very scandalous report of me, by asserting that I have given information against several people, and my neighbours in particular, to the lieutenant of the press gang.' Other wrongdoers exploited the press gang's presence in York for their own financial gain:

> Last week a pretended press gang seized several men at Tadcaster and extorted money from them to set them at liberty; they even went so far as to take some men out of their beds. The press gang here being informed of this, a party of them set out to visit their officious brethren there; but the pretenders sheer'd off before their arrival.

(*York Courant*)

———◆———

**2011:** A railway sign displaying the famous 'Platform 9¾' was placed outside York Minster to mark the start of the National Railway Museum's 'Wizard Week'. The platform features in J.K. Rowling's *Harry Potter* books as the boarding point for student wizards heading for Hogwarts Castle, and the road-train transported members of the public to the museum for the nine-day Harry Potter celebrations. (*Yorkshire Post*)

# *February 15th*

**1216:** On this day, King John made one of many visits to York and on this occasion, he fined the city £1,000 for alleged sympathy with rebel forces. (After signing the Magna Carta at Runnymede in June 1215, John campaigned throughout the country, causing destruction that has been compared with William I's punitive activities.) During March 1216, John returned to the south of England and northern rebel barons, led by De Ros, Percy and Bruce, recaptured York and held it against the King. King John's first visit to York had been in March 1200, and during the early part of 1201 he and his twelve-year-old bride had journeyed as far north as Carlisle. On their return southwards they called at York. Further visits by John followed in 1204 and in each of the four following years. He called twice in 1210 and again in June 1212 and 1214. (Knight, C.B., *A History of the City of York*)

———— • ◆ • ————

**1907:** A letter appeared in *The Yorkshire Evening Press* under the heading 'Object lesson for York', at a time when the vexed question of the city's tramways was under consideration. The writer drew attention to losses being made by a similar system in Halifax, but a take-over of the scheme by York Council went ahead. (*Yorkshire Evening Press*)

# February 16th

**1922:** Faith Brook was born on this day in York, into a family of actors who soon moved to Hollywood, where she spent her childhood. At the age of eighteen, she returned to England and, after studying at RADA, completed a season at the Old Vic. Her first credited film appearance was *The Jungle Book* in 1942 and her career has included around thirty-five films, forty-six plays and six television series, as well as numerous television appearances. In recent years she has appeared on stage in *The Colour of Poppies* and, in 2008, *Uncle Vanya*. (www.filmreference.com)

---

**2011:** The death of York City's all-time record goal scorer, Norman Wilkinson, was reported on this day. He had lived until the age seventy-nine. He scored 143 goals in 401 league and cup appearances during a twelve-year career at Bootham Crescent (May 1954 to May 1966). Born in Alnwick, he played for Hull City before signing for York City. He was the youngest member of the team at York and they reached the FA Cup semi-final (after he had scored twice in the fifth round victory over Tottenham Hotspur). By profession he was a cobbler. Norman Wilkinson took great pride in wearing well cared for, decent boots. (*Yorkshire Post*)

# February 17th

**1891:** On this day, Rowntree & Co. opened a private freight siding with three trains running daily. It remained until 1971. (Edgington, J. & Gilks J.S., *Trains from York*)

───◆───

**1908:** During 1906, the Liberal government passed the Education (Provision of Meals) Act. Accordingly, in February 1908 the Education Committee began providing 'Meals for Necessitous Children', consisting of soup and bread worth 1½d. In one week, the *Yorkshire Evening Press,* dated 17 February 1908, reported that 2,912 meals were given to 753 children. Funding came from the equivalent of a half penny rate, and the same newspaper reported, 'Nearly one thousand children are being fed every week day in York by the school committees and voluntary helpers… It is a staggering total, for behind these figures lies concealed a vast amount of poverty and misery.' (*Yorkshire Evening Press*)

───◆───

**2011:** It was reported that York Museum Trust withdrew its plan to bring a giant observation wheel back to York, in the face of conservation concerns over bats. Ecologists indicated that further investigation was needed to establish the level of bat activity around the proposed site in the city's Museum Gardens. The scheme aroused widespread opposition from English Heritage, and the Dean of York, Keith Jones, expressed severe concerns that the wheel would ruin views across to York Minster. (*Yorkshire Post*)

# February 18th

**1510:** A York printer was working on the first York edition of the *Directorium Sacerdotum* (a guide for priests), which was nicknamed the *Pica* (Latin for magpie), as the text, like a magpie, was black and white. Each one of the 234 pages took at least a full day to arrange by hand. After checking the letters were composited into text on a metre-long 'galley', they were arranged in a 'forme', which held enough words to print four pages. At this point it was tightly bound into a square to hold the letters in place. Copies were collected from the printer in a loose form and each individual parish was responsible for binding their own copy. Most books would have been in simple form with a vellum or paper cover. The *Pica*, which was assembled by Robert Avissede, a priest at St Gregory's Church near Micklegate, served as an ecclesiastical calendar by providing dates of saints' days and feasts. Only two known copies exist – one in Sidney Sussex College, Cambridge and the other in York Minster Library. (www.yorkpress.co.uk)

# February 19th

**1846:** On this day, George Shaftoe died at the age of thirty-three and was buried in the small graveyard of St George's, where the notorious highwayman Dick Turpin was buried in 1739 after his execution. The Shaftoe family has lived in the York area for more than three centuries and the earliest mention of an ancestor appears in 1381, when Robert de Shafton was living in the parish of St Mary Bishophill Senior. Early members of the family were arrow makers and others seem to have been walkers (or fullers) of woollen cloth. By 1650, pipes were being manufactured in York and Hull, and as the price of tobacco came down, pipe makers made larger bowls. During 1678, Richard Shafton was established in the centre of the city and during the early eighteenth century, the type of pipes and their quality improved. Pipe making continued in the Shaftoe family and George, who was born on 7 April 1812 to parents George and Hannah, was eight when his father died. He worked for his mother in the pipe-making business until 1840, when she handed over the business to him, but he died in his early thirties. (Shafto, R., *Shaftoes of York*)

# February 20th

**1859:** At shortly after 1 a.m. on this day, the landlord of a beer house was confronted by police. During the mid-nineteenth century, beer houses gained a notorious reputation and the premises in Black Horse Passage, leading to Wesley Place, was no exception. The landlord in the 1850s had regular brushes with the law. On this occasion, Sergeant Ingram hammered on the door. Landlord David Dixon refused three times to allow his house to be searched, but magistrates stated that it was already proven that it was a base for thieves and prostitutes and Dixon was fined 5s. Six weeks later, Sergeant George Sykes managed to force an entry into the beer house, where he found fifteen men of bad character drinking ale. Reports of criminal behaviour continued into 1860, when a Mrs Coulson reported that her husband had been robbed of banknotes and £3 10s in gold while drinking there on 17 December. (*York Herald*)

———◆———

**1931:** The printing company Sellingtons (York) Ltd was formed on this day by Percy McDermid; Edwin J. McDermid of London; William Temple, licensee of the Golden Lion Hotel in St Sampson's Square; and William Wright, bookbinder of 137 Haxby Road, York. But within three months the three York-based partners had left the business. The company continued doing business but changed hands several times in the next few years. (Sessions, W. & M., *Printing in York*)

# February 21st

**1907:** Wystan Hugh Auden was born in York. After graduating from Oxford University in 1928, he visited Germany before returning to England to become a teacher. Auden's first volume of verse, *Poems*, was published in 1930 and this was followed, in 1932, by *The Orators*. A year later *The Dance of Death*, a satire on decadence, was published. During 1935 he married Erika Mann, daughter of the German novelist Thomas Mann. Two years later, political sympathies drew him to Spain to closely observe the Civil War. At this time he received the King's Poetry Medal, and following visits to China and the United States, Auden emmigrated to America in 1939. During 1946, he took American citizenship and held teaching posts at several American colleges and universities. He was awarded the Pulitzer Prize for the poetical work *The Age of Anxiety* (1947) and worked with Kallman on the libretto for Stravinsky's opera *The Rake's Progress* (1951). Between 1956 and 1961, he was professor of poetry at Oxford University, but following a period of ill health he died at a property he owned in Austria on 29 September 1973. (www.bbc.co.uk/history/historic_figures; Hartley, M., & Ingilby, J., *Yorkshire Portraits*)

# February 22nd

1807: John Carr died on this day. His career in architectural design work had spanned more than sixty years, having got hundreds of commissions covering locations in Scotland and Oporto in Portugal. Born at Horbury near Wakefield on 15 May 1723, he was educated at Wakefield Grammar School and then worked with his father, Robert, a quarry owner and building surveyor, until his father's death in 1760. During 1746, John Carr married Sarah Hinchcliffe and by 1750, he had worked on alterations at Askham Hall and built Kirby Hall, Ouseburn. His design for a grandstand on York's Knavesmire brought him more recognition, and when he designed Harewood House for Edwin Lascelles in 1759, his fame was sealed. A whole series of projects followed: Lytham Hall near Preston; Abbot Hall near Kendal; Heath Hall, Wakefield: and in 1762, the high point of his Palladian style, Constable Burton Hall near Leyburn. As principal surveyor to bridges of the North Riding during the 1770s, he built the beautiful Greta Bridge near Barnard Castle, and in 1778 Carr began work on the Crescent at Buxton for the Duke of Devonshire. With a house and office in Skeldergate at York, John Carr was twice Lord Mayor of the city and a Justice of the Peace for the West Riding. In 1791, he rebuilt the church at Horbury at his own expense. He died at Askham Richard near York. (www.countrylife.co.uk)

# *February 23rd*

**1719:** York's first newspaper was published by Grace White, who had inherited her husband's printing house in Coffee Yard, off Stonegate. By 1724, the business had passed into the ownership of Thomas Gent. His first issue for the week 16 to 23 November in that year appeared under the new title, *The Original York Journal or Weekly Courant*. Some four years later, he renamed it *The Original Mercury, York Journal or Weekly Courant*. It appeared in print until at least 1739. Thomas Gent moved his press to Petergate in 1742, but since 1725 there had been serious competition from *The York Courant*, which had been printed by John White from a press near St Helen's Church. In 1734, the business was sold, first to John Gilfillan and then to Alexander Staples, who relocated the press in premises on Coney Street, almost opposite St Martin's Church. During Ann Ward's ownership in the late eighteenth century, the *Courant* had links with some of London's coffee houses. Business was arranged with places such as St Paul's Coffee House, Chapter Coffee House in Paternoster Row and the Edinburgh Coffee House at the Royal Exchange. In January 1820, the new owner, Henry Cobb, renamed the paper *The York Courant and Original Advertiser* and it continued under that title until 27 April 1848. (York A.D. 7–1971, *Yorkshire Evening Press* supplement)

# February 24th

**2011:** Candlelit tours of Fairfax House in Castlegate offered a rare insight into life at an eighteenth-century household after nightfall. The York Civic Trust restored the building to its former glory in the early 1980s and it was reopened to the public in October 1984. The tours first started during the 'Illuminating York Festival' of 2010 and included the library with a stucco ceiling that celebrates the work of Milton, Locke, Addison and Pope, and items of furniture collected by Noel Terry between 1925–79. There are more items from Noel Terry's collection in the form of barometers along walls of the hallway (with the earliest example being a freestanding ivory stick barometer of 1695), while the dining room has elegant cabinets on either side of the fireplace, housing a collection of mid-eighteenth century blue and white 'Nankin' porcelain, rescued from the wreck of the *Geldermalsen* in 1985. The Lower Staircase's most prominent feature is a superb long-case clock, which was made in Liverpool by Robert Anderson in 1775. Between doors stands a walnut chair dating from 1715. In contrast, the Great Staircase has a fine ceiling by Giuseppe Cortese and a Venetian window at the halfway point as you reach the upper floor. (*Yorkshire Post*; *Fairfax House: An Illustrated History and Guide*)

# February 25th

**1941:** The first Feast of the York Butchers' Gild took place in Davy Hall, Davygate; the beginning of a new era for this long-established trade guild. Guilds can be traced back to Saxon times, when there were frith guilds, and by 1066, guilds' merchants were in existence to protect and regulate trade. In the twelfth century, more guilds were organised to safeguard the interests of members of individual crafts and trades. There were also guilds for social and religious purposes, such as the Guild of Corpus Christi, founded in 1408. The Butchers' Gild controlled issues to do with hygiene, weights and measures, meat restricted days, periods of fasting and foreign (non-gild) butchers. York's Shambles is well known as the butchers' street, but their trade area extended over St Andrewgate and St Saviourgate. Membership of the Butchers' Gild dropped from thirty or forty in 1812 to just two in 1929, and only one in 1940. At that point, new members were sworn in and, since then, membership has continued to grow with gild members drawn from a wider geographical area (including the first three female members in 2002). Along with other guilds, they worship in All Saints' Church, Pavement. (www. yorkbutchersgild.com)

# February 26th

**1834:** On this day, Richard Richmond was drinking with his brother at the Leopard in Pavement, York, when the landlord, William English, requested that they leave. He had worked as a servant in the Dringhouses area, but was often to be found at this alehouse. They moved on, but only along the yard to a brew house, where they spent the next four hours drinking more. A brazier's premises next door had been locked up and secured for the night, but when the owner, a Mr Nelson, returned the next day, a piece of copper valued at 50s had been stolen. Thieves had forced open a window to gain entry. The copper was found under a beam in Richard Richmond's lodgings, in a hay loft at Dringhouses, and when he appeared in court at the Guildhall on the following Tuesday a guilty verdict was returned and a sentence of six months' imprisonment passed. (*York Herald*)

---

**2011:** A group of archaeologists, 'On-Site Archaeology', were finalists at the Current Archaeology Live conference at the British Museum on this day. Their short-listing for an award followed excavation of a mass burial site at All Saints' Church, York. A total of 113 members of Oliver Cromwell's parliamentary force were probably victims of disease as archaeologists found no battle injuries. (*Northern Echo*, 19 August 2010 and 7 January 2011)

# February 27th

**1390:** According to the historian Drake, a curious incident took place on this Monday 27 February. A gathering of notable citizens in the council chamber on Ouse Bridge included Robert Savage, Mayor of York; John de Hoveden and John de Doncaster, bailiffs; and Ralph del See. As they were talking, a local man, Robert de Ellerbeck (a mercer by trade), arrived in the chamber with head and feet uncovered. He promptly knelt and then prostrated himself at the feet of Ralph del See, before exclaiming, 'I beseech thee, Ralph, for the love of Our Lord Jesus Christ, who redeemed mankind by his precious blood on the Cross, that thou wilt pardon and remit to me the death of Richard del See, thy father.' Many of those present prevailed on Ralph to forgive him and, taking pity, Ralph addressed Robert de Ellerbeck: 'In reverence to God, and at the entreaty of these worthy men, and for the sake of the soul of the said Richard, I remit and release unto thee for ever the death of Richard del See, my father.' Drake indicates that the death of Richard del See must have been accidental and, though there are discrepancies in the detail, it remains an intriguing tale. (Knight C.B., *A History of the City of York*)

# February 28th

**1631:** On this day, Richard Neile was elected Archbishop of York and, following Royal Assent, he was enthroned on 16 April of the same year. On 24 November 1633, he played a part in the baptism of James, Duke of York and during 1635, he successfully defended the right of the Archbishops of York to visit Queen's College, Oxford when this was disputed by Thomas Laud. While he was not noted for great intellect, Richard Neile displayed considerable powers of application and concentration, as well as an ability to organise and guide the work of others around him. He earned a reputation for a commonsense approach towards implementing doctrines and policies prepared by others. Archbishop Neile continued to be active in political as well as ecclesiastical circles up to his death on 31 October 1640. He died at the mansion house belonging to the Prebend of Stillington. He was buried at the east end of the Minster in the chapel of All Saints. (*Dictionary of National Biography*)

# February 29th

**1868:** The last public execution at the gallows near the Castle Wall, opposite St George's Field and known as the New Drop, took place on this day. Soon afterwards, the gallows were removed and subsequent executions were carried out, without publicity, inside the castle precincts. Before 1801, York's gallows were located on the Knavesmire, but visitors to the city objected to their closeness to one of the area's main highways and this outcry led to their repositioning close to the castle. A small doorway in a corner of the museum wall still marks the route that prisoners took from the condemned cell to the 'new drop'. Nearby, on the bank of the River Foss, a public house named The Windmill did a roaring trade on a Friday afternoon when executions took place. Executions within the castle walls continued from 1868 until December 1896, when August Carlsen was found guilty of murder and taken to the gallows. Following his execution, the black flag was raised above the castle walls for the last time. (www.york-united-kingdom.co.uk)

# March 1st

**1682:** Sir Thomas Herbert died on this day. He was born at a property on Pavement, York in 1606 and went on to become a traveller and adventurer typical of that period. Between 1626 and 1629, he journeyed with the Earl of Pembroke on a visit to the Shah of Persia, where he was given a Persian costume and a black page boy. These feature prominently in a portrait of Thomas Herbert which was lost for many years, only to re-appear in about 1926, when it was bought by a descendant, George E. Herbert. Initially, he supported the parliamentary cause, but during 1647 Herbert became a committed Royalist and for the next two years was a personal attendant to the King. Though he remained in London until after the restoration of Charles II, his later years were spent in York at No. 9 High Petergate, where he wrote his memoirs. On his death, Sir Thomas Herbert was buried beside his ancestors in St Crux Churchyard. (www.yorkconservationtrust.org)

———— • • ————

**1730:** The foundation stone was laid for York's Assembly Rooms on Blake Street. Designed and built by Richard Boyle, 3rd Earl of Burlington, the structure has been termed 'the earliest neo-classical building in Europe'. These most elegant rooms were used for fashionable balls in Georgian times. (www.yorkhistory.org.uk; www.britannica.com)

# March 2nd

**1882:** The funeral took place of George Leeman, who died in Scarborough after a lifetime of work in the city of York and surrounding area. Born in York, he qualified as a solicitor and set up a legal practice in the city during 1835. During the following year, he became a liberal councillor for Castlegate Ward and in 1839 for the Guildhall Ward, before serving as an alderman for twenty-eight years from 1850. The highlights of Leeman's political career came with terms as Lord Mayor of York in 1856, 1860 and 1870, and as member of parliament for York between 1865–8 and 1871–80. George Leeman is better known for his contribution to the growth of the railway network. Having replaced George Hudson as chairman of the York, Newcastle and Berwick Railway in 1849, he facilitated mergers that created the North Eastern Railway Co. in 1854. It became one of the wealthiest railways in the country and Leeman served as chairman from 1874 to 1880. At national level, he was chairman of the Railway Association of Great Britain, and during 1875 he presided over celebrations to mark the fiftieth anniversary of the opening of the Stockton–Darlington line. A statue of Leeman by local sculptor G.W. Milburn celebrates his contribution to York's development. (www.historyofyork.org.uk)

# March 3rd

**2011:** An exhibition, 'The Great Lost Library of Alcuin's York', opened on this day in York's Old Palace, which houses the current York Minster Library. During the eighth century AD, Alcuin assembled a massive library featuring works on topics including astronomy, arithmetic, religion and natural history. Working with his teacher, Aelbert, Alcuin is thought to have gathered books and manuscripts between the years 730 and 780, to such an extent that York gained a reputation as one of the most influentially intellectual cities in Europe. Students arrived in the city from as far afield as the Netherlands and Ireland. Invading Viking forces are believed to have destroyed the library during sustained attacks on York and parts of Northumbria during AD 866 and 867, but some manuscripts survived after being taken abroad by missionaries before the onslaught. These precious documents are now located throughout Europe and even in America. The exhibition, which has been assembled over the last year by Dr Mary Garriston from York University's Department of History, features calligraphy and photographs of manuscripts preserved across Europe and North America. Funding has been provided by the Yorkshire Philosophical Society, the Sheldon Memorial Trust, York Decorative and Fine Arts Society and York University. (*Yorkshire Post*)

# March 4th

**1228:** King Henry III granted to the Dominicans of Black Friars the King's Chapel of St Mary Magdalene on the King's Tofts as well as land lying between that of William Malesoures and Robert Fitz Baldwin. In 1237, the King provided them with forty oaks from the Forest of Galtres, to be used in building the priory. During a visit to York on 3 September 1268, he granted them permission to enclose land containing a public well, on condition that the prior set up another well for public use. (Benson, G., *An Account of the County and City of York*)

———◆———

**1903:** The Annual General Meeting of York Women's Suffrage Society was held and one of its main speakers was the Lady Mayoress – Mrs Edwin Gray. In her speech Mrs Gray pointed out that although women could not vote in parliamentary elections, they could, with appropriate qualifications, vote for county councillors, for guardians and for parish councils. She also highlighted the fact that women on the Isle of Man already had a parliamentary vote. Reflecting her position as a Liberal, Mrs Gray's campaigning zeal extended into other areas of social reform including housing and living conditions. (*Yorkshire Evening Press*)

# March 5th

**1433:** A sub bailiff of Sir Henry Bromflete, High Sheriff of York, arrested William Gyllam of Whixley within the liberty of the city of York – an area of land which included the walled city and some city parishes to the north and east sides, as well as open tracts of land such as Knavesmire and Bishops Fields on the south and west. He was on the high road from Holgate to York, between the windmill on the east or York-side of the village and a bridge at the east end of the village. The next day the Under Sheriff for the county came before William Ormshered, the Lord Mayor, and released the prisoner, acknowledging that he had been wrongly arrested and that the place where the arrest took place was within the liberty of the city of York. (Knight, C.B., *A History of the City of York*)

---

**1921:** It was reported that another picture house was to be added to York's growing list of entertainment venues. Located in Castlegate, it was named as St George's Super-Cinema, with a seating capacity of 1,340 (including 450 in the balcony). The screen would measure 22ft by 18ft and the orchestra would be that of Harold Croke. An advertisement for the first show called the cinema 'St George's Hall' and prices for the first film, *Three Men in a Boat*, ranged from 1s 6d to 8d. (*Yorkshire Evening Press*, 5 March 1921)

# March 6th

**1917:** Francis Alick Howerd was born in York on this day. He first appeared on the stage at the age of thirteen, but ambitions to become a serious actor floundered when he failed to get an audition at RADA. He began entertaining during army service in the Second World War. His professional career got underway in summer 1946 with a touring show, *For the Fun of Howerd*, and his radio debut at the beginning of December the same year, in the BBC *Variety Band Box* programme. Frankie Howerd's popularity increased through the late 1940s and into the 1950s, often with material prepared by Eric Sykes, Galton and Simpson, and Johnny Speight. He also featured regularly in the comic *Film Fun*, but although he experimented with different formats, the late 1950s brought a downturn in his fortunes. After suffering a nervous breakdown in the early 1960s, his career revived with shows such as *A Funny Thing Happened on the Way to the Forum* and *The Frankie and Bruce Christmas Show* with Bruce Forsyth. Seemingly off-the-cuff remarks characterised his shows for the BBC and also Thames Television in the 1960s and '70s, and in 1977 he was awarded an OBE. During the later years of his career, Frankie Howerd developed a cult following among student audiences, but in 1991 he suffered respiratory problems and died on 18 April 1992. (www.screenonline.org.uk; www.frankiehowerdcom)

# March 7th

**1379:** York Tyburn was erected, with the gallows taking their name from those used in London. They remained in use for some 422 years. Several other locations had gallows and they were often controlled by church authorities. The Archbishop of York had a gallows on Foss Bridge, and the scaffold in Burton Stone Lane was under the command of the abbot of St Mary's Abbey. The Dean and Chapter of York controlled a similar set of apparatus at the junction of Wigginton and Haxby Roads. Another gallows, owned by St Leonard's Chuch, was located at Green Dykes, now named Garrow Hill (where a nearby route named Thief Lane marks the last journey made by convicted criminals). When St Leonard's gallows were dismantled, Tyburn was the only place of execution. (Naismith, J.S., *Tales from the York Scaffold*)

———— • ✦ • ————

**1905:** The High School for Dancing at 8 Stonegate, York staged a 'Japanese Carnival and Fancy Dress Ball':

Dress Japanese or Oriental preferred but optional. Subscription including refreshments 2/6 each. Dancing at 8.30. Carriages at 2 am. Novel Parasol, Lantern and Fan dances by Pupils in Japanese Costumes.

(*Yorkshire Evening Press*)

# March 8th

**1807:** On this day, Thomas Cooke was born at Allerthorpe, near Pocklington. His formal education consisted of two years at an elementary school, before he taught himself navigational and astronomical skills in preparation for a career as a sailor. Persuaded by his mother to develop a land-based career, he moved to York in 1829 as a mathematics teacher and then set up his own business during 1836. An interest in optics led Cooke to a career in making telescopes and time-pieces, with the first of these – a refracting telescope – using the base of a tumbler, shaped to form its lens. His first shop was at 50 Stonegate, York, before a move to larger premises in Coney Street. Cooke's first telescope was built for William Gray and, as an excise tax on glass inhibited the making of refracting telescopes, he was one of the pioneers of making such instruments in this country. Thomas Cooke's mechanical skills led to him manufacturing turret clocks for church towers, and after founding the firm T. Cooke & Sons, he moved to larger workshops – the Buckingham Works at Bishophill in York. One of Cooke's finest achievements was the construction of a 25 inch 'Newall' refractor for Robert Stirling Newall. He also made telescopes for the Royal Observatory at Greenwich and another for Prince Albert. He died on 19 October 1868 and is buried in York Cemetery. (Feinsten, C.H., *York 1831–1981*)

# March 9th

**1793:** An insight into operations of a pawnbroker – and in this case also a licensed auctioneer – is provided in a newspaper advertisement from the *York Herald* on this day:

> Unredeemed Pledges to be Sold by Public Auction.
> On Wednesday the 17th day of April next, at ten o'clock in the forenoon at the house of Mr George Fettes, licensed auctioneer, in Lady Peckett's Yard, Pavement, York.
> Several LOTS of UNREDEEMED PLEDGES, consisting of PLATE, WATCHES, WEARING APPAREL etc…
> Those who are interested in this notice, may apply before the day of sale and either pay off the interest or redeem their goods.
>
> GEORGE FETTES, Auctioneer.

———◆———

**2011:** Offers were invited by 12 noon on 9 March for Penn House, with a guide price of £1,500,000. In 1852, Joseph Rowntree senior, a grocer and tea and coffee merchant, had the house built for his retirement at the corner of Bootham and St Mary's in York. In a gazebo in the back garden he wrote tracts on Temperance, in keeping with his Quaker beliefs. At the turn of the twentieth century, Seebohm Rowntree used Penn House as the hub for a survey into living conditions among York's poorer class. His book, *Poverty: A Study of Town Life*, informed politicians and helped to lay the groundwork for the welfare state. (*Yorkshire Post*)

# March 10th

**1787:** On this day, William Etty was born in Feasegate, York, the son of a baker and confectioner. After an early education, with no artistic guidance, he took up an apprenticeship with a busy printing firm in Hull during 1798. With ambitions to be an artist, Etty moved to London in 1805 and, two years later, he became a student at the Royal Academy. His uncle also paid for a year-long period of tuition under the established artist Sir Thomas Lawrence, but recognition and success remained elusive. During 1811, his first piece of work was accepted by the Royal Academy and in the 1820s he began to achieve critical acclaim. Yet William Etty's work divided opinion throughout his lifetime, largely because of his paintings of the female nude. In 1842 he established the York School of Design, which later became the York School of Art. He also played a part in conservation of the city walls. William Etty died in 1849 and was buried in St Olav's Church. A statue of him was erected in front of the city's art gallery in 1911. (www.historyofyork.org.uk)

---

**1800:** George Hudson was born at Howsham. He moved to York in 1815 as an apprentice to Nicholson and Bell, drapers and silk mercers. His political career saw him become Lord Mayor of York in 1837, 1838 and 1846, but he is best known as 'the Railway King'. (Edgington, J. & Gilks J.S., *Trains from York*)

# *March 11th*

**2011:** A three-day festival called 'Spookfest' began in York after the city had been named 'Europe's most haunted city' by *National Geographic* magazine. Activities included ghost walks, horror films shown at the City Screen, and a series of talks at Bedern Hall on topics ranging from vampires to contacting the dead. There was also a guest appearance by Ciarán O'Keeffe, star of *Most Haunted*, at the Treasurer's House. (Press cuttings; www.spooksfest.co.uk)

———•❖•———

**2011:** York Festival of Science and Technology was staged from 11 to 20 March. Held on an annual basis within the UK's National Science and Engineering Week, the festival celebrated its fourteenth year. A range of activities included Dr Marty Jopson's exploration of the crazy early history of communication devices; St Peter's School's explanation of 'Bloodhound SSC' (a supersonic car); a public debate on the subject 'Energy for Our Future! Have Your Say'; and an appearance by Ortis Deley and Pollyanna Woodward from Channel Five's *The Gadget Show*. (www.scy.co.uk)

# March 12th

**1482:** At a council meeting on this day it was agreed, '...the common crane shall be kept by the chamberlain and a clerk in the year ensuing...' Some four years later, on 31 January 1486, the council leased the common crane to William Jackson for a term of ten years, for ten marks annually. Part of the agreement was that Jackson was to 'stand and bear at his proper charges all manner casualties and misfortune of anything coming or happening to the said crane... and also sustain and bear at his proper costs and expenses all manner of slings, cables and hooks.' It seems clear that the crane was the property of the Corporation at that time and certainly into the nineteenth century. During the early 1800s, a wharf at the southern end of Skeldergate still had the name Old Crane Wharf, until a bonded warehouse was constructed on the site. (Knight, C.B., *A History of the City of York*)

———◆———

**1920:** Councillor J.T. Clarke raised the question of levels of rent to be paid by residents on the new housing development at Tang Hall estate. Initial plans for the scheme had been adopted by the council in the latter weeks of 1919, but despite widespread unemployment in the York area there were lengthy delays in the housing programme. During October 1920, the rents for Tang Hall properties were fixed at 10s, 11s 6d and 13s. (*York Herald*)

# March 13th

**1902:** Press reports stated that cases of smallpox were breaking out in York and the question of vaccinating children against the disease was causing considerable heated debate between the vaccination officer, Mr M. Wrigglesworth, and the vaccination authority, which was the Board of Guardians and local politicians. The outbreak of smallpox began in London and then spread to Leeds and York, where it was still prevalent in 1903. (*Yorkshire Evening Press*)

———•◆•———

**1929:** Henry Scott Tuke died after a lengthy career as a painter and photographer. He was born into a well-known Quaker family based in Lawrence Street, York on 12 June 1858, and although previous generations had played major roles in the fields of psychiatry and social improvement, Henry (or Harry, as he was known by family and friends) showed no interest in medical matters. He was encouraged from an early age to draw and paint and, in 1874, moved to London where he enrolled at the Slade School of Art. After further periods of study in France and Italy, he joined the Newlyn School of Painters in Cornwall and, after an exhibition of his work at the Royal Academy of Art in London, he gained several lucrative commissions. Henry Tuke is widely remembered for his oil paintings of young men, but his collection of over 1,300 works includes as many sailing ships and maritime settings as human figures. (Emmanuel, C., *The Life and Work of Henry Scott Tuke*)

# March 14th

**1586:** Margaret Clitherow was brought from prison to attend court in York's Guildhall. This was a time of great religious turmoil. Born towards the end of Mary Tudor's reign, Margaret was brought up as a Protestant and married John Clitherow, who owned a meat business in the Shambles. Soon after her marriage, she converted to Catholicism and though her husband remained Protestant, he continued to offer support by paying her fines for not attending Protestant church services and tacitly accepting the shelter she offered to priests in their home. Their property also housed a secret cupboard containing vestments and wine and bread for Mass. During 1586, severe measures were taken against Roman Catholics in the north, and Margaret Clitherow's involvement was betrayed by a child. In the courtroom she was asked to enter a plea, but she steadfastly refused and the judge, Sir John Clenche, pronounced her guilty of 'having harboured and maintained Jesuits and Seminary Priests, traitors to the Queen's majesty and her laws.' Margaret Clitherow was put to death ten days later in the most barbaric manner: a board was placed over her and huge stones piled on top. Following her execution, Queen Elizabeth I wrote to the citizens of York expressing her horror at the treatment of a fellow woman. (www.sacred-destinations.com; www.suite101.com)

# March 15th

**1813:** John Snow was born in North Street, York. He studied in the city until the age of fourteen, when he moved to Newcastle-upon-Tyne as apprentice to a surgeon. After working as a colliery surgeon, he practised in Burnopfield, County Durham and then in Pateley Bridge, North Yorkshire, before enrolling as a student at the Hunterian School of Medicine in Great Windmill Street, London, in 1836. During the following year, he began working at Westminster Hospital and was awarded membership of the Royal College of Surgeons on 2 May 1838. Membership of the Royal College of Physicians followed in 1850. John Snow was one of the first physicians to calculate dosages of ether and chloroform for use as a surgical anaesthetic. He personally administered chloroform to Queen Victoria during the birth of her last child. (*Cholera, Chloroform and the Science of Medicine: A Life of John Snow*)

———— • ◆ • ————

**1940:** Frank Gordon Dobson was born in York on this day. He was educated locally, before gaining a BSc degree from the London School of Economics in 1962. During the 1970s, he emerged as group leader of Camden's London Borough Council and was elected as MP for Holborn and St Pancras in 1979. Promotion to the front benches saw him hold several important posts from 1982. In recent times he has advised the coalition government about levels of poverty in modern Britain. (Press articles: *The Times,* the *Guardian* and the *Independent*)

# March 16th

1190: Widely regarded as one of the most shameful episodes in York's history, the death of around 1,500 Jews on this day was the culmination of a chain of events linked with the coronation of King Richard I at Westminster. Richard ordered that no Jew was to be allowed to enter Westminster Abbey or Westminster Hall, and some who did arrive there were roughly handled and ejected. Serious anti-Jewish rioting followed and a leading Jew from York, named Benedict, was fatally injured in the capital. His companion, Jocenus, escaped and fled to York, where events took an even more sinister turn. Jocenus and fellow Jews took refuge in York Castle, but when the constable left the building on personal business, the terrified Jews were convinced that he was about to hand them over to the mob. They refused him entry and the High Sheriff ordered an assault on the castle. For several days, the Jews held out against a full-scale siege, but after their offer to buy their release had been refused they reached a terrible decision. Many destroyed their goods and treasure before each man killed his own family members and then themselves. Others appealed to the mob for mercy, but in vain. They were massacred to the last child. (York A.D. 71–1971, *Yorkshire Evening Gazette* supplement)

# March 17th

**1909:** Seebohm Rowntree spoke about a diet chart at the annual meeting of the York Health and Housing Reform Association. The chart had been prepared for use by poorer sections of the city's community. It claimed to explain how 'a working man' could 'supply all bodily needs' for himself, his wife and three children for 12s 9d per week. Arguments in support of the chart were put forward by the *Daily News* and a number of individuals, and others, such as W.A. Fowler of Heworth, led the criticism. Rowntree pointed out some misunderstandings about the chart and explained that it represented only a guide to the best way of spending 12s 9d per week. (*Evening Press*)

———•◆•———

**1909:** The question of slave labour in overseas cocoa plantations that supplied chocolate-making companies in England became a major issue during the early 1900s. Cadbury's of Birmingham had involved Fry of Bristol and Rowntree of York in their investigations, and W.H. Cadbury and a Quaker named Joseph Buritt reported, on this day, that 'no adequate steps' had been taken 'to remedy the evils already proved to exist', and that Messrs Cadbury, Fry and Rowntree would cease buying 'cocoa produced in the islands of San Thomé and Principe'. (Peacock, A.J., *York 1900 to 1914*)

# March 18th

**1858:** Two army recruits arrived at the 'Square and Compass' in the Garden Place area of York and were given permission by the landlord, Thomas Garnett, to lodge on the premises. At around 6 p.m. one of the recruits, by the name of Valentine, returned to the inn with a mutton chop and requested that it should be cooked. Mrs Garnett, however, said he could not remain at the inn and should only return at bed time, 'for tradesmen and others who come here with gold pins and studs will not sit with such a ragamuffin as you.' With her words ringing in his ears, he moved on to other lodgings, before reporting the incident to Sergeant Atkinson the next day. At the inn, Mrs Garnett informed the sergeant, 'I will not have the recruit, neither for good nor bad.' At a hearing in the Guildhall the following week, the landlord complained about the sergeant's insulting behaviour towards his wife, but the sergeant denied causing offence. The Lord Mayor ruled that publicans were obliged to provide overnight lodgings and daytime accommodation for those billeted on them. He also stated that the landlord had misunderstood the law and fined him the minimum amount of 40s. (*York Herald*)

—•◆•—

**1915:** At 9.54 p.m. a Midland train derailed at Chaloner's Whin Junction during a snowstorm. (Edgington, J. & Gilks J.S., *Trains from York*)

# March 19th

**1891:** The enthronement took place of William Connor Magee as eighty-first Archbishop of York. He was already in his seventieth year of age and died on 5 May 1891 in London, following a serious bout of influenza. William Magee was buried at Peterborough, where he had served as Bishop for many years and left an impressive reputation as an orator in both church and parliamentary circles. (Knight, C.B., *History of the City of York*)

———— • ✦ • ————

**1904:** Unemployment and hardship was widespread in the York area when, on this day, the *Evening Press* published an article under the heading 'York Cabby, His Work, His Hours, His Wages', which explained that there were 200 of these workers (170 full time) in the city. Their wages were 18*s* per week and the report continued, 'Most of the men are married and the fact that they only earn about two thirds of what is now admitted on the authority of Messrs Booth and Rowntree shows that they must often have a very hard struggle to keep the wolf from the door… and… the cab trade is very bad in York now.' It was a similar story from the York City Hairdressers' Association, whose members' wages varied from 18*s* to £1 per week. The building trade was also reported as 'slack'. In response to these difficult conditions, York Soup Kitchen was opened in the New Year of 1904, 'in consequence of the great sickness… in the city and the number of people out of employment.' (*York Evening Press*)

# March 20th

**1357:** The company of Merchant Adventurers of York was granted a charter of incorporation on this day. By royal licence, thirteen York merchants were allowed to acquire property in York to the annual value of £10, and in 1430 Henry VI incorporated the Mistery of Mercers in the City of York, with powers to elect a governor and two wardens. Elizabeth I formally constituted the Society of Merchant Adventurers of York by charter in 1581. Membership was offered to merchants with ten years' service, or those who had served seven years' apprenticeship, and the society was given a monopoly over goods and merchandise shipped into York, apart from salt and fish. (www.nationalarchives.gov.uk)

---

**1776:** Elizabeth Boardingham was the last woman to be burned at the stake on 20 March 1776 (before the sentence was abolished in 1790). Born in Flamborough in about 1742, by 1775 she had been married to John Boardingham and had given birth to five children. During 1775, while her husband was in York prison, she took in a lover, Thomas Aikney, and after her husband's release she moved to Lincolnshire with Aikney. Some three months later, she returned to the family home and all seemed well, but on 13 February 1776 Aikney arrived at about 11 p.m. and stabbed John Boardingham to death. Elizabeth denied any involvement in the murder but was convicted of petty treason. (Research paper by Dr K. Prior)

# March 21st

**1905:** William Shaw of St Ann Street was prosecuted for unlawfully selling 'certain intoxicating liquor, to wit a pint of beer… not in cask or bottle, and… not in a quantity less than half a pint, in a certain measure not marked according to the imperial standard…' Shaw's court appearance followed a visit to his premises by a weights and measures inspector, who ordered a pint and got a pint and a half. The whole controversy became known as the 'long pull'. It stemmed from the terms of the Licensing Act of 1872, which stated that all intoxicating liquor of a half pint or over that was not sold in a cask or bottle should be sold in measures marked according to imperial standards. William Shaw's punishment was a fine of *2s 6d* with costs. (*Yorkshire Evening Press*)

———•◆•———

**1910:** A newspaper report from this day stated that on one Sunday in March, eleven tram cars had travelled 790.66 miles and taken £71 *2s 1d* in fares from 13,230 passengers. Sunday travel was obviously extremely popular in the York area, but the introduction of trams on the Sabbath during late January had aroused considerable hostility. Opposition was led by local Methodist churches, but a debate in the council narrowly approved continuation of Sunday tram services. (*Yorkshire Evening Press*)

# March 22nd

**1792:** The trial of Spence Broughton got underway in York when he was accused of robbing the Sheffield to Rotherham mail coach on 9 February 1791. Following the robbery, Broughton and his accomplice, John Oxley, went their separate ways – Broughton to Mansfield and Oxley to London – but when stolen notes were traced to the capital, Oxley was arrested along with Thomas Shaw, who had assisted with planning of the robbery and concealment of stolen cash in his garden. Broughton was also taken into custody and, after questioning, the three robbers were detained in different prisons. Somehow, although he was clamped in leg irons, Oxley managed to escape and was never recaptured, but Shaw's evidence ensured Broughton's conviction. Following his execution, Broughton's body was removed from the scaffold and hung from a gibbet. He was the last condemned man to suffer this punishment in Yorkshire. (*York Tales From the Scaffold*)

---·◆·---

**1824:** York's streets were first lit by gas on this day and it was also supplied to some shops and 250 private subscribers in their own homes. Customers could choose from three different types of lamp and were charged at half yearly rates, which varied with the daily period of supply. Improvement Commissioners were responsible for paving, lighting and cleaning the streets, until their replacement by a Board of Health in 1850. (www.localhistories.org)

# March 23rd

**1743:** Lancelot Blackburne died on this day after a controversial and colourful life, which included spells as Archbishop of York and as a pirate. Born in London on 10 December 1658, he was educated at Westminster School and Christ Church College, Oxford. After graduating in 1680, he was ordained as a priest and then spent the next few years in the West Indies, where he was based in Nevis for a time. One popular account of his activities suggests that he spent three years sailing with buccaneers, either as a chaplain or as a pirate. There is no conclusive evidence in support of either theory, but a document dating from 1681 shows that he was paid £20 by King Charles II for secret services. Returning to England in 1684, he married Catherine Talbot. During 1724, Lancelot Blackburne was installed as Archbishop of York and held this post up until his death. His career was controversial, for he seems to have carried out few confirmations and stopped ordaining priests after ten years. Rumours persisted that he had secretly married George I to his mistress and he was ejected by John Disney, vicar of St Mary's Church, Nottingham, after a confirmation service when he asked for his pipe, tobacco and ale. As one writer states, 'His behaviour was seldom of a standard to be expected from an archbishop... In many respects it was seldom of a standard to be expected of a pirate.' (*Oxford Dictionary of National Biography*)

# March 24th

**1732:** William Tuke was born in York to a prominent Quaker family and in adulthood, he joined the family's tea and coffee merchants business. A few years later, in 1755, he took over the business (which became part of Twinings Tea Company in the mid-twentieth century). Apart from his business interests, William Tuke campaigned for abolition of the slave trade and on the local front, he founded a private Quaker asylum, the York Retreat, in 1796. As director of the asylum, Tuke pioneered an approach known as 'moral treatment', which placed great importance on patients' basic needs and comforts, and his methods influenced practices in other European asylums during the nineteenth century. Philippe Pinel, a French physician, adopted Tuke's approach and is remembered for work such as unchaining mental patients in the Paris asylum. In later life William Tuke continued his involvement with the family's tea business and in running the York Retreat, as well as setting up several Quaker schools. His son and grandson continued the family's involvement with 'The Retreat' and publication of his approach in book form ensured recognition of William Tuke's contribution to the treatment of mental illness. (www.sciencemuseum.org.uk)

# March 25th

**1586:** Catholic martyr Margaret Clitherow's shrine is set in a single room of No. 10 the Shambles, where a plaque on the wall explains the story of her life. A statue of her and a priest is set behind an altar. (It is now believed that her actual home stands on the other side of the street – the only property to contain a priest hole.) Margaret Clitherow's daughter became a nun and both of her sons became priests, while in subsequent years many schools in England have been named after her. In 1970, Margaret was made a saint by Pope Paul VI, who referred to her as the Pearl of York. (She was one of forty new saints, who were described as 'the forty Martyrs of England and Wales'.) Her feast day in the current Roman Catholic Calendar is 26 March. The story of Margaret Clitherow's martyrdom is also depicted in stained glass at the Church of Our Lady and the English Martyrs in Cambridge, while an elaborate memorial to Sir John Clenche, the judge who sentenced her to death, is in the Church of All Saints at Holbrook in Suffolk. (www.sacred-destinations.com; www.suite101.com)

# March 26th

**1908:** Passions were aroused throughout the country in response to H.H. Asquith's Licensing Bill, which he introduced during a speech on 27 February 1908. The details of his scheme would see the loss of more than a third of the pubs and beerhouses of England and Wales and the Tory party campaigned strongly against Asquith's Bill. In York, however, there was considerable support for the scheme, with the city's Wesleyan members and workers, based at the Central Mission at Peaseholm Green, coming out in favour on 26 March. Two days later, the York Free Church Council announced their support and the Society of Friends acted similarly, while the Liberal party claimed, 'The Licensing Bill is a bold and statesmanlike endeavour to cope with a gigantic evil, which, whatever be the fate of it, does honour to the government that introduced it.' The Bill had its third reading in the House of Commons on 20 November 1908, but just a week later, after three days of debate, the Bill was defeated in the House of Lords by 272 votes to 96. (*Yorkshire Evening Press*)

# March 27th

**1643:** On this day, John Bartendale, a piper and local citizen, was found guilty of felony and hung from the gallows on Knavesmire. Reports suggest that after about an hour he was taken down and buried close by. Several hours later, a gentleman named Vavasour was riding past the location when, to his amazement, the earth began to move. He gave instructions for his servant to bring a spade and further investigations led to John Bartendale's emergence from the ground. He was given water and soon recovered sufficiently to sit up and enquire where he was, as a group of incredulous spectators looked on. He was taken back before the same judge that had ordered his execution, but this time the instruction was to free him. Bartendale became known as 'Honest John' and led a happy life as an ostler, or publican, in the city, while people came from all parts to listen to the story of his remarkable survival and to drink to his continued health. (www.theoriginalghostwalkofyork.co.uk)

---·◆·---

**1908:** Lord Wenlock spoke at the first meeting of the North Eastern Railway League of Riflemen and made it quite clear that, in addition to entering local competitions, he hoped that members would spend part of their leisure time practising an appropriate drill. This would, he continued, make them 'more useful to their country'. (*Yorkshire Evening Press*)

# March 28th

**1788:** A dispensary opened on this day in a small building on St Andrewgate. Baines' Directory of 1823 reported that it was 'of the same nature as the County Hospital though unconnected with it', and continued:

> Its objects are to dispense gratuitously advice, medicine and surgical assistance, to those who are unable to pay for them.
>
> This establishment has continued to flourish over thirty four years and has, out of 42,488 patients, effected cures upon 28, 851 of them. (Note: medical and chirurgical [surgical] attendance are given every Monday, Wednesday and Friday at eleven o'clock and medicines dispensed gratis to all proper objects, recommended by an annual subscriber of half a guinea or upwards, or by a donator of ten guineas or upwards. Patients incapable of attending in person are visited at their own homes.)
>
> The expense of this establishment last year amounted to £433 and the number of patients admitted and remaining on the books was 2,054, exclusive of 648 children inoculated without cost for the cowpox.

('A History of York', *Baines' Gazetter*, 1823)

# March 29th

**1935:** A letter dated 29 March 1935 from a regular patron, calling himself 'Observant', praised the virtues of the Zotofoam Baths in York. Installed by the York Corporation Parks Committee, the foam and tonic baths (at St George's Baths Building) were said to be a treatment for rheumatism and obesity and were officially opened by the Lord Mayor on 2 October 1934. Two cubicles had been installed at a cost of £26 per cubicle and members of the public could use them for a twenty-minute period at a cost of 2s 6d. The treatment involved running fairly hot water into an ordinary slipper bath and then forcing air into the bath once a person has entered, before squeezing a tube of Zotofoam into the water. This resulted in a bathful of white foam which would act as a body massage to 'eliminate unwanted secretions from the pores of the skin'. [In some ways the Zotofoam bath was the predecessor of whirlpools, which now feature in health spas, and such a bath was once described as being 'like a Jacuzzi on steroids'. Use of these baths continued well into the 1960s.] (*Yorkshire Evening Press*; www.victorianturkishbathorg)

# March 30th

**1955:** York City FC became the first 3rd Division club to feature in an FA Cup semi-final replay, on 30 March 1955, against Newcastle United. They had already defeated Scarborough, Dorchester Town, Blackpool (who had won the competition two seasons earlier), Bishop Auckland, Tottenham Hotspur and Notts County in previous rounds, before meeting Newcastle. The first semi-final encounter resulted in a 1–1 draw, but in the replay, York City were beaten 2–0 by the eventual winners. York's FA Cup campaign was notable for Arthur Bottom's total of eight goals. (www.yorkpress.co.uk)

---

**1972:** Her Majesty Queen Elizabeth II distributed Maundy Money at York Minster, and the flagged walkway beside the Minster was named 'Queen's Path' in honour of her visit. Maundy Thursday is the day before Good Friday and in recent times the Queen has followed a traditional role of handing out Maundy Money to a group of pensioners. Since the fifteenth century, the amount of Maundy coins handed out and the number of people receiving the coins has been directly linked to the years of the sovereign's life. Men and women who receive the coins are all retired pensioners recommended by clergy of all denominations, in recognition of their service to their church or community. (www.visityork.org)

# March 31st

**1829:** The formal trial of Jonathan Martin began on this day, following the destructive fire at York Minster in early February of the same year. Investigations into the cause of the blaze were assisted by information provided by Jonathan Martin's landlord and by Martin himself, who posted threatening letters to the Minster Clergy complete with his own signature. With a clear suspect in mind, the manhunt got underway and 'wanted' posters were issued, along with coverage of the investigation in northern newspapers. Jonathan Martin had travelled through Easingwold to Thirsk and then to Northallerton, where he hitched a lift on a coal cart to Darlington. From there he headed towards Hexham, but a sheriff's officer, William Stainthorpe, had seen posters and so arrested him at his lodgings. From Hexham jail, Martin was secretly transferred back to prison in York and, when brought before magistrates, admitted all charges. While held in jail, he spoke of angels trying to help him escape. Early stages of the trial were held on 23 March at the County Court (now York Crown Court), before an adjournment led to the trial proper getting underway at 9 a.m. on 31 March 1829. Within minutes the jury had reached a verdict of 'guilty due to insanity'. (The judge directed the jury to adjust this to 'not guilty on grounds of insanity'.) From York Castle he was moved to the Criminal Lunatic Asylum at St George's Fields in London, where he died on 27 May 1838. (Naismith, J.S., *Tales from the Scaffold*)

# April 1st

**1914:** A regatta was staged on the Ouse on this day, to celebrate Skeldergate Bridge being formally declared free from tolls. Construction work on the bridge spanned 1878 to 1880 and the first pedestrians were allowed to cross on 1 January 1881. A small arch, close to the former toll house at the east end of the bridge, was originally designed to lift in order to allow tall ships to reach quays between the Skeldergate and Ouse bridges. The opening mechanism was last operated in 1975 and winding gear has since been removed. During 2006, a Belgian speciality coffee house was opened in the former motor house of Skeldergate Bridge, with a bistro area bordering the Tower Gardens on one side and the River Ouse on the other. Across the river in St George's Field, the ducking stool was operated in earlier times. Initially, it was used for females who used false measures or brewed bad beer, but later it accommodated 'flysters or scolds'. (www.historyofyork.org.uk)

---

**1922:** North Eastern Railway absorbed the Hull and Barnsley Railway prior to the grouping arrangement of 1 January 1923, when the North Eastern finally lost its identity. (Appleby, K., *Britain's Rail Super Centres: York*)

# April 2nd

**1694:** During the night of 2 April, a highly destructive fire swept along High Ousegate. The close proximity of properties, one to another, and the nature of roofing and building materials meant that such an event was always a danger. One report states that it lasted around eight hours and destroyed some thirty houses (and this accounts for the absence of any medieval timber and plaster houses on High Ousegate opposite All Saints' Church). An estimate of the damage puts the total at £20,000, but fortunately no lives were lost in the blaze. (The Church of All Saints, Pavement, York)

---

**1830:** The trial of William Shaw began on this day. He faced a charge of murder. A few days earlier, twenty-two year old Rachel Crosley had left home at just after 10 p.m. and was never seen alive again. Initial searches of the area around her home near Kirkburton were unsuccessful but when daylight came, the whole community was stunned by the discovery of her body at the bottom of a mineshaft close to the family home. William Shaw was pinpointed as the main suspect, and witnesses soon provided compelling evidence that he was the last person to be seen with Rachel before her death. At his trial, Shaw was found guilty and the death sentence was carried out within days of his conviction. (Naismith, J.S., *Tales from the Scaffold*)

# April 3rd

**1902:** The Education Bill, which abolished school boards and made county borough councils, such as York, the local authorities for all secondary and technical education, aroused heated debate in the city. Non-conformists opposed the Bill, which was sponsored by A.J. Balfour, but support came from Roman Catholics, the Conservative Association and, as reported on 3 April, from the Convocation of York. (*Yorkshire Evening Press*)

---

**1938:** The new island platforms 15 and 16 became partially operative at York station (with platform 16 not fully operational until 1951 because of the war years). (Edgington, J. & Gilks, J.S., *Trains from York*)

---

**1952:** The last of forty-two houses completed under York Master Builders' Apprenticeship Training Scheme, which began in 1945, were opened at Gale Lane Estate, Acomb. The Lord Mayor (Alderman J.H. Kaye) unveiled a plaque which read 'York Master Builders' Training Scheme 1951' and was made by a joiner instructor, H.G. Shepherd. The apprentice scheme was initiated because of a shortage of joiners in the war years and York was one of the first cities in the country to take up the scheme. (Press cuttings)

# April 4th

**1868:** Frederick Parker was the last condemned prisoner to be publicly executed at York following his conviction for murder. Parker and a fellow prisoner, Daniel Driscoll, had been released from the 'Beverley House of Correction' after serving sentences for minor offences. They had then spent the day in alehouses at Bubwith before setting out for Hemingbrough. Early the following morning, an estate worker found clothing, a builder's trowel and a hedge stake covered with blood. Further investigation uncovered the partly hidden body of Daniel Driscoll. Police enquiries quickly established robbery as the motive for Driscoll's murder, with Parker as the prime suspect. He was arrested and taken to York Castle. The outcome of his trial was never in doubt and a crowd of 5,000 to 6,000 onlookers witnessed Parker's execution. (Naismith, J.S., *Tales from the Scaffold*)

---

**2008:** York Minster became the first cathedral to have a carillon of bells, with the arrival of twenty-four bells to supplement the existing 'Nelson Chime'; they ring out to announce Evensong at about 5 p.m. each day. (The carillon comprises a total of thirty-five bells, which are played through a baton clavier instrument. The change means that many different hymns can be played.) The newly-installed bells were tested with a performance from expert carilloneur Trevor Wakeman. (www.yorkminster.org)

# April 5th

**1557:** The Master, Robert Johnson, and the chaplains of the Hospital of Our Lady in the Horsefair, formally granted the hospital to the Dean and Chapter. The deed states that the hospital was no longer fulfilling the purpose for which it was established and that the Dean and Chapter propose 'as soon as it is possible, to found a Grammar School, where poor and needy youths and boys shall be taught the art of grammar and receive free maintenance therefore.' (Knight, C.B., *History of the City of York*)

———◆———

**1764:** A law of this date defined regulations relating to fellies (the width of wheels):

That the width of wheels of every wagon, cart or other carriage of the like kind, kept or used for carrying goods or other things for hire, within the said city, suburbs or liberty and the wheels of every waggon, cart or other such carriage in which bricks, tiles, stones or gravel shall be carried... or in which coals are carried from the river Ouse or any coal yards in the said city... and the wheels of every dray, rully or other carriage of the like construction... shall after the 5th day of April 1764 be made of fellies six inches broad at the least...

(Hargrove, W., *History of the City of York*)

# April 6th

**1776:** Robert Iredale of Bank Bottom, Southowram in West Yorkshire was executed at Tyburn, York, for having coining tools in his possession. He denied involvement in coining activities, but admitted counterfeiting York Bank guinea notes. Following the execution, his corpse was brought home with the noose still around his neck and, according to reports, his wife charged people one penny to view the body. The widespread activities of coiners in West Yorkshire were highlighted in the late 1760s by a government enquiry into the practice of clipping and coining. There is evidence of much earlier coining in Yorkshire, which was exposed when William Burnley, a fletcher, and John Burnley, both from Halifax, took sanctuary in the church during 1499. In 1529, Laurence Holdsworth of Sowerby was implicated and in the late 1600s Edmund Robinson, a clergyman based at Holmfirth and Haworth, was hanged at York for his coining crimes. Coining activity took different forms. It could involve forging gold and silver coins or 'diminishing' coinage, which meant clipping and filing the coins. Amounts of these clippings were then melted down to make counterfeit coins, which were then added to the genuine coins in circulation. (*The Yorkshire Coiners 1767 to 1783*)

# April 7th

**1739:** Dick Turpin was executed at Tyburn on York's Knavesmire, after being convicted on a charge of stealing a black mare and a foal at Welton. Born in 1706, he was the son of John Turpin, an innkeeper at Hampstead in Essex – opposite which a circle of nine trees is still known as 'Turpin's Ring'. In his early years, Turpin was apprenticed to a butcher in Whitechapel, but then embarked on a career of crime which included cattle stealing, smuggling and then violent robberies. Lonely farmsteads were targeted and robbed, the occupants often suffering torture. A reward of fifty guineas was increased to a hundred to capture the criminal, as the robberies continued. During February 1735, Turpin began a criminal partnership with Tom King, but as officers of the law closed in on him, he fled to Yorkshire where he assumed his mother's name of Palmer. Some four years later he was committed to York Assizes and faced trial, on 22 March 1739, for the theft of the black mare and foal at Welton. A guilty verdict meant that he was sentenced to death. After the execution, Dick Turpin's body was kept in the Blue Boar Inn, Castlegate, before burial in St George's Churchyard, where his grave can still be seen today. (Naismith, J.S., *Tales from the Scaffold*; *Oxford Dictionary of National Biography*)

# April 8th

**1769:** Tate Wilkinson, manager of theatres in York and Hull, obtained a Royal Patent for these venues at a cost of almost £500, and the York Theatre opened as the Theatre Royal on 8 April 1769. During 1744, building work on the theatre site covered the ruins of the medieval St Leonard's Hospital and there was a phase of rebuilding in 1765 to provide seating for 550 patrons. Many London-based stars of the theatrical world appeared in York during the summer Race and Assize Weeks, with acts at the Theatre Royal including Ned Shuter, a comedian, in 1773; Mrs Yates, who specialised in roles as a heroine in classical tragedies during 1785; and Miss Elizabeth Farren, with her portrayal of 'fine ladies' in comedy productions of 1789. Improvements to the Theatre Royal include redesigned frontages in 1835 and 1880 (when decorative carved heads were added, representing characters from Shakespeare plays) and refurbishment of the interior in 1901, 1967 and 1994. During 2007, the theatre was awarded Investors in People Standard – at that time the only producing theatre in Yorkshire to achieve this accolade. (www.yorktheatreroyal.co.uk)

# April 9th

**1639:** Although there is no definitive proof, it is extremely likely that on this day, the Royal Press was located in York when it printed King Charles I's statement 'for the suppression of various monopolies', as the proclamation carries the acknowledgement, 'at our manour in York'. Its intention was to demonstrate the monarch's care and providence for the public good of the people. On this occasion, Charles I stayed for almost four weeks at the King's Manor as he headed north to Scotland. Three years later, the King spent around five months in York – and again it seems that the royal printing press was brought with the royal party. By now, though, the King's Manor was empty and unfit to house royal visitors, so the King and his group lodged in the spacious and luxurious mansion of Sir Arthur Ingram, which was located in Dean's Park, close to the north side of the Minster. A large number of items were produced by the Royal Press at York, including a catalogue dated 5 August 1642, and in spite of difficulties caused by temporary arrangements, the documents are composed of neat and accurate printing. (Stacpoole, A., *Noble City of York*)

# April 10th

**1771:** For one night only, at the Merchant Taylor's Hall in Oldwork (Aldwark), a talented Mr Pittard, described as 'late comedian at the Theatre Royal, Covent Garden and formerly of the York Theatre', presented *The Temple of Taste or The Impromptu.* His intention was to 'entertain his audience with an entire new lecture on Hearts, which will be taken off in a peculiar manner…' (Press reports)

---

**2001:** York's Lord Mayor opened the city's Millennium Bridge. Completed at a cost of £4.2 million, its design was based on the spokes of a bicycle wheel, as the bridge was intended to provide a strategic crossing place for York's countless cyclists. With a total width of approximately 150 metres, and an 80 metre inclined main arm-span, the bridge extends over the River Ouse to the south of York and links Hospital Fields Road and Maple Grove in Fulford with Butcher Terrace on the South Bank. This spectacular crossing point soon attracted more than 2,000 users per day, with more than half of these cyclists. (www.lucas.com; www.vryork.com/millennium_bridge_york)

# April 11th

**1907:** A new craze was sweeping the country and it seemed that every home had to have a gramophone. Records advertised for sale on this day included musical performances by a notable York personality and famous piccolo player, Eli Hudson, along with others by Dame Nellie Melba, Adelina Patti, Caruso and Clark's London Concert Band. Music of a rather different type was available from Olly Oakley (whose real name was James Sharpe) with his banjo performances. He had started to make recordings in 1903 and performed any number of ragtime compositions during the Edwardian era. The first edition of the *Yorkshire Evening Press* in 1908 included advertisements for gramophones and one of these – by Pathephone – offered a model with an unwearable sapphire needle at a price of 45s. Sales of gramophones had already been boosted by a free concert at the Exhibition Buildings in July 1907. It was arranged by J. Gray & Sons of Coney Street, York. During the Edwardian era, and as the First World War loomed closer, people had more disposable income and most homes had a gramophone. (*Yorkshire Evening Press*)

# April 12th

**1706:** On this day, a new service began in York:

> York Four Days Stage Coach.
> Begins on Friday the 12th of April 1706.
> All that are desirous to pass from London to York, or from York to London, or any other place on the road, let them repair to the Black Swan in Holbourn in London, and to the Black Swan in Coney Street in York. At both which places, they may be received in a stage coach every Monday, Wednesday and Friday, which performs the whole journey in four days (if God permits). And sets forth at five in the morning... Allowing each passenger 14lb. weight, and all above 3*d* a pound. Performed by Benjamin Kingman, Henry Harrison, Walter Baynes.

(Haslehust, E.W., *York*)

———— ◆ ————

**1976:** The official closure date for seven public conveniences passed by almost unnoticed, after a review of York's essential services. Lack of usage, costs of supervision, maintenance and repair, as well as vandalism, prompted the Corporation to propose closure of urinals at Baile Hill, Blue Bridge Lane, Dennis Street, Fourth Avenue, Melrosegate, Micklegate Bar and Walmgate Bar. A three-month period was allowed for objections, but in fact only eight objections were received and the closures went ahead as planned. (Murray, H., *Where to Go in York*)

# April 13th

**1885:** George Leeman's contribution to the civic and industrial life of York and area was marked by the unveiling of a statue in Station Road (re-named Leeman Road at the same time). The life-sized standing figure of Leeman, sculpted in white marble, is displayed on a pedestal of red granite with a moulded top section and base. An inscription on the west side of the pedestal has the words 'GEORGE LEEMAN', while the east side provides information stating that the statue was erected by public subscription. A curious and fictitious story claims that the Leeman statue was in fact a statue of George Hudson ('the Railway King'), which was stored away when he 'lost all credibility' and later re-worked as Leeman. The statue was the focus of a thorough cleaning exercise under the guidance of William Anelay, before Her Majesty Queen Elizabeth II's visit to York for Royal Ascot. Scaffolding was erected around the statue to allow close inspection, before a mixture of DOFF and TORC processes was applied to the figure of Leeman. On 24 June 1983 the George Leeman statue was given Grade II listed status. (www.britishlistedbuildings.co.uk; www.yorkpress.co.uk; www.williamanelay.co.uk)

# April 14th

**1516:** On this day, York's Mayor and Corporation welcomed Margaret, Queen Dowager of Scotland, on her journey southwards to visit her brother Henry VIII. This was her second visit to the city and she stayed overnight at St Mary's Abbey, before travelling by water to the pike garth, where she was entertained by Sir John Carr, High Sheriff. On 16 April, the Mayor, aldermen and other officials escorted the Queen and her entourage as far as St John's Church, Micklegate as she set out for Pontefract. Returning to Scotland the following year, Margaret Tudor was again entertained at St Mary's Abbey during the Whitsuntide period. (Benson, G., *An Account of the County and City of York*)

---

**1919:** According to newspaper billings, a new musical craze, in the form of jazz, was making an appearance in York. At the Empire, John, Harry and Burt Lester were listed to perform, featuring the latest London and American craze, 'The Jazz Band'. A reviewer stated that the show at the Empire was of a good standard. He said the act provided by John, Harry and Burt Lester 'is a novelty to York audiences in as much as they introduce the jazz band and dances which were exceptionally well received.' (*Yorkshire Evening Press*)

# April 15th

**1777:** Sarah Siddons was appearing at York Theatre Royal for a month-long engagement during the early stages of her acting career. Born on 5 July 1755 at Brecon in Wales, she was the eldest daughter of Roger Kemble, an actor-manager with his own travelling company of players which included most members of his family. Acting was only just becoming a respectable profession for a woman and she had to overcome initial doubts from her family about her choice of profession. A first appearance at Drury Lane in 1775 had proved to be a failure and from 1777, she spent some six years with provincial companies (particularly in Bath and York). Tate Wilkinson, manager of York Theatre Royal at that time, said later, 'I never remembered so great a favourite, as a York actress, as Mrs Siddons was in that short period.' With a growing reputation, she returned to Drury Lane on 10 October 1782 and became an immediate sensation. For the next twenty years she was probably best known for her portrayal of Shakespeare's Lady Macbeth. Returning to York in 1786, she played eleven nights between 29 July and 28 August. One performance as 'Belvidera' in Otway's *Venice Preserved*, on 3 August, resulted in takings of £192, prompting Tate Wilkinson to state that it was 'the greatest receipt... she ever acted to at any theatre, at that time out of London'. (www.bbc.co.uk; 'The Theatre Royal', *York – York History,* No. 4)

# April 16th

**1570:** Guy Fawkes was baptised at the Church of St Michael-le-Belfry in Minster Yard. In his early years he attended St Peter's School in the city. At some point in his youth, he became a Roman Catholic and worked for the 1st and 2nd Viscount Montagu before moving to the continent as a soldier. Fighting under Sir William Stanley, an English Catholic who had switched sides to support Spain, Fawkes was a junior officer at the siege of Calais in 1596, before travelling to Spain in order to gain support for a Catholic rebellion in England. During 1604, Fawkes got involved with a small group of English Catholics led by Robert Catesby, whose aim was to assassinate James I and install Elizabeth as monarch. The conspirators acquired the lease on a property with an undercroft directly below the House of Lords' Chamber in parliament and barrels of gunpowder were stored there during the summer of 1605. Guy Fawkes was made responsible for lighting the fuse in the cellar when parliament re-assembled on 5 November 1605, but the plot began to unravel when a letter was sent to Lord Monteagle warning him of events on 5 November. The letter was shown to the King and, during a search of the cellars, Fawkes was detained and confessed to his involvement in the plot. The trial of eight of the plotters began on 27 January 1606, but the outcome was never in doubt: Fawkes and three others were executed in Old Palace Yard on 31 January 1606. (Fraser, A., *The Gunpowder Plot*)

# April 17th

**1851:** Ann Turner and Ann Robinson appeared in court on a charge of being common prostitutes and fighting in the Bedern area of York. A fifteen-year-old youth, Oswald Barker, was also charged with assaulting Ann Hunter at about 10.30 on the same evening. In evidence, it was said that she slapped his face but this led to him hitting her in the face with a half brick. The Lord Mayor saw no excuse for Barker's behaviour and sentenced him to twenty-one days' hard labour at the House of Correction. Five months later, plans were announced to improve Bedern, which, along with the Walmgate area of the city, had gained a reputation for crime and disorderly gatherings. (*York Herald*)

———— • ◆ • ————

**1903:** Licensing magistrates in York and elsewhere were turning down large numbers of applications, and moves were made to compensate licence holders who lost their livelihood through no fault of their own. On this day, the city's MP, John George Butcher, spoke to the Primrose League about a 'Licensing Law Compensation for Non-renewal Bill', which would give the full value of the licence from a compensation fund, either by a levy on the trade or by the proceeds of taxation. (*Yorkshire Evening Press*)

# April 18th

**1703:** A stagecoach service between York and London began on this day. Stage coaches were introduced into England in about 1625, but it was some time before they came into widespread use. The stagecoach could be a stagecoach proper, a mail coach, road coach and private coach. Drawn by four horses, there was seating for four or six people inside and up to twelve on the roof. Stages were arranged at about 10 mile intervals so that horses could be changed. By the end of the seventeenth century, there were only services on three of the country's principal roads though stagecoach services developed during Charles II's reign. The usual fare in the middle of his rule was a shilling for every 5 miles, with some 40 or 50 miles travelled each day. (Knight, C.B., *History of the City of York*; http://yourarchives. nationalarchives.gov.uk)

# April 19th

**1885:** The first Military Sunday at York Minster was held on this day in accordance with arrangements made by the Dean, the Very Reverend A.P. Purey-Cust, as a memorial service for General Gordon, who had been killed in Khartoum the previous January. This service was subsequently repeated as an annual event until the outbreak of the Second World War in 1939, and was usually attended by all the regular and territorial troops stationed in the city. The spectacle of the parading soldiers before and after the services caused the event to gain extraordinary popularity. The city would be crowded with thousands of visitors arriving by rail and road, and bicycles were greatly in evidence. Pedestrian parties from considerable distances, many of whom walked through the previous night, were a notable development. (Knight, C.B., *History of the City of York*)

———◆———

**1920:** The Ministry of Health outlined its reasons for turning down proposals by the city council and York Dispensary to buy Acomb Hall and 53 acres of land at a cost of £12,000, for use as a maternity hospital. (*York Herald*)

# *April 20th*

**1768:** Formed on 20 April 1768, the Ancient Society of York Florists claims the record as 'the world's longest running horticultural show'. The foreword to the rules states, 'Happiness being the ultimate end of Society... and the cultivation of flowers, from their beautiful forms, lively tints and graceful odours regale the senses... and so the arts of sculpture, architecture and embroidery borrow assistance from foliage and flowers.' Records date back to 1768 and indicate that cash prizes and, later, silver medals, spoons and goblets were awarded to the grower of the best hyacinth, auricula, polyanthus, tulip, ranunculus and carnation. Added to the classes of entries were, gooseberries from 1785 to 1848, in 1826 geraniums and in 1829 dahlias. The Society held its shows and feasts at the Sand Hill, Colliergate and at Baynes Coffee House in Petergate, York, and although they allowed the introduction of new plants, they did not become a specialist society, but instead increased the number of shows to cater for the new range. Documents and official papers of the society still display the Royal Coat of Arms from the Queen Anne period, and King Edward VII and Queen Alexandra were patrons for many years up to their deaths. Current shows are held in the Conference Hall at Askham Bryan College. (www. ancientsocietyofyorkflorists.co.uk)

# April 21st

**1911:** A winding-up order was made against the owners of York's Sycamore Rink, the Victoria Pier Syndicate, when liabilities were stated to be £190. The rink's location outside the city contributed to its failure, but a rival venue in Fishergate fared little better and closed some three months later. The craze for roller-skating had turned out to be short term, as in most other places, with a large majority of people preferring to visit venues that showed movies. (*Yorkshire Evening Press*)

———◆———

**1913:** Suffragette activity in York was blamed for the discovery of a bomb – 'an infernal machine' – in the doorway of offices of the *Yorkshire Evening Press* in Coney Street. It was a timed device containing an accumulator and gun cotton which closely resembled those found on railings of the Bank of England in London. A potentially serious explosion was averted by the actions of a patrolling policeman, but it represented the most serious militant action in York. Suffragettes had already been blamed for the destruction of mail in the city by posting letters containing combustible liquid, labelled with the slogan 'Votes for Women'. (*Yorkshire Evening Press*)

# April 22nd

**1878:** The Lord Mayor of York laid the foundation stone of a building to house the Fine Art and Industrial Exhibition, in a ceremony preceded by a long procession from the Guildhall. The main party included aldermen and councillors, the city Sheriff, mayors of several Yorkshire towns, clergy and volunteers. A public luncheon was held in the De Grey Rooms after the ceremony. The exhibition catalogue described the front of the building as 'in the Italian style of architecture' and design work was credited to the York-based architect Edward Taylor. The square in front of the building was laid out at the same time. It continued in use as the Yorkshire Fine Art and Industrial Institute from its opening in 1880 until 1892, when it was sold to the council. The original building was about the same size as the present gallery, as it had a 'Great Exhibition Hall' at the rear. This large room was about six times the floor area of the present main gallery. It staged events such as boxing matches, but it was hit by a bomb during the Second World War and was demolished in 1942. (www.historyofyork.org.uk)

# *April 23rd*

**1938:** York Castle Museum opened on St George's Day 1938 in the city's former prison buildings. The Lord Lieutenant of the East Riding of Yorkshire performed the opening ceremony for period rooms, which showed everyday objects in context rather than in glass cases. The collection of objects had been assembled by Dr John Lamplugh Kirk – a young country doctor based in Pickering during the early 1900s. His assorted items, or 'bygones' as he termed them, included everything from furniture, farm equipment, fireplaces and shop fittings, to policemen's truncheons and Valentine's cards. He had offered his collection to other Yorkshire towns and cities but it was York, with prompting from Alderman J.B. Morell, that agreed to convert the old female prison. Highlights of the museum are undoubtedly the period rooms and two streets reconstructed indoors – one, a Victorian street complete with Hansom cab, pawnbroker's premises and tallow-candle factory, within the prison's open-roof exercise yard, and the other an Edwardian courtyard. Seventy years later, on Saturday, 26 April 2008, anniversary celebrations included activities such as making a birthday badge and decorating cakes with icing in the new Kitchen Studio, as well as viewing a new gallery – 'The Sixties'. (York Castle Museum press release; *AA Pocket Guide to York*)

# April 24th

**1904:** A red and white heifer being driven from York market to a butcher's shop at Micklegate Bar enlivened an afternoon when it escaped from its driver. The cow set off down Fishergate, Piccadily and moved on to Walmgate and then Fossgate, where it sought sanctuary in Messrs Slater's provision shop, wrecking the glass door as it charged in. The counter assistant fled into the back room, leaving the heifer in the shop, where it smashed a considerable amount of crockery. It was eventually driven out with the assistance of PC Covill and some bystanders, but rather than being caught, it set off on the rampage again, this time trying to gain access to Mr Whitehead's shop on Foss Bridge. In the process, 'taking two unoffending foot passengers from behind', it 'tossed them off their feet'. Next, it headed out of Walmgate towards Hull Road, scattering pedestrians in its path, knocking over two small boys and one woman carrying a pitcher of water, before the cow finally found her driver. Possibly recognising him, the heifer made a determined charge, using her horns to assist his passage over a wall. The heifer did not have a happy ending to her escapades. Driven to a field near Tang Hall Lane, she was slaughtered to prevent a 'second reign of terror'. (*Yorkshire Evening Press*)

# April 25th

**1816:** The first steam packet that ever came to York appeared in our river. It came from Selby and was called 'The Waterloo Steam Packet'. It commanded much attention and the new walk was crowded to behold it. According to Benson, in *The City and County of York*, vessels carrying 150 tons traded regularly between London and York, and others of half that burden between Hull and York, and others from York to Boroughbridge and Ripon. A packet from Newton, and another from Selby and Cawood, arrived and returned each Saturday, as well as a steam packet from thence to Gainsborough. Coal was brought up the Ouse in barges from Flockton, Haigh Moor and Silkstone. The Foss was navigable to Stillington. (*A New Guide for Strangers and Residents*, 1838)

———◆———

**1912:** *The Titanic on her Fatal Voyage* was the film showing at York's Victoria Hall on this day, at a time when cinema-going was extremely popular. During the following month, a feature film on the Crimean War was accompanied by an invitation to the city's veterans to attend the showing, and as an added attraction 'The Electric' began to employ a violinist as well as a pianist. (*Yorkshire Evening Press*)

# April 26th

**1662:** King Charles II issued the Royal Charter of Incorporation of the Company of Merchant Taylors of the City of York. The first reference to Taylors was in 1273, when they were called 'Tayleurs' and were licensed to export wool, but the earliest mention of a guild organisation appears in ordinances and registers of members dating from 1387. During the medieval period, the tailors were closely linked with the religious brotherhood of St John the Baptist and it was this organisation that built the present hall. York tailors wielded considerable influence in social and economic aspects of the city's business and played an important part in the well-known sequence of York Corpus Christi mystery plays. Apprentice registers dating from 1605 indicate that about one fifth of boys were from the city and nearly all others were from adjacent villages. Until the 1830s, the Merchant Taylors' Co., which had a few women members, was primarily a working body of middle-ranking master tailors and their hall continued in use for a range of social, educational and theatrical uses. During the Victorian period the hall was used as an elementary school and since the late 1930s, the Great Hall and the Little Hall have been systematically restored to their earlier splendour. (www. merchant-taylors-york.org)

# April 27th

**1769:** On this day, the first mass was held in Mother Aspinal's new chapel beneath its magnificent neo-classical dome, but it was not until 1791 that the chapel obtained a licence as a public place of worship, following the second Catholic Relief Act of 1791. The community of nuns who currently reside at the Bar Convent belong to the Congregation of Jesus, which was established by the Yorkshire woman Mary Ward (1585–1645) and the Bar Convent itself was established in 1686 by Frances Bedingfield. He was an early member of Mary Ward's institute and responded to Sir Thomas Gascoigne's statement that 'We must have a school for our daughters', by purchasing a modest seventeenth-century property for the sum of £450. Initially, it was a boarding school for Catholic girls, but in 1699 it became a free day-school. The community survived persecution and poverty in early years, before their debts were cleared by Ann Aspinal, who joined the community in 1727. During the 1760s, Mother Aspinal and the architect cooperated on the demolition of the original house and the construction of the Georgian property. Members of the community ran the school for 299 years, but in 1985 it was transferred to the Diocese of Middlesbrough and became part of the All Saints' Catholic School. The Bar Convent is still home to Mary Ward's religious order, the Congregation of Jesus, and the Grade I listed buildings continue to be open to the public as a museum. (www.bar-convent.org.uk)

# April 28th

**1770:** David Hartley, widely known as 'King of the Coiners', was executed along with an accomplice, James Oldfield, at Tyburn on the outskirts of York. During the mid-eighteenth century, much of the coining activity in this country took place in the Cragg Vale district of Calderdale in West Yorkshire, where the acknowledged leader was David Hartley. It is believed that he gained his know-how as a coiner in Birmingham and, back in the remote setting of Bell House in Cragg Vale, was assisted by his brothers, Isaac and William. The first evidence against the Cragg Vale coiners appeared in a letter written in October 1767 by a William Hutchinson, but it was some two years later that a government enquiry reported on the practice of clipping and coining in the Calderdale area. A new Supervisor of Taxes, William Deighton, was appointed and he soon enlisted the aid of a known coiner, James Broadbent of Sowerby. David Hartley was arrested at the Old Cock Inn at Halifax on 17 October 1769 and taken under close guard to York Castle, along with a person named Jagger. Some six months later, in April 1770, Hartley was sentenced to death for clipping and diminishing the gold coin. (*Leeds Mercury*; Roth, H.L. *The Yorkshire Coiners 1767 to 1783*)

# April 29th

**1942:** For more than an hour, some forty German aircraft dropped a mixture of incendiary and high explosive bombs around the city, becoming known as the Baedeker Raid. York Minster was not seriously damaged, but Rowntree's original North Street factory, along with large supplies of sugar, burned fiercely and the Guildhall was soon reduced to a burnt-out shell. Telecommunications in the city were wrecked and even though the nearness of the river provided fire fighters with a constant supply of water, the railway station was also severely damaged by fire. Outside the city, the airfield suffered severe bomb damage. Before this sustained air raid, York had received 780 alerts, but only four people had died (on three separate occasions), when stray bombs had been dropped. Public shelters had remained largely unused during these previous raids. There had been a possible indication of an impending raid on York with the earlier raids on Bath and Norwich, but the so-called Baedeker Raid claimed ninety-two lives and many more were injured. (Rothrie, N., *Baedeker Blitz*)

— • ◆ • —

**1992:** A commemorative plaque was unveiled in the National Railway Museum, where the bombs of 29 April 1942 fell in the running shed of the York North Depot, destroying two depots. (Appleby, K., *Britain's Rail Super Centres: York*)

# April 30th

**1648:** Extremely unpleasant events took place at a house in the Clifton area of York, known by the sign of the 'maypole', in the late 1640s. Two young sisters had already been executed for their part in the poisoning of two men on the premises. Then another woman, Grace Bland, for some unknown reason, burned the house of the 'maypole' to the ground on this day in April. She went to the gallows on the same day. Six other women were found guilty of various crimes and fourteen men were convicted of rebellion. (Naismith, J.S., *Tales from the York Scaffold*)

---

**1919:** Plans were announced for a new picture palace to open, to be called 'The Grand'. Impressive dimensions included a 'hall' measuring 120ft by 40ft with a capacity for 1,000 patrons, as well as shops and a café at the entrance. On the floor above there was to be a ballroom (73ft by 30ft) with a maple sprung floor. This entertainment venue, with an entrance on Clarence Street, was also to be 'one of the most hygienic houses in the country'. The Grand opened on 10 November 1919. (*Yorkshire Evening Press*)

---

**1992:** The redesigned layout of St Sampson's Square, incorporating a new lavatory with access on street level, was opened by Councillor Bob Fletcher, chairman of the planning committee and Hugh Bayley, MP for York. (Murray, H., *Where to Go in York*)

# May 1st

**1946:** Sir Edward Cuthbert Bairstow, an English organist and composer, died in York on this day. Born on 22 August 1874, his training as an organist included tuition with John Farmer at Balliol College, Oxford and Walter Alcock at Westminster Abbey. He became a Bachelor of Music in 1894 and Doctor of Music in 1901. After spells in London, Wigan and Leeds, Edward Bairstow became organist at York Minster in 1913 and remained there until his death. He was knighted in 1932. Bairstow soon built a reputation for plain, direct comment, which was not always well received. When asked if he would follow the example of York's previous organist, Thomas Tertius Noble, by moving to the United States of America, he replied that he 'would rather go to the Devil'. With his roots firmly established in Yorkshire, Edward Bairstow built a close friendship with Dr Moody, organist at Ripon Cathedral, and declined the offer to succeed Frederick Bridge at Westminster Abbey. Most of Bairstow's compositions were church music, including twenty-nine anthems. He also composed instrumental pieces, mainly for the organ. Of the twelve that were published in his lifetime, the 1937 'Sonata in E flat' is probably the most highly regarded. He also composed a small amount of chamber music, including a set of variations for two pianos and another set for piano and violin. (Jackson, F., *The Life and Works of Edward C. Bairstow*)

# May 2nd

**1916:** The horrors of modern warfare were brought home to North Yorkshire with Zeppelin raids on coastal targets during December 1914, but it was some time later that York came under attack, with the most serious of raids on the city on 2 May 1916. At about 10.30 p.m. the slow-moving shadow of a German airship was picked out in the night sky above York. During the next ten minutes, eighteen bombs were dropped, causing nine deaths and forty more injuries. Among the casualties were George and Sarah Avison, who were killed instantly by a direct hit on their home in Upper Prince Street. Full details of this raid, and two other Zeppelin attacks in 1916, were withheld because of war-time censorship measures (they were only released on 2 May 1956), but there was widespread fear of further raids. A number of local people were subsequently prosecuted for showing lights at night. (www.historyofyork.org.uk)

# May 3rd

**1961:** Stephen McLaren was born on this day in the Fulford area of York. He attended Nunthorpe Grammar School, on the opposite side of the city, in order to develop his range of sporting activities. As a professional soccer player, McLaren was a midfielder with clubs in the lower English leagues, most notably with Hull City, where he played 178 games and scored sixteen goals. When his playing career ended in 1992, Steve McLaren began a coaching career that took him to Oxford United and Derby County, before he joined Alex Ferguson at Manchester United. United won 'the treble' of titles and McLaren gained a reputation as a fine tactical coach, before moving to Middlesbrough FC as manager in 2001. The high-point of his managerial career came on 1 August 2006, when he was appointed as England manager. His tenure of the post lasted just eighteen games in sixteen months. In June 2008, Steve McLaren became manager of Twente in Holland and, after winning their first championship, he was named 'Dutch Manager of the Year'. During 2010, he left Twente to join the German side Wolfsburg, but on 7 February 2011 a poor run of results resulted in his sacking. (BBC press reports, 2000–11)

# May 4th

**1684:** A wealth of folklore surrounds the life and career of Will Nevison, who was hanged at Knavesmire on this day. Born in the 1630s or 1640s, he seems to have had a number of names, ranging from John Nevison or Nevis to Johnson, and is said to have been dubbed 'Swift Nick' by King Charles II. Nevison's exploits are bound up in ballads and folklore, but after becoming a villain at an early age in this country, he moved to the Netherlands, where he was imprisoned for theft. After escaping from captivity, Will Nevison fought with English regiments before returning to England to continue his criminal career. Back in Yorkshire he soon earned a reputation as an extortionist, murderer and highwayman. His exploits assumed even greater proportions and there were reports that he made an epic journey of 220 miles from Kent to York in just one day. This escapade ensured his acquittal on a charge of robbery in Kent, but he was finally betrayed at an inn, The Magpie, in Sandal Magna. Arrested by Captain William Hardcastle, Will Nevison was taken to York Castle and, following a trial, was hung on the Knavesmire on 4 May 1684. (www.jss.org.uk; Holmes, S., *Nevison the Highwayman*)

# May 5th

1873: Some projects involving river crossings are lengthy and complicated, but provision of a bridge to replace the Skeldergate ferry across the Ouse at York was relatively speedy. On 5 May 1873, York City Council set up a committee to consider the question of a bridge. At the meeting, some three months later on 4 August, the committee produced a report in which they supported the planned bridge. The next step involved making application to parliament for appropriate powers to begin work. It was decided that Thomas Page, engineer of the Lendal Bridge, should be approached about the new project. The anticipated cost of the Skeldergate Bridge scheme was about £20,000 and Mr Page visited York in October and November for preliminary tours and to inspect the site. When the lease of the ferry expired in February 1874 the council retained it, and by the following month Thomas Page had prepared plans for a 'fixed' bridge with a single arch spanning 150ft. Representation by river users on 6 May 1874 led to a revised plan for a bridge with an opening span and this was ratified by ratepayers at a public meeting on 25 September 1874. (Knight, C.B., *History of the City of York*)

# May 6th

**1708:** Wool merchants had long since disappeared from street scenes in York, when the wool market was revived in St Anthony's Hall on 6 May 1708. A wool fair was also held in Peaseholme Green every Thursday from Lady-day to Michaelmas, where fleeces from the north and eastern areas were sold in large numbers to customers from western parts. In a similar vein, a leather fair was held on the first Wednesday in March, June, September and December. (*Baines' Gazetteer*, 1823)

———◆———

**1832:** Fire had swept through the choir area of York Minster during 1 and 2 February 1829, but a large public subscription raised funds towards the £65,000 repair project, and the newly-restored choir was opened on this day in May. During the blaze, the roof, woodwork and walls above arches of the choir were either destroyed or seriously damaged, while the organ was burnt out and communion plate melted. Restoration work was completed under Sir Robert Smirke's direction. Another result of Jonathan Martin's arson attack was that the Chapter decreed that 'henceforth a watchman shall be employed to keep watch every night in and about the cathedral' and, in addition, the Minster Police was established. (www.sacred-destinations.com)

# May 7th

**1574:** An order was made stating that none of the inhabitants of Huntington would have any dung or manure from within the city suburbs, or liberties, nor any citizen suffer any inhabitant of Huntington to carry and bear away any dung or manure, on pain of 3*s* 4*d* for every default. This legislation was passed because the inhabitants of Huntington impounded certain cattle belonging to free citizens of York as they were going to Stockton Common. (Knight, C.B., *History of the City of York*)

———◆◆———

**1844:** In April 1887 T.S. Noble, secretary of the Yorkshire Philosophical Society, cited a Deed of Arrangement dated 7 May 1844, when he reminded the council that they had covenanted not to construct any building on the Esplanade near Lendal Tower. During the 1860s and '70s, urinals had been completed: at the Cattle Market in 1862, at Castle Mills Bridge during 1865, and at Victoria Bar in 1866. Another was completed during 1866 at a newly-created breach in the medieval defences. In spite of Mr Noble's objection, the network of urinals was completed with a building on the Esplanade, near Lendal Tower, and those near the walkway on the walls were fitted with a modesty screen in the form of a roof. (Murray, H., *Where to Go in York*)

# May 8th

**1348:** References to murage grants differ for individual townships, with taxation of different articles varying according to the local trade or peculiar local circumstances:

1348 May 8th: To the mayor and bailiffs of York. Order to supersede the demand made upon William De Dunolm, the King's merchant for 16d a sack on 281 sacks 15½ stones 3 pounds of wool, in the name of toll and murage, and to de-arrest without delay the wool arrested for that cause, permitting William or his attorney to take the wool to the port of Kyngeston-upon-Hull, as the King charged William to take the said wool of counties Cumberland and Westmoreland to that port and thence to Flanders and to do the King's pleasure there with the same, and the King has learned that the mayor and bailiffs exact 12d murage and 4d for toll on each sack of that wool, passing through that city to the said port, and have arrested the wool for that cause, and the King has not hitherto been bound to pay any toll or custom to his subjects on his wool or any other of his things.

(Cal. Close Rolls 1343–1346, p. 101)

# May 9th

**1153:** William Fitzherbert, a nephew of King Stephen, was installed as Archbishop of York on this day. He possessed the unusual distinction of having been Archbishop twice, both before and after his rival, Henry Murdac. Deposed in 1147, William Fitzherbert worked hard to achieve his second term of office as Archbishop following Murdac's death in 1153. During the procession for his enthronement, a wooden bridge over the Ouse collapsed, but there was no loss of life. This was attributed to the prayers of Archbishop William. However, he lived for only thirty days following his enthronement; allegedly he was the victim of poisoning. From 1177, miracles were reported at this tomb, and in the year 1227 he was declared a saint. (www. historyofyork.org.uk)

———•◆•———

**1943:** On this day, Vince Cable was born in York. He attended Nunthorpe Grammar School before studying economics at Cambridge University, where he was president of the Students' Union. After holding a number of advisory posts, including work with the Kenyan government and Commonwealth Secretary General, he became Liberal Democrat MP for Twickenham in 1997. Between 2003 and 2010 he was the main Liberal Democrat economics spokesman and in May 2010, he was appointed Secretary of State for Business, Innovation and Skills in the coalition government. (BBC press articles)

# May 10th

**1257:** Sewal de Bovill, Archbishop of York, died on this day. In his early life, he was a pupil of St Edmund Rich at Oxford and during 1240, he was appointed both Dean of York and Prebendary of Fonton. Fifteen years later, he was elected as Archbishop and although the King initially refused to sanction his appointment on account of his illegitimacy, the Pope granted a dispensation and he was consecrated by de Cantilupe, Bishop of Worcester. Very soon de Bovill clashed with the Pope over the nomination of an Italian, Jorden, to the Deanery of York and this resulted in his initial suspension and then excommunication. Apart from serving on a commission attempting to negotiate an agreement between Alexander of Scotland and his nobles, he played no part in politics and built a reputation for his knowledge in areas such as science, law and theology. Following his death, Sewal de Bovill was buried in the south transept of York Minster. (Hart, A.T., *Ebor: The Archbishops of York*)

# May 11th

**1840:** A major railway landmark was achieved when the first direct train ran from York to London on this day in May. George Hudson, 'the Railway King', convinced George Stephenson of the merits of building the line through York rather than bypassing it, and the impact on the city was considerable. Travel by stage-coach declined, but other aspects of York's business and trade were rejuvenated. People and products were transported to and from York more rapidly than ever before and new markets opened up for entrepreneurs. By the 1850s, thirteen trains each day were carrying 341,000 passengers every year, and this facilitated a dramatic increase in tourism. Within two years of the first train steaming into York, there were excursions to York from Manchester, Nottingham and London, while theatre-goers converged on York's Theatre Royal from miles around. Huge numbers of people also attended two fine art exhibitions, one in 1860 and the other 1879, at York Art Gallery. Apart from boosting heavy industry in York, railways brought less obvious benefits as well, such as two postal deliveries each day (leading to the building of a main post office in Lendal in 1884). (www.historyofyork.org.uk)

# May 12th

**1791:** It seems that it was not until the late eighteenth century that the principal of the 'encore' was established in England and the first occasion was in York – on 12 May 1791. A performance was being given for the theatre doorkeeper's benefit and the last item on the bill was 'The Conjuring Song' by a Miss Reynolds. During this rendition, a cake, a leg of lamb and a lawyer in a sack were conjured in sequence with the words of the song, and at the end the audience demanded an encore. The singer thought it was absurd to repeat the routine and left the stage before the curtain was brought down. Members of the orchestra then left the theatre, but instead of calming the scene, matters got worse. Tate Wilkinson, the theatre manager, appeared on the stage in an attempt to placate the audience, only for a volley of candlesticks, branches and flaming candles to be thrown at his head with shouts of 'knock the insolent fellow down'. This chaotic scene was only resolved when the band returned to their places and the song was re-sung, among debris including grease and broken brass pieces. (Heape, R. Grundy, *Georgian York*)

# May 13th

**1809:** Beilby Porteus, Bishop of London, died on this day after a life-time of service in the Anglican Church. Born in York on 3 May 1731, he was the youngest but one of nineteen children and after schooling at Ripon, he studied at Cambridge University. Soon after his marriage in 1756, he became rector of Hunton in Kent and held a number of other posts before becoming Bishop of Chester in 1776. Some eleven years later, he succeeded Dr Lowth as Bishop of London. During his time as Bishop of Chester, Porteus gained a reputation for campaigning against slavery. Apart from preaching about the 'plight of West Indian Negro slaves', he also took part in many debates in the House of Lords on the subject. With a reputation as a scholar and fine preacher, he used an invitation to preach the anniversary sermon of the Society of the Propagation of the Gospel in Foreign Parts to explain his views. He criticised the church's lack of action over the plight of slaves on its Codrington Estates in Barbados and outlined ways in which the prospects of slaves at that location could be improved. (*York and its Vicinity for the Resident and Tourist*, Porteus research project)

# May 14th

**1850:** Joseph Murgatroyd earned a distinctly scandalous reputation in York during the early 1850s. On this day, he appeared before magistrates at the Guildhall following an incident during the previous evening, a Monday, in the Shakespeare Tavern near the Minster. He had sampled the landlord's rum and then requested food, 'in the shape of teas and other good things'. Landlord William Braithwaite was probably aware of Murgatroyd's notorious reputation and refused to serve him. At this point, Joseph Murgatroyd smashed three squares of window glass. In court he admitted to previous court appearances, but could not remember which of his names he had used. Unable, or unwilling, to pay the 6s damages, he was sentenced to two months' hard labour. Sadly, Joseph Murgatroyd's behaviour did not improve and he came before the court again in September 1852 and November 1855, when he received similar sentences of hard labour. (*York Herald*)

———•———

**1989:** The opening of the new York Integrated Electronic Control Centre meant closure of signal boxes at York Yard South, York Yard North and Skelton, and interfacing with other power boxes at Doncaster, Church Fenton and Selby, to the south and Tollerton, Poppleton and Strensall. (Appleby, K., *Britain's Rail Super Centres: York*)

# May 15th

**1953:** The Borthwick Institute for Archives was officially opened in the fifteenth-century St Anthony's Hall on Peaseholme Green. It represents one of the largest archive repositories outside London and includes probate and parish records for the Diocese of York, local Health Trust papers, records of local families and the University of York Archive. It is now housed in a new purpose-built property adjacent to the J.B. Morrell Library on the University of York's Heslington Campus. (Borthwick Institute for Archives)

———•◆•———

**2006:** York Cold War Bunker opened its bomb-proof doors to the public for the first time. Now under the management of English Heritage, the bunker was built in 1961 and operated by the United Kingdom Warning and Monitoring Organisation. It was staffed by the Royal Observer Corps, who would record, monitor and disseminate information on nuclear attacks. The bunker was decommissioned in 1991 after the signing of a non-aggression treaty between NATO and the Warsaw Pact countries. Apart from the Operations Room, the other rooms (officers' room, telephone exchange and dormitories) are open for viewing by members of the public. (www.english-heritage.org.uk)

# May 16th

**1889:** Thomas Pumphrey, an inspector of cruelty to children, called at the Waggon and Horses early on this day and requested a room for the night, as he was feeling fatigued. The landlord, Thomas Thompson, showed him to a room and later joined him for drinks. When Mr Pumphrey handed over money for the drinks, the landlord noticed blood on his hands and then more around a jagged wound on his neck. It became clear that he needed help and Thomas Thompson took him to the county hospital, where checks showed that the wound measured 2ins in length and was half an inch deep. He spent several days in hospital and a week later, he was charged with attempted suicide. Thomas Pumphrey's defence was that he was suffering serious stress from a broken engagement and from his mother's illness. He was safely held in custody until his brother arrived a week later to care for him. (*York Herald*)

———◆———

**1906:** An Education Bill provoked a storm of opposition from members of the Church of England in York. Canon Argles chaired a meeting at which W.F.H. Thompson, the Liberal Unionist, declared, '...of all the Bills that were ever before the country... this is the most astonishing, most impudent and most impossible.' (*Evening Post*)

# May 17th

**1984:** The Jorvik Centre in the city's Coppergate area was officially opened by the Prince of Wales. During 1972, a small-scale excavation by York Archaeological Trust provided evidence of early settlement in the Coppergate area, and in May 1976 aspects of the Viking era were exposed. The area under excavation was widened to cover 1,000 square metres and between 1976 and 1981, teams of archaeologists were able to carefully trowel their way through 2,000 years of York's history. A total of around 40,000 archaeological contexts were recorded by the York Archaeological Trust. Apart from establishing the construction and layout of buildings in which townsfolk lived and worked, the site provided clear evidence of how people bought and sold goods, of their diet, and of how they spent their leisure time. Jorvik Viking Centre reproduces aspects of tenth-century life through a series of tableaux, illustrating shops, street scenes and daily life. It then shows how the site was investigated by archaeologists before exhibiting actual artefacts. (Jorvik Viking Centre press material)

# May 18th

**1812:** This advertisement was featured in a local newspaper:

Fashionable Millinery Rooms
MRS MORGAN
Respectfully informs the Ladies of York and its environs,
that her Elegant and Fashionable Assortment of Millinery,
Dresses etc. adapted to the present season, will be ready for
inspection in the course of next week. Mrs Morgan begs to
assure her friends, that as every attention has been paid in
selecting the most fashionable articles, she flatters herself
they will meet general approbation. An early inspection will
be esteemed a favour... Coney Street, May 18th 1812.

(*The York Herald*)

———— ◆ ————

**2010:** Peter Gibson OBE, former Superintendent of Works at
York Glazier's Trust, received Honorary Freemanship of the
city for services to York churches, particularly the Minster.
Born within Minster Close, he joined the glazier's workshop in
1945 and became an expert on conservation of medieval stained
glass. In 1967, he became the first superintendent of the newly
formed Glazier's Trust and held the post until his retirement
in 2003. The most challenging phase of Peter Gibson's career
came in July 2004, after fire destroyed much of the Minster's
South Transept and caused severe cracks in the Rose Window.
(www.bbc.co.uk/news)

# May 19th

**1633:** King Charles I made several visits to York during the Civil War period and on this day, the order of the council stated, 'And now it is ordered there be Trumpeterrs on the out syde of Micklegatebarr yf they can be gotten and cornettes on the insyde to sound at His Maiesties entrance into the Cittye.' Following the King's visit on 19 May, there was reference to '…the waites sounding and playing on their Cornettes on both sydes of the gaite…' but there is no word of trumpeters. (Merryweather, J., *York Music*)

———◆———

**1889:** Suspicious behaviour outside the Wool Pack Inn on this Sunday morning in May, caused PC Alp and Blackburne to question a woman who was hiding an item under her apron. It transpired that the landlady, Elizabeth Milner, had given her the tin bottle of beer the previous night. Mrs Milner appeared at the Guildhall the following Wednesday on a charge of selling intoxicating liquor outside permitted hours. She explained that during her fifteen years at the Wool Pack, there had been no complaints against her or her husband and the case was dismissed. (*York Herald*)

# May 20th

**1878:** The imposing, five-storey Royal Station Hotel opened for business on this day, one year after the new station opened (and replacing the earlier Station Hotel that stood adjacent to the first station). Within the yellow Scarborough brick walls there were spacious banqueting rooms and a hundred large bedrooms, each at a cost of 14s per night. A twenty-seven roomed west wing was added in 1896 and given the title 'Klondyke', after the US gold rush of that time. Following a visit by Queen Victoria on her way to Balmoral, the designation 'Royal' was added to the original name. (www.historyofyork. org.uk)

———— •◆• ————

**2010:** York's main library on Museum Street re-opened after a major alteration and refurbishment programme. The scheme was a result of a partnership between York Council and Aviva, which saw £540,000 invested to convert the space into a state-of-the-art 'Explore Centre'. Figures released in February 2011 showed nearly a 60 per cent increase in children's fiction borrowing during the eight months since the alterations were completed. (*Yorkshire Post*)

# May 21st

**1864:** Violence erupted at the Queen's Head in Fossgate when an Irishman, Thomas Palfreman, approached a table where four labourers were sitting and offered to fight any of them for a shilling. As one of the labourers stood up to get a light for his pipe, Palfreman landed a blow on his face and then kicked him in the ribs as he fell. Witnesses stated that another of the group around the table, John Foy, struck Palfreman in the face and a general meleé ensued. A dramatic conclusion was reached when Palfreman stumbled with a severe stomach wound. The police arrived on the scene and everyone at the inn was arrested. The next day, a long-bladed knife was discovered in the kitchen where the stabbing had happened and John Foy was convicted of manslaughter, with twenty years' penal servitude following Palfreman's death from his injuries. (*York Herald*)

———— ◆ ————

**1913:** Victoria Hall, one of York's extremely popular picture houses, showed a local sporting event: the York City versus Rotherham United football match. (*Evening Press*)

# *May 22nd*

**1913:** The controversial issue of Sunday opening for shops exercised many minds, and the Wesleyan minister, Reverend Stanley Parker added fuel to the debate by announcing, from the pulpit of Wesley Chapel, 'Sunday openers are nothing more nor less than blacklegs.' In 1902, the council had passed a resolution that shops in York should close on Sundays and that any offenders would be prosecuted, but no further action had followed until, in 1913, a group of sabbatarians presented a petition with 1,187 signatures and called for action on the matter. A vote by the council showed a large majority in favour of Sunday closure and the measure was implemented. Support for this move had come not only from councillors connected with groups such as Wesleyans and Quakers, but also from others who argued that shops should close on Sundays so that workers got a day of rest. On the other hand, some locals saw this development as a planned conspiracy by larger shopkeepers against small businesses. Prosecutions for Sunday trading were made and the issue continued to feature prominently in York's local government circles until November 1913. (*Evening Press*)

# May 23rd

**1823:** 'As two troops of soldiers were assembling in Thursday Market one of the horses became unruly and whilst plunging their hooves the pavement gave way and exposed a deep well built round with stone. It was traced back to 1688 along with the old Market Cross and Guard Room which stood there...' (*New Guide to the City of York for Strangers and Residents*, 1838)

———— • ◆ • ————

**1919:** A canteen providing food and drink to servicemen travelling through York railway station closed on this day, having opened on 15 November 1915. It represented an aspect of the war effort in the city during the First World War. An internment camp was established in the Castle Yard with another in a field adjacent to Leeman Road. The Cattle Market was adapted as a horse depot and considerable numbers of horses passed from here to Holgate railway dock. Among other local wartime measures, public buildings including chapels, schools and the Railway Institute were requisitioned for military use, while about 700 Belgian refugees were lodged, mainly in private houses. (Benson, G., *An Account of the County and City of York*)

# May 24th

**1834:** Joseph Rowntree was born in York on this day. He attended Bootham School in the city and at the age of fourteen, journeyed with his father to Ireland and witnessed the resulting distress of the potato famine. This experience is said to have provided a basis for his political views and business approach in later life. After starting as an apprentice in his father's business, Joseph took over the running of the company with his brother, John Stephenson Rowntree. In 1869, he joined another brother, Henry Isaac Rowntree, who owned a chocolate factory in York, and when Henry died in 1883, Joseph became owner of the company. He employed his own progressive ideas in setting up and then running a new factory that opened in 1881. These included the introduction of one of the first occupational pension schemes. Rowntree's company expanded from thirty to in excess of 4,000 employees by the end of the nineteenth century. A merger with John Mackintosh & Co. in 1969 was followed by take-over by Nestle in 1988. Joseph Rowntree's schemes to improve the quality of life for his work force included provision of a library, free education and the services of a dentist, doctor and social welfare officer. Three trusts were also set up: Joseph Rowntree Village Trust, the Charitable Trust and the Social Services Trust. ('Joseph Rowntree Biography' – *The Joseph Rowntree Foundation*)

# May 25th

**1379:** 'William Mynne, a shipman of Beningborough, fell from a ship in the River Ouse opposite St Mary's Abbey and was rescued in a dying condition. His rescuers, hoping that the Blessed Virgin might work a miracle on his behalf, hastened with him through the great gates of the Abbey at the bottom of Marygate, carried him into the chapel and laid him before the altar. Immediately they got him there he died and his soul was commended to God.' (Knight, C.B., *History of the City of York*)

———— •◆• ————

**1547:** A house of Treasurers of York Minster was surrendered with the post to the Crown on this day. It had been built in 1419 and continued as a home for the treasurer until 1547, when it was sold to Archbishop Holgate and then passed to Archbishops Heath and Young. During 1720, the building was divided into two, leaving Gray's Court, with its fine courtyard and twelfth-century foundations, separate from the current Treasurer's House. Frank Green carried out further alterations between 1897 and 1930, when he handed it over to the National Trust. Today the building contains a fine collection of medieval and seventeenth and eighteenth-century furniture and is well known for the sightings of ghostly legionaries in the early 1950s. (www.britainexpress.com)

# May 26th

**1642:** A document printed by Robert Barker, 'Printer to the King's most excellent Majestie', gives a brief insight into the working day of Charles I. It reports on a visit by Sir Edward Hyde to the King at York:

> When he came to the court, being about four of the clock in the afternoon, the King was at council upon the publishing his answer to the Declaration of the twenty-sixth of May; which though it contained eight or nine sheets of paper, he brought to the Board in his own handwriting; having kept the promise he had made at Greenwich to that hour, in writing out all the papers himself which had been sent to him; which had been a wonderful task he had imposed upon himself; so that he always spent more than half the day, shut up by himself in his chamber, writing: which was the most the Houses heard of him in London and which perplexed them very much.

(Parl. Hist. Vol. xi, p.138)

# May 27th

**1918:** William Steele Savage, holder of the Military Medal, died in action on the Western Front on this day in May. His name is inscribed on the Soissons Memorial, which commemorates those who died in the Battles of Aisne and Marne. Born to William and Rebecca Steele Savage of 6 Galtres Place, Townend Street, York, he was a member of the Army Cyclist Corps during later phases of warfare on the River Aisne. The original British Expeditionary Force had crossed the Aisne in August 1914 to the east of Soissons, and then re-crossed it on the western side in September. During the next three and a half years, this section of the battlefront was held by French troops, but the city remained within range of German artillery. At the end of April 1918, five divisions of Commonwealth forces were posted to the area, but during a fierce and sustained German attack they were pushed back across the Aisne, suffering 15,000 fatal casualties. The IX Corps was replaced by XII Corps, who took part in a successful counter-attack to regain lost ground. The Soissons Memorial was unveiled by Sir Alexander Hamilton-Gordon on 22 July 1928. It commemorates almost 4,000 British soldiers who died in the battles of Aisne and Marne and have no known grave. (www.commonwealthwargravescommission; *Yorkshire Evening Press*)

# May 28th

**1888:** The Markets Committee reported that a covered market could be erected on the site of the police-station premises in Silver Street for about £3,000. It was objected in the council meeting that the scheme was too small and that a site in Davygate could be obtained and utilised without any cost to the ratepayers. The question of sites remained unsettled and the subject was shelved for a later date. (Knight, C.B., *The City of York*)

---

**1920:** Delays in York's post-war housing programme were causing serious concern and the Lord Mayor and Councillors Petty and J.B. Inglis reported to the council on progress at Tang Hall on this day. If extra funding was not made available, Councillor Inglis forecast that work could slow to a halt. Government funding was not available, so a bonds scheme had been introduced with bonds bearing 6 per cent interest. They 'were issued in portions of £5 and upwards, repayable at par in five, seven or ten years'. Support for this scheme soon came from the Yorkshire Insurance Co. the Rowntree Co. and Sir John Butcher. (Peacock, A.J., *York 1918 to 1920*)

# May 29th

**1839:** In the early days of railway development, the Leeds and Selby line did not connect with any other railway. On this day in May, it was joined at York Junction (now Gascoigne Wood Junction) by the York and North Midland from York. This momentous occasion began with a breakfast 'of the most sumptuous description' at the Guildhall in York, where the directors of the North Midland Railway and the Great North of England Railway were invited guests. The Guildhall York and North Midland directors and guests formed a procession to a temporary station outside the city walls, close to the present Queen Street Bridge, as the station inside the walls was incomplete. (Hoole, K., *Regional History of the Railways of Great Britain, The North East,* Vol. 4)

---

**1906:** A civic procession provided a most undignified element to York's Military Sunday. The Lord Mayor, Robert Horton Vernon Wragge, invited the Lord Mayor of Sheffield as his guest and stated that the dignitary 'should have the position of honour behind the civic mace', with the Sheriff and senior Aldermen, as well as the Deputy Lord Mayor, following behind. The Sheriff did not accept this ruling and 'would not waive his claim to walk beside the Lord Mayor of the city, with the result that the three gentlemen walked abreast, the two Lord Mayors and the Sheriff.' (*Evening Press*)

# May 30th

**1885:** The Society for the Protection of Ancient Buildings held a meeting in the Corn Exchange to protest against what it described as 'the proposed destruction of certain churches in the city of York'. The basis of the protest was a scheme put forward by Archbishop Thomson to unite the following parishes: St Crux with All Saints, Pavement; St Sampson's with Holy Trinity, Kings Court, or Christ Church; St Mary, Castlegate with St Michael, Spurriergate; St Martin, Coney Street, with St Helen; All Saints, North Street with St John, Micklegate; and Holy Trinity, Micklegate with St Martin cum Gregory. The intention was to augment the value of the joint livings, not to destroy ancient buildings, although the fate of St Crux (demolished in 1887) gave some point to the society's protest. The Archbishop's scheme was subsequently considerably modified and only the first three of the proposed amalgamations were effected at that time. (Knight, C.B., *History of the City of York*)

# May 31st

**1982:** On this Monday, Pope John Paul II visited York and thousands of people gathered on the racecourse for the event. Estimates put the number of onlookers at about 210,000 as Pope John Paul arrived by Sikorski helicopter from Manchester for the visit, which lasted about one hour and twenty minutes. The earliest arrivals made their way to the racecourse from midnight, and at 8 a.m. the Bishop of Leeds, Right Reverend Gordon Wheeler, celebrated Mass for the many thousands of people who had already arrived at York to take up their places in the several dozens of enclosed areas positioned on the grass. The entire visit of Pope John Paul was based on the Seven Sacraments of the Roman Catholic Church and in York he celebrated 'Marriage and Family Life'. During his sermon he made reference to 'the hopes and ideals that sustain the Christian vision of marriage and family life'. Following the service at York, Pope John Paul was flown to Leeming Bar and then went by fixed-wing aircraft to Edinburgh as part of his pilgrimage through Scotland and then Wales. (www.bbc.co.uk)

# June 1st

**1863:** The death was reported of Tom Holtby, driver of the Edinburgh mail coach that arrived in York for the last time in 1842. (Development of the railway network had brought an end to mail-coach services up and down the country.) This occasion was celebrated with appropriate ceremonial trappings as the mail coach flew a black flag from its roof and Holtby passed the reins to Lord MacDonald. His lordship completed the drive into York with Holtby acting as guard. When he died, Tom Holtby was in his seventy-second year and his lengthy career in coaching had seen him rise from early employment as a stable hand at the Rose and Crown in Easingwold. His next position was as post boy and then box on a cross-country coach, before his skills with the whip saw Holtby gain a place on the London to Edinburgh *High Flyer* and then on the mail coach. A thrifty outlook during his coaching career left him comparatively wealthy and, in spite of losses through unfavourable investments, he left in excess of £3,000 at his death. (Harper, C.G., *The Great North Road, the old mail road to Scotland*)

# June 2nd

**1832:** The first case of cholera was reported in York on this day. As the density of the population increased in townships during the middle decades of the nineteenth century, outbreaks of cholera became a more frequent occurrence. Increased numbers of deaths, and the need to bury victims as soon as possible, put pressure on graveyards such as St Cuthbert's. The sheer volume of burials led to a rise in the height of the ground. Shallow graves gave off an appalling stench and as more soil was heaped on the burial areas the ground rose even further. Until the mid-nineteenth century, few houses had a piped water supply and householders relied on wells in yards or cellars, which were often beside the graveyards. A victim of the water-borne diseases, typhoid or cholera would be buried in the graveyard and infection would seep from their remains into the water supply. Water drawn from the well would be contaminated and the fatal disease would spread through members of the household. (www.visityork.org)

———— • ◆ • ————

**1902:** During the period 1900–1902, the authorities waged a 'crusade against motor cars', with a number of successful prosecutions for 'motor scorching' including J. Suggitt, who was convicted of driving above the legal limit of 12 miles per hour on this day. (*Yorkshire Evening Press*)

# June 3rd

**1642:** During the early summer of 1642, King Charles I was based in York and at the end of May he issued a proclamation ordering all ministers, freeholders, farmers and substantial copyholders to gather on Heworth Moor outside York on 3 June. Large numbers of people responded to the King's instruction, though contemporary estimates of tens of thousands of supporters are most probably grossly exaggerated. The King arrived on the moor with large numbers of retainers and a fully armed force of 800 foot soldiers and 500 horsemen. He addressed the gathering with a call for loyalty and support from his subjects. The crisis between Charles I and parliament had been developing for some time. On or around 20 May 1642, the King made arrangements for the next session of parliament to be transferred to York, but this was rejected by a vote in the House of Commons itself. A number of members from both Houses of Parliament travelled to York in support of Charles and, as the situation worsened, he organised the gathering on 3 June. Matters were brought to a head on 12 August when Charles issued a proclamation from 'Our Court at York', declaring his intention to raise his standard at Nottingham on the 22nd of the month. (Knight, C.B., *A History of the City of York*)

# June 4th

**1465:** George Neville, younger brother of the Earl of Warwick, was 'translated' to the See of York (meaning he was transferred from his previous post as Bishop of Exeter to become Archbishop of York). His actual enthronement as Archbishop took place in September 1465 at Cawood Castle in front of a huge number of guests, made up of clergy, nobility and family members. It was obviously of great importance for the Neville family to demonstrate their wealth and status by preparing a feast of enormous proportions. Guests are said to have consumed a whole range of poultry and wild birds including pigeons, peacocks, cranes, quails and swans, along with 608 pikes and bream, twelve porpoises and a number of seals. There were sheep, calves, pigs and capons, along with hot and cold venison pies, 4,000 dishes of jelly and a similar number of baked tarts, sugared delicacies and cakes. Guests also consumed some 300 tuns of ale and 100 tuns of wine at this grand feast. (www.britannia.com)

# June 5th

**1732:** Margaret Mason's Hospital in Colliergate, York, was founded under the terms of the widow's will. The three-storey building originally housed six poor widows who received £1 per year under the original benefaction, and a further 50s from the benevolence of the Countess of Conyngham (adding up to an annual total of £3 10s). The building was repaired in 1786, and during 1946 it was converted to five bed-sitting rooms. The hospital closed and became derelict in 1958. (www.british-history.ac.uk; *Baines' Gazetteer 1823*)

———◆———

**1911:** When the 'Electric' opened in York in the early days of June 1911, the city could boast four venues showing films on a regular basis, but on 5 June, one of these, Victoria Hall, suffered a serious fire. In addition to this blaze, there were other major fires at around this time in the Gas Company's property in Little Stonegate, at Boyes' Stores on Ouse Bridge and at a mill in Skeldergate. (*Yorkshire Evening Press*)

# June 6th

**1912:** On this day, the new lecture theatre was opened at the Yorkshire Museum by Dr T.G. Bonney. He was presented with his portrait, which had been painted by Mr William Orpen ARA. Opened in February 1830, the Yorkshire Museum was founded by the Yorkshire Philosophical Society to house their geological and archaeological collections, which had previously been stored in Ousegate. Four permanent collections at the museum have English designated collection status, which means that they are 'pre-eminent collections of national and international importance'. The biology collection contains 200,000 specimens, the majority of which are insects. The geology collection contains over 112,500 specimens of rocks, minerals and fossils, and most of the astronomy collection is kept in the observatory in Museum Gardens. The archaeology collection is made up of almost one million items that date from around 500,000 BC to the twentieth century. In 1992, the Yorkshire Museum paid £2,500,000 for the Middleham Jewel, a diamond-shaped pendant dating from about 1460, engraved with a picture of the Christian Trinity on the front and the Nativity on the back. This fine museum building has Grade I listed status and the lecture theatre is now known as the Tempest Anderson Hall. (www.yorksphilsoc.org.uk)

# June 7th

**1840:** During the first half of the nineteenth century, the Bedern area of York had some of the city's poorest housing set around half a dozen public houses, and often there were scenes of rioting and disorder. In the early hours of 7 June, noise from the Slipper public house wakened members of the Swales family in an adjacent property. From her bedroom, Mrs Swales could see through a window of the inn that a group of men were brawling. The next day the landlord of the Slipper, William Smith, appeared in court on a charge of allowing drunkenness on his premises. Giving evidence, Mrs Swales told the court that she had seen one of the accused, Thomas Pullen of Coffee Yard, waving a pair of fire tongs in the pub yard before leaving later with a woman who appeared to be drunk. Another key witness, George Hall, admitted he and four friends had been drinking heavily in the Cross Keys before seeking further refreshment in the Slipper. The landlord refused their demands for more ale and that is when the violence broke out. The Lord Mayor found the case against the landlord unproven, but gave him a warning about future trouble at the Slipper. (*York Herald*)

# June 8th

**1961:** On this day, the Duke of Kent married Katharine Worsley at York Minster, in a ceremony conducted by Dr Ramsay, Archbishop of York (who went on to become Archbishop of Canterbury). It represented the first royal wedding at York Minster since that of Edward III some 633 years ago. The reception was held at Hovingham Hall, in the bride's family home, and following the marriage she was styled as 'Her Royal Highness the Duchess of Kent'. Katharine Worsley was born at Hovingham Hall, the only daughter of Sir William Worsley and his wife, Joyce Brunner. She was educated at Queen Margaret's School near York and became a talented musician, playing the piano, organ and violin. The Duke of Kent performs royal duties on behalf of the Queen and is also president of the Wimbledon All England Lawn Tennis Club, as well as Grand Master of the United Grand Lodge of England, the governing body of Freemasonry in England and Wales. Although the Duchess has converted to Catholicism, the Duke retains his position in line of succession to the throne of England. (www. theroyalforums.com)

# June 9th

**1762:** An interesting insight into the life and times of the occupants of Fairfax House, Castlegate, in York can be found in receipts held by the decorator of Anne Fairfax's bedroom, Samuel Carpenter. On 9 June 1762 and 21 June 1763, he received the amounts of £9 and £21 as payment for his painting and decorating work at Fairfax House. The invoices also included payment for 'mock India paper' for the 'misses Bedchamber at 1s 3d yard'. A portrait of Anne is displayed above the fireplace in the bedroom. Painted in 1742 by Phillip Mercier, a French artist, it portrays her as a shepherdess. Anne was twice engaged to affluent Catholic gentlemen, but it seems that in both cases religious difficulties brought an end to the relationships. Anne's bedroom has on display a four-poster bed designed by Francis Johnson, in 'Chippendale' style, and some particularly impressive dressing chests and secretaires, which may have originated from Chippendale workshops. Also prominent are items of porcelain, including a pair of bowls showing the arms of the Dutch East India Co. (VOC) and a pair of *famille verte* plates from about 1725. (*Fairfax House, York*, York Civic Trust)

# June 10th

**1890:** Yorkshire County Cricket Club 1st XI played a match against Kent at the Wigginton Road ground on 9 and 10 June. It was Yorkshire's only first-class fixture to be played in the city, although the county's second team continued to play at this ground from 1920s to the late 1950s. (Yorkshire won the match by eight wickets after dismissing Kent for forty-six runs in their first innings. Three Kent players were noted as 'absent, injured' when they failed to arrive at the ground.) The Wigginton Road ground, originally known as 'Clarence Street', was prepared in time for the 1864 season by the newly formed Yorkshire Gentlemen's Cricket Club. It had cost between £700 and £800 for necessary work and annual rent was £50. A pavilion was constructed at the southern end of the ground and, later, a bowling green and tennis courts were completed at the Wigginton Road side. In the early 1960s, hospital authorities announced that they were ending the lease on the ground and the last cricket match was played between York 'A' and Bridlington CC in an East Yorkshire Cup match. The northern section of York Hospital now covers the site. (*York C.C. 1784–1984*, York Cricket Club; Draper, S., *Cricket Grounds of Yorkshire*; *White Rose Magazine*, August 1993)

# June 11th

**1788:** George Shaftoe was born on this day. Although his father was a mariner, George decided to return to the family trade of pipe making. As well as the long churchwarden pipes, clay pipes were also being made in a range of designs, with some bowls moulded to show inns and regiments. At the age of fourteen, George Shaftoe was apprenticed to Mark Hesp of Monkgate. His seven-year apprenticeship ended when he was twenty-one and a few weeks later, he married Hannah Gowland at All Saints, Pavement. They lived for a time in Petergate and then Goodramgate, during which time George worked as a journeyman pipe maker, but after a move to Walmgate he set up his own pipe-making business in Barleycorn Yard. George Shaftoe became a freeman of the city in 1814, but he died in 1821 at the age of thirty-two and was buried in the churchyard of St Denys, Walmgate. Following his death, his wife, Hannah, continued to run the pipe-making business for another seventeen years. (Shafto, R., *Shaftoes of York*)

# June 12th

**1899:** This poster appeared in the local press in June 1899:

Every Afternoon and Evening at 3 & 8 pm.
A series of
LECTURES
Upon OBJECT LESSONS, consisting of
The Actual Instruments of Torture
Now sanctioned by the Roman Church, used by the
Romanizing Clergy in the Church of England viz.
A SPIKED IRON CAGE
From the Kilburn Sisterhood, used for the Incarceration of
Children in their Orphanages
HAIR SHIRTS, ROPE, STEEL WHIPS
Armlets, steel with sharp points; Cinctures, steel with sharp
points to be worn round the waist, etc.

Models of the Rack, Stake, Iron Maiden
The lectures will be given by
Mr D. STEVENTON HYSLOP & MR. C.L. CLARKE
(of the Protestant Alliance, London)
Admission Free. Collection to defray Expenses
A few reserved seats, one shilling.
Questions may be submitted in relation to the subject at the
close of each lecture.

(Printed at the Yorkshire Herald Office)

# June 13th

**1910:** An interest in skating swept through York in the late Edwardian era, but by 1910 rinks were rapidly losing their appeal to members of the public. The Sycamore Skating Rink closed on 3 June 1910 and its rival in Fishergate continued in business only until summer 1911. Reports in local newspapers also suggested that the City Roller Skating Palace was experiencing difficulties and on 13 June 1910 an application was made for a licence 'to enable musical entertainments to be held there in place of roller skating'. In spite of this seeming change of direction, it reopened in September with space for 700 to 800 skaters and 5,000 spectators, but this seems to have been an optimistic move, for a month later it was reported that 'Kardoc, the Handcuff King and Jail breaker' was making an appearance at the venue. Such shows made little difference and when the enterprise folded, there were assets totalling just £8. There was yet another twist in the Palace's active life when it was purchased from the liquidator and re-opened during the late summer of 1911 to stage rink hockey matches. (*Yorkshire Evening Press*)

# June 14th

**2005:** The Royal Ascot Meeting was staged at York between 14 and 18 June 2005 and the Duke of Devonshire, the Queen's representative, reflected on the five days' events by stating, 'We are delighted to have staged such a successful, popular and high quality Royal meeting at York this year while Ascot's £185 million redevelopment is taking place.' The oldest race is the Gold Cup, which was first run in 1807 when it was won by 'Master Jackey', a three-year old who had already won a race at Ascot twenty-four hours earlier. In order to stage races like the Gold Cup over 2½ miles and the Queen Alexandra Stakes, the Knavesmire track had to be lengthened with a fully cambered and drained three furlongs. (www.racingbetter.co.uk)

---

**2007:** At an awards ceremony in Athens, York was voted 'European Tourism City of the Year', beating 130 other cities, including Gothenburg (second) and Valencia (third place). A panel of judges said they were impressed by York's 'world class attractions, distinctive shopping, festivals and events'. Over the previous ten years, York had seen a 52 per cent increase in visitor spending and in 2006, there were nearly four million visitors. (www.bbc.co.uk/news)

# June 15th

**1612:** Sir Robert Watter, twice Lord Mayor of York, 'by his will proved 15th June 1612, appointed that a hospital should be erected out of his houses in Nowt-gate, which should be for the perpetual maintenance of ten persons; to consist of a reader or governor with £3 per annum and certain brothers and sisters to each of whom £2 per annum was to be allowed out of the lordship of Cundale.' By the time *Baines' Gazetteer* was compiled in the early 1820s, the number of dwellings had been reduced to seven and the reader 'no longer existed while only £14 was paid to the institution instead of 20 guineas annually'. (*Baines' Gazetteer*, 1823)

———— ◆ ————

**1912:** Plans to set up a professional football club in York moved slowly in the early months of 1912, but in June a prospectus of the new organisation was published. It was also decided that capital of £2,000 should be raised through 5s shares and a public meeting took place in June to improve sales, which had only reached £180. Directors stated they would only allot them when they had 2,000 subscriptions and the number of shareholders rose dramatically in the next few days. (*Yorkshire Evening Press*)

# June 16th

**1644:** St Mary's Tower is prominent at the corner of Bootham and Marygate and has occupied this position since 1325. Following the closure of the abbey by Henry VIII's commissioners in 1539, it was used to store documents and records of many Yorkshire monasteries, but during the early months of 1644, York was in the throes of a siege. At noon on this day in June, a mine was exploded beneath the tower by besieging forces under the command of the Earl of Manchester. The outer half of the structure collapsed, fatally injuring some of the defenders and destroying documents, although some were salvaged by Roger Dodsworth and lodged in York Minster Library. The tower was rebuilt in similar form to the original, using materials from a ruined section of the Manor, but the join is clearly visible on external stonework. It was given Grade I listed status on 14 June 1954 – almost exactly 310 years after its dramatic role in the English Civil War. (Butler, R.M., *Bars and Walls of York*)

# June 17th

**1800:** William Parsons, third Earl of Rosse, was born on this day in York. Following early schooling at Trinity College, Dublin, he graduated in 1822 from Magdalen College, Oxford University, with a first-class honours degree in Mathematics. Among public offices that he held, Parsons was MP for King's County from 1821 to 1834, president of the Royal Society (1848–54) and Chancellor of Trinity College, Dublin (1826–7). But he is probably best known for the construction, in 1845, of a 72-inch telescope, 'Leviathan', at Birr Castle, Parsonstown, in County Offaly. It was twice the size of his earleir telescope and took three years to complete. Until the Hooker 100-inch telescope came into use at Mont Wilson, California, Parson's telescope was the largest in the world. He made use of it to observe and catalogue many galaxies, including the Whirlpool Galaxy. He died in 1867. (Wikipedia, 'William Parsons, 3rd Earl of Rosse')

# June 18th

**1839:** On this Tuesday, a gathering of sergeant majors and sergeants met in the Black Swan Inn to celebrate the twenty-fourth anniversary of the Battle of Waterloo against Napoleon's forces. The soldiers were from the Royal Regiment of Dragoons and the 7th Queen's Own Hussars and were based at the local barracks. Three of those present had fought at Waterloo on 18 June and proudly wore their medals. A whole range of seasonal items were served, along with a fine selection of quality wines. Toasts were drunk to many individuals including Queen Victoria, the Dowager Queen Adelaide and the Duke of Wellington. (*York Herald*)

——◆——

**1912:** Press reports from this day explain that initial moves to establish a professional football club in York had happened slowly but, following the sale of shares, a ground was found in Burton Stone Lane with a tenancy of five years. A player/manager, Peter Boyle, was appointed and after the pitch had been levelled and drained, terracing and stands were completed to provide a ground capacity of 10,000. (*Yorkshire Evening Press*)

# June 19th

**1823:** The foundation stone was laid for a new prison to serve the city of York on 19 June 1802. It was completed in 1807 and covered part of the site of an early castle known as the Old Bayle, near Skeldergate postern. Perimeter brick walls enclosed an area of about three-quarters of a square mile, with the three-storey prison building in a central position. Within the surrounding courtyard the cupola and vase were visible from other areas of the city. Common criminals were held on the ground floor, with debtors imprisoned on the second and third floors. George Rylah was appointed governor with an annual salary of £150 and outbuildings, which included his lodgings, also contained a chapel where the chaplain, Reverend William Flower, preached a sermon on alternate Sundays and led prayers with prisoners on Thursday evenings. The appointed prison surgeon was George Champney. Executions were infrequent but, when required, a scaffold was installed outside the wall close to the Old Bayle Hill. (*Baines' Gazetteer*, 1823)

# June 20th

**1668:** Richard Shaftoe married Sarah Hanworth at Holy Trinity Church in Micklegate. In 1675, he became a freeman in York by paying twenty nobles (a noble being 6s 8d) and established himself as one of the city's first clay tobacco pipemakers. (Shafto, R., *Shaftoes of York*)

---

**1833:** Philip Knapton died at York on this day. Born into a musical family on 20 October 1788, his father Samuel (1756–1831) was a renowned cellist and became known as the 'Father of the Musical Society'. Philip received his musical education at Cambridge from Dr Hague and then returned to York, where he became a partner in his father's Coney Street music business. He was also a much-loved church organist at St Saviour's Church, a fine pianist and well-respected composer. Among his musical works, Philip Knapton composed several overtures, pianoforte concertos and other orchestral works, as well as arranging numerous pieces for pianoforte and harp. His song entitled 'There be none of Beauty's daughters' enjoyed long-term popularity. He also served as an assistant conductor at the York Festivals of 1823, 1825 and 1828. (www.townwaits.org.uk)

# June 21st

**1960:** York Guildhall was re-opened by the Queen Mother on this day, following extensive building work in the late 1950s. An earlier guildhall or 'Common Hall' is mentioned in a charter of 1256 and work on the present building dates from 1445 (with accounts still in existence). A council meeting was recorded as being held there during May 1459. The building was badly damaged by incendiary bombs on 29 April 1942, and the shell of the Guildhall was left as a stark reminder of the wartime blitz until 1956, when renovation work got underway. In the last five and a half centuries, the Guildhall has witnessed any number of dramatic events, ranging from the persecution of Catholics during the reign of Elizabeth I and the trial of Margaret Clitherow in 1586, to the counting out of a £200,000 payment to Scottish forces for the support of parliament against Charles I. Today, the roof has a range of amusing bosses with grotesque animals and faces, while the upstairs council chamber has fine panelling and original furniture. (www.aboutbritain.com)

# June 22nd

**1860:** John Shaftoe, builder and city councillor, tendered for the stone and brickwork of a new iron-girder bridge over the Ouse. His tender of £9,390 was the lowest of three and it was accepted on 22 June 1860. Just a week later, however, he withdrew his tender because of an error in the calculations. He was declared innocent of any wrongdoing, but withdrew from council activities and did not seek re-election in the next elections. The following year, the incomplete Lendal Bridge fell into the Ouse and a cast-iron bridge, designed by Thomas Page, was constructed in its place. (Shafto, R., *Shaftoes of York*)

* * *

**1887:** Queen Victoria's Jubilee celebrations included a knighthood for Joseph Terry, the city's Lord Mayor, and on 22 June he presented her with an album of York views. Her Majesty 'turned over a few of the leaves to look at the contents, and bowed her acceptance with stately courtesy and affability', before shaking hands with the Lady Mayoress, but there is no mention of her speaking a word. (Kightly, C. & Semlyen, R., *Lords of the City*)

* * *

**1897:** Businesses closed for the day and Museum Gardens were open all day free to the public as celebrations of Queen Victoria's diamond jubilee took place throughout the city. (Knight, C.B., *History of the City of York*)

# June 23rd

**1942:** Martin John Rees, Baron Rees of Ludlow, was born in York. He was educated at Shrewsbury School, before graduating with a first-class Honours Degree in mathematics from Trinity College, Cambridge. After completing his doctorate under Dennis Schiama at Cambridge, he held research posts in Britain and the United States. From 1992 to 2003, Martin Rees was Royal Society Research Professor and from 2003, Professor of Cosmology and Astrophysics. With more than 500 research papers to his name, he has made major contributions to the origin of cosmic microwave background radiation, as well as to galaxy clustering and formation. Between 2005 and 2010 he was president of the Royal Society and on 22 July 2005, Rees was elevated to a life peerage. Less than two months later, he was created Baron Rees of Ludlow. Among the many awards he has received are the Balzan Prize 1989, Bower Award 1998, Michael Faraday prize 2004 and Crafoord Prize, 2005, but he has also contributed books on astronomy and science for the lay public. (www.bbc.co.uk/news; www.royalsociety.org.uk)

# *June 24th*

**1925:** On this day, the future King and Queen of England visited York to unveil the war memorial and the restored Five Sisters' Window in the Minster. At that time, the royal couple were Duke and Duchess of York and, as well as unveiling the memorial, they also visited York County Hospital in Monkgate. There was an amount of behind-the-scenes controversy resulting from Lord Mayor, Sir Robert Newbald Kay's application for a grant towards the cost of entertaining the royal couple. Opponents suggested that a sub-committee should determine the nature of hospitality, but Sir Robert was adamant that he alone should make the decision. In the event, he was allowed a grant of £75 and, as he insisted, there were no alcoholic drinks on offer. (Kightly C. & Semlyen, R., *Lords of the City*)

---

**2011:** An exhibition showcasing the work of one of York's most famous artists, William Etty, opened in the city's art gallery. With works drawn from the Tate, the Royal Academy and Manchester Art Gallery, as well as York's own collection, the exhibition attempts to examine Etty's equivocal status from stalwart of the Royal Academy to exclusion from the artistic elite because of his supposed 'perverse' passion for the voluptuousness of the female nude. (*Yorkshire Post*)

# June 25th

**1877:** York's first railway station was a temporary wooden structure on Queen Street, outside the city walls, and served the York and North Midland Railway from 1839 to 1841, when the city's old railway station was completed inside the walls. Trains travelling between London and Newcastle had to reverse out of the old station and this unsatisfactory procedure stopped with the construction of the present station. Constructed between 1873 and 1877, it stands on the site of a Roman cemetery and was designed by North Eastern Railway architects Thomas Prosser and William Peachey. When opened on 25 June 1877, it was claimed to be the largest in the world, with a total of thirteen platforms. A curved roof of glass and iron, some 48ft high, covers the main platforms. York is an extremely important junction on the British railway network, at about the halfway point between London and Edinburgh and the point at which the southbound Leeds branch diverges. It is also a terminus for some Trans-Pennine routes. (Pevsner, N., *York and the East Riding*; *AA Pocket Guide to York*)

# June 26th

**1533:** The Priors of Drax and Durham appeared in York Court on charges of erecting fishgarths in the River Ouse. Their case was heard by the Lord Mayor, Recorder and two aldermen, and both priors claimed that they had left sufficient space beside their barriers. The court's decision went in their favour and certificates along these lines were issued to the King's Bench. Fishgarths had caused problems for a considerable time, but from the 1540s there were fewer difficulties, largely because of the closure of monastic sites and improved methods of farming, as well as better facilities for distributing sea fish. (Knight, C.B., *History of York*)

———•◆•———

**1902:** On this day, the following advertisement appeared in newspapers:

> 26 June 1902
> Minster Festival of the Coronation of their majesties
> King Edward and Queen Alexandra
> Offertory for York County Hospital Programme 1d.

(Programme of events and local press coverage)

# June 27th

**1642:** The enthronement of John Williams as the sixty-fourth Archbishop of York took place on this day. With his home at Cawood Castle, he soon became embroiled in issues relating to the Civil War. He criticised the actions of Sir John Hotham during King Charles' visit to Hull and, not long after his enthronement, Archbishop Williams was warned that Captain Hotham, Sir John's son, was about to attack Cawood Castle, with the intention of exacting revenge. According to reports, Archbishop Williams made a rapid departure from Cawood Castle and returned to Wales. He never returned to his diocese of York and died at Golthaeth in Carnarvonshire on 25 March 1650. Following his death, the See of York was vacant for ten years. (Knight, C.B., *A History of the City of York*)

---

**1706:** On this day, a special sermon was preached in the the Cathedral and Metropolitical Church of St Peter in York:

> Being the Day of Thanksgiving for the late signal and glorious victory obtained by the Forces of Her Majesty, and those of her Allies; under the command of His Grace the Duke of Marlborough over the French army in Brabant... By Samuel Terrick, Canon Residentiary of the Church of York and Rector of Wheldrake...

(Item printed by John White for Francis Hildyard)

# June 28th

**1476:** John Bailey, a water leader of York, was appointed by the council to take the 'metres and measures' of all sorts of grain, salt, coals and all other measurable items arriving by water for sale in the city. The appointment was for a five-year term, during which he paid the city 26s 8d each year. His income was provided by charges paid by vessels arriving in the river. The rate was one penny for every twenty quarters of grain and coal, and one penny for five quarters of salt. Failure to cooperate with measuring would result in a fine of 3s 4d. (Knight, C.B., *History of the City of York*)

———— • ◆ • ————

**1913:** The annual general meeting of York City Football Club took place. It was the end of its first season in the Midland League and they had a tenth-place finish position, but had accrued considerable debt. Closer analysis showed that £2,000 had been spent 'on the field' and, in overall terms, expenditure of £2,224 had exceeded income by £627. One cause of this shortfall was the club's failure to find jobs promised to players, which resulted in payments of an extra £1 per week. Also it was said that the club had compounded its problems by employing 'several players who were colloquially known as "good old has-beens"'. (*Yorkshire Evening Press*)

# June 29th

**1895:** A gymnasium for St Peter's School at Clifton was opened by Major General Reginald Thynne GOC, North Eastern District (1894–1902). The new building was completed during 1894–5, on ground between the chapel and the main road, with building work by T.P. Barry of York, using designs by the architect Francis W. Bedford of Leeds and Westminster. An anonymous donor, who was eventually identified as former scholar Reverend H. Bloomfield, provided funds for the project. The cornerstone had been laid on 2 August 1894 by Mrs Handford, wife of Reverend G.T. Handford, the headmaster. The gymnasium was first used in September 1895. (Murray, H., *Heraldry and Buildings of York*)

———— • ◆ • ————

**1903:** During the early months of 1903, there was a considerable amount of debate about the choice of a Labour candidate for York and at a selection meeting in the Kendrick Rooms, Spen Lane, a former postman, George Harold Stuart, came out on top. His adoption meeting was held on 27 February, and in subsequent rallies, one of which took place on 29 June, he spoke on both national and local issues to gain support from uncommitted constituents and Liberal supporters who were yet to select a candidate. (*Yorkshire Evening Press*)

# June 30th

**1644:** Throughout the month of June 1644, parliamentary forces besieged the city of York, but the situation took a decisive turn on 30 June, when news reached commanders that Prince Rupert was at the head of an army of 20,000 men intent on relieving the siege. Royalist forces were expected to pitch camp in the Knaresborough-Boroughbridge area, and it was decided to intercept Prince Rupert's army on their approach to York. Besieging armies withdrew from York on 1 July and marched along Boroughbridge Road as far as Marston, where they formed battle lines. In the meantime, Prince Rupert's forces had crossed the River Ouse near Nun Monkton and marched towards York, before halting close to Overton. Prince Rupert arrived in the city and consulted with the Marquis of Newcastle, before deciding to do battle with parliamentary forces at the earliest opportunity. Accordingly, with his own army reinforced by numbers from the city garrison, he left York to face parliamentary troops who were still in position on Marston Moor, between the villages of Marston and Tockwith. (Knight, C.B., *History of the City of York*)

# July 1st

**2003:** A plaque on the wall of the Blue Bell in Fossgate reads, 'National Inventory of Historic Pub Interiors. This is to certify that the Blue Bell, York, has been included in CAMRA's National Inventory in recognition of the outstanding historic importance of the little-altered interior as at 1st July 2003'. Each of York's many pubs and bars has points of interest, but the two rooms of the Blue Bell have a very special atmosphere. The Edwardian interior remains exactly as it was after a refurbishment in 1903, with a small bar at the front with nine beer pumps. Behind a glass screen is the Smoke Room, served through a hatch. Ceilings and walls are of polished wood and a passage leading to the Smoke Room at the rear also has a serving hatch with adjacent folding seats. Preservation of the Blue Bell is the work of the Robinson family (George, his wife and daughter, Edith, who were licensees for most of the twentieth century). Since 1 October 2000, it has been run by Jim and Sue Hardie. (Thomas, P., *Yorkshire's Historic Pubs*)

———— ◆ ————

**1972:** More than 2,000 Friends of York Minster assembled to celebrate the 500th anniversary of the great church. The Archbishop of Canterbury, Dr Michael Ramsey, preached at a special service in the Minster. (*The Observer*)

# July 2nd

**1644:** Having arrived in York on the previous day, Prince Rupert mustered Royalist forces in the city and marched out to confront enemy forces on 2 July 1644. Some of his troops crossed a bridge of boats at Poppleton and he then gathered forces on Hessay Moor. The vanguard of his troops caught up with the rear of parliamentary forces near Long Marston and both sides took up battle lines. Royalist forces based themselves on the north side of the moor while parliamentary troops occupied higher ground between Tockwith and Long Marston. An artillery duel at about 3 p.m. signalled the start of the Battle of Marston Moor, which involved the highest number of troops of any battle in the English Civil War. Rupert commanded 11,000 foot soldiers and 7,000 cavalry, who faced parliamentary forces numbering around 27,000 men, of whom about 9,000 were cavalry. Fighting really began at about 6 p.m. and, although it seemed at times that Royalists would triumph, Oliver Cromwell's actions seem to have contributed to parliament's victory by late evening. Prince Rupert fled the battlefield and made his way to Lancashire through Wensleydale, while the Earl of Newcastle fled to Scarborough, where he joined a ship to the Continent. (Singleton, F.B. & Rawnsley S., *A History of Yorkshire*)

# July 3rd

**1876:** The city council made the first move in what became a protracted series of proposals for improving the area of York between Nessgate and Tower Street. By a majority of two to one, approval was given for the larger of two schemes under consideration, which involved clearing and improving unsanitary conditions in the 'Water Lanes' district. The estimated cost of the scheme was £32,000 and the council, meeting in December 1876 and on 10 January 1877, scaled down the proposed improvements to encompass more or less the smaller scheme that had been rejected on 3 July 1876. On 7 March 1877, a Local Government Board Inspector held an inquiry into the application and the cost of improvement was estimated at £16,148, but at a meeting of the council on 2 October 1878, it was decided to refer the whole question back to the Sanitary Committee for further deliberation. All the initial plans were reviewed but the council instructed the city surveyor to prepare another amended scheme. On 1 January 1879, the council was requested to approve an application to the Local Government Board for powers to implement the scheme prepared some three months earlier, but a majority voted against this move. Finally, on 3 September 1879, a modified scheme was accepted and approved and re-development work went ahead over the next two or three years. (Knight, C.B., *History of the City of York*)

# July 4th

**1936:** York City Aerodrome was officially opened by Lord Swinton, Minister for Air, on the outskirts of the city. The first aeroplane to arrive in York had landed on the Knavesmire in February 1913, with Captain Langcroft of the Royal Flying Corps at the controls, but it was not until 1931 that York had its own aircraft factory. Airspeed Ltd was co-founded by Neville Shute, who later carved out a career as a novelist. His company was based in Piccadilly bus garage. In the early years the company designed aircraft and gliders, but as business grew and alternative premises were not available in York, the operation was moved to Portsmouth. Soon after this, Yorkshire Aviation Services Ltd were given assistance in finding land at Clifton and they were able to offer flying lessons at 40s per hour, with an air taxi available for hire at a charge of 6d per mile. When war broke out in 1939, the airfield became a base for RAF bomber aircraft and three new runways and a number of ancillary buildings were constructed. The airfield site suffered serious damage during air raids in April 1942 and, after returning to civilian use, the land was sold for housing in the 1950s. (www.historyofyork.org.uk)

---

**1983:** BBC York first went on air at 6.30 a.m. on this day. It was the only station in North Yorkshire for its first nine years of broadcasting. (www.bbc.co.uk/york)

# July 5th

**1649:** Sir Christopher Croft, an influential figure in York during the first half of the seventeenth century, died on this day. He married Elizabeth Harrison, daughter of Alderman Sir T. Harrison on 21 November 1613 and some five years later, he held the office of Sheriff of York, before becoming Lord Mayor in 1629. During 1641, he entertained King Charles I at his home. In November of the same year, he was awarded a knighthood. (*Burke's Peerage, Baronetage and Knightage*)

* * *

**1918:** Throughout the period of the First World War, members of the York branch of the Independent Labour Party (ILP) maintained their opposition to warfare and voiced their views strongly on a number of other issues. When the Lord Mayor Foster Todd was knighted and J.G. Butcher, the Tory MP became a baronet, labour members of the council congratulated the recipients, but on 5 July 1918 the ILP wrote to the local papers disassociating itself from the congratulations, 'believing that the conferring of titles makes an invidious distinction between one person and another, and is against the best interests of the community as a whole.' (*York Herald*)

# July 6th

**1755:** John Flaxman was born in York on this day, the son of a well-known moulder and seller of plastercasts. He had little schooling and was largely self-educated. The family moved to London and the young John Flaxman developed his interest in drawing and modelling, along with a close study of classical literature. He soon formed close friendships with artists William Blake and Thomas Stothard, and after 1775 Flaxman began to work for the potter Josiah Wedgwood. During 1787, he travelled to Rome to continue his studies and received enough commissions to stay until 1794. On his return to London, John Flaxman designed a large monument to the Earl of Mansfield in Westminster Abbey and established his considerable reputation as a sculptor. He became a member of the Royal Academy in 1800 and its first professor of sculpture in 1810. He completed a wide range of works after 1800, ranging from small monuments in relief to very large commissions in the round (such as the Nelson monument in St Paul's Cathedral), and designs for silversmiths (including the Shield of Achilles). John Flaxman died on 7 December 1826. (www.britannica.com)

# July 7th

**1845:** On this day, the railway line from York to Scarborough was opened, with thirty-five carriages drawn by two engines, *The Hudson* and *The Lion*. After breakfast in the Guildhall, under the presidency of George Hudson, a procession led by a band made its way to the station and the train left at half past ten. It arrived in Scarborough at thirty-five minutes past one in the afternoon, and 'the company proceeded to an elegant luncheon which had been laid out in the temporary station.' This was followed by a procession around Scarborough, before re-boarding the train for York at quarter to four in the afternoon. On arrival in York, the railway company provided dinner for around 700 guests in the Guildhall, where George Hudson presided over proceedings as president of the railway company. (Hoole, K., *Regional History of the Railways of Great Britain, The North East*, Vol. 4)

———◆———

**1871:** Seebohm Rowntree was born in York on this day. Between 1897 and 1941, at different times, he was both director and chairman of Rowntrees Ltd, the cocoa and chocolate firm in York. He put into practice new concepts of the employment of labour based on his own sociological studies. (Hartley M. & Ingilby, J., *Yorkshire Portraits*)

# July 8th

**1780:** Workmen clearing away an amount of rubbish from behind the courthouse in York unearthed a human skeleton, lying about a yard away from the wall and with the leg bones enclosed in double irons. During his trial for murder, which began on 3 August 1759, Eugene Aram had made reference to the sudden and unexplained disappearance of a thief named William Thompson during June 1757 and now, more than twenty years later, it was widely believed that this was the skeleton of Thompson. Most of the speculation suggested that he was attempting to escape and had reached the roof of the old courthouse by using a ladder, before falling to the ground. It seems that Thompson either died instantly or that his injuries proved fatal and, over time, vegetation covered his body. It was only after a considerable lapse in time that the human remains, presumably those of William Thompson, were accidentally uncovered. (Hargrove, W., *History of York*, Vol. II)

# July 9th

**1984:** A massive fire swept through large areas of York Minster causing damage estimated at £1 million. The alarm was raised shortly after 2 a.m. and 150 fire fighters from across North Yorkshire spent two hours bringing the blaze under control. The fire was concentrated in the thirteenth-century south transept and the roof was burned out, but staff battled through heavy smoke and flames to salvage priceless artefacts. The Archbishop of Canterbury had conducted a service the previous day and, when he visited the scene after the fire, he commented, 'There's a certain obvious poignancy which makes one a bit lost for words.' After further investigation, the fire brigade reported that the most likely cause of the fire was a lightning strike. Modern fire alarms were installed in the new roof at a cost of £350,000. Hundreds of people gave support, ranging from cash donations to oak trees and, after considerable discussion, the south transept roof was rebuilt with a hand-carved wooden replica. Glass in the rose window was painstakingly restored with added reinforcement. (www.news.bbc.co.uk)

# July 10th

**2006:** The Privy Council approved a request from St John's College to become a fully-fledged university, to be known as York St John University. Originally founded in York as the diocesan teacher-training college for men, St John's College opened its doors in 1841. During 1975, it merged with the women's teacher-training college, which had moved from York to Ripon in 1862 to create the College of Ripon and York St John. After a comprehensive strategic review in 2001, York St John vacated the Ripon site in order to extend and enhance provision on the site in Lord Mayor's Walk at York. The title of York St John University was adopted from 1 October 2006 and it offers degree courses at undergraduate and postgraduate level. The first chancellor is the Archbishop of York, Dr John Sentamu, who was installed at a ceremony in York Minster on 7 March 2007. (www.thestudentroom.co.uk/wiki/York_St_John_University)

# July 11th

**1913:** Yorkshire has provided any number of famous international cricketers, but perhaps the least well known is Paul Antony Gibb, who was born at Acomb on this day. At Cambridge University he gained 'a blue' in his first summer and also scored his highest innings for Yorkshire on his debut at Bramall Lane, Sheffield in 1935. Yorkshire's playing strength, and the disruption of the Second World War, meant that he never gained a county cap, but Paul Gibb had the honour of captaining Yorkshire on their first overseas tour to Jamaica in 1935–6. The 1938 season was his best, with a score of 1,658. He was also chosen to tour South Africa in the following winter. On his test debut at Johannesburg, he scored 93 and 106, making him the first Yorkshire man to score a century on his test debut. Following a career that produced 12,520 runs and 548 wicket-keeping dismissals, he became an umpire and also coached in South Africa. Paul Gibb died at Guildford, Surrey on 7 December 1977. (*One Hundred Yorkshire Greats*, Yorkshire CCC)

———— • ✦ • ————

**2010:** The Eighth York Rotary Dragon Boat Challenge took place over a 250-metre stretch of the River Ouse. The nominated charity for 2010 was St Leonard's Hospice and in the previous seven events, a total of £480,000 had been raised. (www.yorkrotary.co.uk)

# July 12th

**1537:** Robert Aske was born into an old-established Yorkshire family at Aughton near Selby. He studied to become a lawyer and was elected a Fellow at Gray's Inn, but found himself opposed to religious reforms of King Henry VIII. In particular, he was against the closure of the monasteries, but when rebellion broke out in York, Aske was still on his way back from London. Soon, however, he was taking a leading role and by the time that much of Yorkshire and parts of Durham, Northumberland, Cumberland and Westmorland were in revolt during October 1536, Robert Aske was widely accepted as their 'chief captain'. On 13 October 1536, he held talks with royal delegates including the Duke of Norfolk. He received assurances of an audience with the King and safe passage to and from the royal court. Following the meeting, Aske was returning to the north when fighting broke out again and Henry VIII changed his mind. Robert Aske was captured and taken to the Tower of London. In court at Westminster, he was convicted of high treason and taken back to York. There, on 12 July 1537, he was hung in chains from a scaffold erected outside Clifford's Tower. ('Aske, Robert', *Dictionary of National Biography*)

# July 13th

**1816:** York County Savings Bank was first opened in New Street on this day, with the intention of providing banking services mainly for the working classes. According to *Baines' Gazetteer* for 1823, 'The Savings Bank is in a flourishing situation and has investments to the amount of £70,923 0s 1d made by 1,854 depositors consisting chiefly of servants and labouring persons.' A notable manager of the York Savings Bank was Robert William Bilton Hornby (1821–1888). Born in York at Heworth Manor, he was admitted to St Peter's School in January 1829 as a 'free scholar', before gaining degrees in theology at Durham University. Following his marriage in 1844, the family settled at Clifton Garth, where they brought up a son and three daughters. William Hornby was also an active director and trustee of the York Cemetery Co. (founded in 1837) and a noted antiquarian with a strong interest in the Minster and other York Churches. His widow placed a window by C.E. Kempe in York Minster in his memory. It is located behind the astronomical clock. (www.bbc.co.uk; *Baines' Gazetteer*, 1823)

# July 14th

**1753:** Magistrates of St Peter's Liberty, York, issued this order:

> Whereas complaint hath been made, that several inhabitants of the Minster Yard, and Bedern, in the City of York, and Liberty of St. Peter York, keep open their shops and sell goods and commodities on the Lord's Day, commonly called Sunday, which is highly offensive both to the laws of God and Man. For the preventing whereof, it is ordered that if any person or persons, shall for the future open any shop or shops and sell or expose to sale, any goods or commodities whatsoever, in the said Minster Yard or Bedern, within the said Liberty, on the Lord's Day, commonly called Sunday, he or she, or they, shall be prosecuted as the Law directs in such case.

(Benson, G., *An Account of the County and City of York*)

———— • ◆ • ————

**1845:** The bell 'Great Peter' was positioned in the Minster, after being drawn on a truck pulled by ten horses from the railway station and over the Ouse Bridge to the Minster's north-west door. It weighed 10¾ tons and measured 8ft 4ins in diameter, at a cost of £2,000. (Benson, G., *An Account of the County and City of York*)

# July 15th

**1503:** Queen Margaret was on her way to Scotland when she was met by the two Sheriffs of York and 100 mounted citizens. In turn, they were joined by Lord and Lady Latimer with fifty retainers of the Neville family; Lord Scrope of Bolton with his son; Lord Scrope of Upsall and retainers; the Sheriff of Yorkshire with his wife Lady Conyers (a member of the Neville family); and considerable members of the household. At Dringhouses, the Earl of Northumberland and 300 horsemen joined the procession. On the Mount, the young Queen who rode on horseback, positioned behind Sir David Owen, dismounted and took her place in a fine litter drawn by horses. After passing through Micklegate Bar, Queen Margaret was welcomed to the city by the Mayor, recorder and aldermen in full ceremonial regalia. Some two hours later, the procession reached the Minster. The following day, the Mayor presented Queen Margaret with a silver gilt cup and cover, engraved with the city coat of arms, and she was present at the installation of Thomas Savage as Archbishop. On Monday, the Queen left York for Newburgh Priory near Coxwold. (Benson, G., *An Account of the County and City of York*)

# July 16th

**1644:** Following defeat at Marston Moor, the Royalist cause in the north of England was doomed, but it was not until 16 July 1644 that the garrison of about 1,000 men marched defiantly out of the city of York. Both Prince Rupert and the Marquis of Newcastle had left the area shortly after the battle, and the garrison was left under the command of Sir Thomas Glemham. He firmly rejected an initial demand for an unconditional surrender and rallied resistance for a further nine days before an armistice was arranged. Under agreed terms, Royalist forces were allowed to march out of York en route for Skipton and the three victorious parliamentary generals made their way to the Minster for a Thanksgiving service. The following day was designated a Day of Thanksgiving and Ferdinando, Lord Fairfax was appointed governor of the city. He and his son, Thomas, are given credit for preserving important aspects of the city's heritage, in particular Minster glass, during this dramatic episode. (Knight, C.B., *History of the City of York*)

# July 17th

**1902:** Magistrates in York were dealing severely with any unlawful activities on Sundays, such as street betting and Sunday gaming (or 'pitch and toss'). Their campaign may have been given impetus by a report from the House of Lords Betting Committee, in 1902, but even before this time raids were being carried out in York under section 1 of the Betting Act of 1863. One of those prosecuted was forty-year-old Thomas Horner, who was given a harsh sentence of a month in prison with hard labour for his transgression. (*Yorkshire Evening Press*)

———◆———

**1979:** Betty's Ltd celebrated its sixtieth anniversary with music in the cafés and a complementary pot of tea and a 'fat rascal' for anyone sharing the same birthday (as evidenced by a driver's licence or birth certificate). Customers who could find any pre-metric coinage were allowed to pay for their tea or coffee at 1919 prices. There was a Diamond Jubilee Ball for 600 staff members, as well as a special Diamond Jubilee bonus, equivalent to three months' pay, for every member of staff. (Wild, J., *Hearts, Tarts and Rascals: The Story of Betty's*)

# July 18th

**1823:** The York Gas Light Co. was incorporated in 1823 by an Act which named 104 citizens as the first subscribing members. On 18 July 1823, a committee purchased 2 acres of land close to the River Foss, in order to build the gasworks. By the following year, gas lighting was in use in streets and shops and there were about 250 private customers, who were charged at half-yearly rates. These rates varied with the daily period of supply and there was a choice of three types of lamp. While replacement of 'the dull and murky glare of oil lamps' with brilliant illumination using gas was warmly welcomed, the high cost caused conflict between the company and York City Commissioners. A rival company, York Union Gas Light Co., was set up in January 1837 and there were problems over mains-laying with the older company. However, an amalgamation in 1844, with six directors from each of the earlier companies, saw the establishment of York United Gas Light Co. Further disputes in 1850 over charges were settled by arbitration and a further name change in 1912 led to the establishment of York Gas Co. After the nationalisation of the industry in 1948, the York works came under the control of the North Eastern Gas Board. (www.british-history.ac.uk)

# July 19th

**1677:** The foundation stone was laid for the brickwork tower at St Martin's Church, Micklegate and building work continued through the later months of 1677. First mentioned in the Domesday Book of 1086, the original eleventh-century church only covered the area of the present nave. The walls of magnesian limestone, with some millstone grit, include a number of re-used Roman stones in the west tower. It was the west tower that was faced in brick during 1677, after a previous rebuild during the early fifteenth century, narrowly escaping demolition in 1548. The interior is almost square in plan and the oldest parts are the twelfth-century nave arcades. A particularly fine reredos in three parts was completed in 1749–51 by Bernard Dickinson. In recent years, the church has housed offices, exhibitions and meetings. (Pevsner, N., *The Buildings of England: York and East Riding*)

———— • ◆ • ————

**1913:** Legislation dealing with Sunday trading caused real problems for magistrates in York during the summer of 1913. A newspaper supplement carried headlines such as 'SEE-SAW LAW AT YORK. DIFFERENT DECISIONS DAY BY DAY' and 'OBJECTIONABLE PROCEEDINGS'. (*York Herald Supplement*)

# July 20th

**1967:** On this day, the York Glaziers' Trust was established. Trusteeship is shared between the Pilgrim Trust and the Dean and Chapter of York. From a workshop base in the former medieval chapel of Vicars Choral, the Bedern Chapel, close to Goodramgate, the Trust offers a wide-ranging set of conservation services. These include conservation of medieval stained glass, enamel-painted glass of the seventeenth century and Georgian-era and Victorian stained glass, as well as preventive conservation, protective isothermal glazing, condition reports, conservation proposals and inspection services. Since its formation, the York Glaziers' Trust has completed around a thousand commissions in cathedrals, parish churches, great houses and museums throughout this country, as well as countless activities at York Minster. Numbered among recent projects are work at the chapter house vestibule in York Minster (1290–1300) and the west window of Beverly Minster, installed by John Hardman & Co. (1859–65). The basic technique of making 'stained and painted glass' has changed surprisingly little over the years and a range of tours at Bedern Glaziers' Studio offer a firsthand glimpse of current projects. (www.yorkglazierstrust.org)

# July 21st

**625:** Paulinus was invested as Bishop of York by Archbishop Justus, following his arrival in England in 604 as a member of a mission. He had been sent by Pope Gregory I to convert the Anglo-Saxon population from paganism to Christianity. After spending a number of years in Kent, Paulinus accompanied Aethelburg, sister of King Eadbald of Kent, on her journey to Northumbria to marry King Edwin of Northumbria. Eventually, Edwin was converted to Christianity along with many of his subjects. Churches were built and Edwin and many of his followers were baptised at York in 627. There is also evidence that, whilst staying with Edwin and Aethelburg at their palace in Yeavering, Northumberland, Paulinus spent thirty-six days baptising new converts in the River Glen. One of the women that Paulinus baptised was a future saint, Hilda of Whitby. After Edwin's death in AD 633, Paulinus and Aethelburg headed south, leaving behind a member of Paulinus' clergy, James the Deacon. Paulinus returned to Kent where he became Bishop of Rochester. Following his death in 644, he was venerated as a saint with a feast day on 10 October. (Yorke, B., *The Conversion of Britain: Religion, Politics and Society in Britain 600–800 A.D*; Kirby, D.P., *The Earliest English Kings*)

# July 22nd

**2008:** Installation and testing of York Minster's carillon of bells had begun on 4 April 2008, but it was more than three months later before the new carillon was played properly on 22 July. Completion of work on the carillon meant that York joined all the major cities of northern Europe in having carillon to enhance the local setting. The bells are played by a carilloneur, using a baton clavier set in the ringing chamber below the bell chamber of the south-west tower. A carilloneur operates the baton clavier by using both hand, batons and feet pedals that resemble a church organ pedal board. The chiming of tunes on the Minster bells dates back to the completion of the building's towers during the mid-fifteenth century. Chiming became less fashionable in the seventeenth century and this led to the removal of the chiming machine in 1750. By adding twenty-four bells to the existing eleven, it became possible to play almost any tune. (www.yorkminster.org)

# July 23rd

**1986:** On this day, Prince Andrew, second son of Queen Elizabeth II and Prince Phillip, was made Duke of York when he married Sarah Ferguson, who became Duchess of York. Born on 19 February 1960 at Buckingham Palace, he is now fourth in line to the throne after Princes Charles, William and Harry. He pursued a naval career and served as a helicopter pilot during the Falklands War (1982–3), before becoming a Commander in 1999. Prince Andrew ended his naval career at the British Ministry of Defence in 2001 and was promoted to Rear Admiral on his fiftieth birthday. 'Duke of York' is a title of nobility in the British peerage and, since it was first granted in the fifteenth century, it has usually been given to the second son of the British monarch. Currently, the Duke of York carries out royal duties and is UK Special Representative for International Trade and Investment. (www.suite101.com/british-royal-family)

# July 24th

**1866:** A first *Yorkshire Fine Art and Industrial Exhibition* was held on a site in the grounds of Bootham Asylum, York. It proved to be extremely popular with members of the public and produced a profit for the sponsoring committee of £1,866. At a meeting on 10 April 1867, the committee was re-elected, with directions to 'apply this surplus in providing some permanent building to be devoted to the encouragement of Art and Industry'. A second exhibition was held on 7 May 1879 and plans were made for a permanent building designed by a local architect, Edward Taylor. It is this building that now houses the York City Art Gallery. (*Architectural History*, Vol. 46: 2003)

---

**1914:** Cases of tuberculosis in York towards the end of June were reported on 24 July: there were eighty-four new patients and 1,237 re-attendances at the TB clinic at Castlegate, giving an average weekly attendance of 101. Poor housing conditions are generally associated with tuberculosis, and although some of York's slum areas had been improved during the Edwardian era, such improvement was limited. As depression affected the city, so the amount of private house building fell away markedly and this was a time of population increase. (*Yorkshire Evening Press*)

# July 25th

**306:** Flavius Valerius Aurelius Constantius was proclaimed Emperor in York on 25 July AD 306. He had travelled to Britain with his father, the Emperor Constantius, in 305 and was proclaimed Emperor by soldiers in York when his father died. Constantine is said to have played a crucial role in uniting the far-flung Roman Empire under one ruler and establishing stability and security throughout the Roman world. He created a new capital at Constantinople (Istanbul) and gave considerable support to Christianity. He is believed to have been converted to the Christian faith in AD 312 and was the first Emperor to allow Christians to worship freely. He later instigated the celebrations associated with the birth of Christ that became known as Christmas. Constantine died on 22 May 337. On 25 July 2006, an exhibition was launched at the Yorkshire Museum, exactly 1,700 years since his proclamation as Emperor. It was organised by York Museums Trust and used a range of items, including rare historic writings, important sculptures and jewellery, to illustrate the story of Constantine's legacy to Europe, the Mediterranean and, eventually, the rest of the world. (www.yorkshiremuseum.org.uk)

# July 26th

**1909:** A major event in York during summer 1909 was the pageant held in Museum Gardens from 26 to 31 July. Many spectators watched proceedings from a 100ft-long temporary stand with seating for 5,000. It was designed by the city surveyor, Mr F.W. Spurr, and took two weeks to assemble, with most of the work completed by workmen from Hungate Saw Mills. Crowds watched a re-enactment of more than 2,000 years of the area's heritage in performances by about 2,500 actors, as well as 250 dancers, two choirs, school children and soldiers. Re-enactment scenes included the mythical founding of York by Greek soldiers in 800 BC and the surrender of Saxon York to William the Conqueror. Master of Ceremonies for the event was Mr Louis N. Parker. Not everything went smoothly, though. Press reports stated, 'The 2,500 performers were all unpaid', and a caption to one photograph, which shows a rehearsal in Museum Gardens reads, '…much to the annoyance of some of the working-class members who struggled to manage the time from work to attend rehearsals.' (*Yorkshire Evening Press*)

# July 27th

**1888:** On this day, the new lock at Naburn was opened by Prince Albert Victor, on the same day that he was presented with the Freedom of the City. Discussion about improving the navigable channel of the River Ouse had taken place for many years before this time. In April 1877, proposals included purchase of a dredger and six barges, as well as a steam boat to tow the barges. At this time the question of improving Naburn Lock was shelved. By 1886, the question of navigational improvements was again under serious consideration when officials of the War Department made a visit on 16 December, with the intention of constructing an ordnance depot and wharf. Five days later, the Navigation Committee toured the river frontage with John Fowler, engineer to the River Tees Commissioners, and they took a close look at Naburn Lock. At the beginning of 1887, Fowler's report to the committee included the recommendation for construction of a new lock at Naburn, in addition to the existing lock. The council voted on 4 February 1887 to carry out the recommendations and the official opening took place on 27 July. (Knight, C.B., *History of York*)

# July 28th

**1518:** The King, by charter on 28 July 1518, granted to the citizens a Common Council to assist and counsel the Mayor, aldermen and sheriffs. The Common Council was to consist of two representatives from each of the thirteen crafts of merchants, mercers, drapers, grocers, apothecaries, goldsmiths, dyers, skinners, barbers, fishmongers, tailors, vintners, pinners and glaziers; and one representative chosen out of each of the fifteen lower crafts of hosiers, innholders, vestment makers, wax chandlers, bowers, weavers, walkers, ironmongers, sadlers, masons, bakers, butchers, glovers, pewterers and armourers. (Benson, G., *An Account of the County and City of York*)

---

**1904:** Distress in York led to the formation of a Citizens' Association, which appointed a committee to set up a labour bureau (as reported on 28 July 1904). Committee members included Seebohm and Arnold Rowntree and, after drawing on information from other cities such as Leeds and Manchester, it was decided that the labour bureau should be run by the York Citizen's Association for Dealing with the Unemployed. (*Yorkshire Evening Press*)

---

**1949:** The royal train for Princess Elizabeth and the Duke of Edinburgh's return to London was stabled at the old station. (Edgington, J. & Gilks, J.S., *Trains from York*)

# July 29th

**1994:** It was announced that the train-making company ABB, which had a factory in York, had lost out on a £40 million order to build high-tech trains for the Heathrow Express rail link. The order had gone to the German company Siemens, and the decision was condemned by the York MP Hugh Bayley. At the same time, Nestlé Rowntree employees were being told that seventy office jobs would have to be lost at the York site over the next eighteen months. These job losses were part of a restructuring exercise involving 450 job cuts in the corporate affairs, personnel and administration departments. (*Yorkshire Evening Press*)

**1994:** York MP Hugh Bayley backed a move to stop discrimination against rugby league players. He had given a pledge to support a parliamentary bill aimed at ending the ban on league players taking part in union matches. For almost 100 years, rugby league players had been banned for life from playing rugby union and the Labour MP for Wakefield, David Hinchcliffe, was tabling a motion in parliament to end the rule. (*Yorkshire Evening Press*)

# July 30th

1994: Three members of the same family were getting married on the same day at York Register Office. Susan Fowler, aged forty-four, of Ratcliffe Street was taken aback when her son Darren, twenty-two, and daughter Amanda, nineteen, told her they were getting married on the same day, but then decided to make it a triple wedding day. Following the ceremonies, there was one huge wedding reception at the Bay Horse pub in Marygate, York. (*Yorkshire Evening Press*)

———◆———

1994: 'A speed boat smashed into the riverbank of the Ouse yesterday afternoon, leaving one of the passengers unconscious. The boat crashed close to the bridge where the A64 York to Scarborough road crosses the river near Bishopthorpe at about 5.30 pm when it careered out of control but the reason for the accident is still unclear.' (*Yorkshire Evening Press*)

———◆———

1994: A York shopping arcade was still half empty and as dingy as ever some two years after plans for extensive refurbishment were announced. Shopkeepers in Davygate were urging the owners, Norwich Union, to tidy up the arcade and put traders back into empty units. (*Yorkshire Evening Press*)

# July 31st

Annually (medieval period): First recorded in the thirteenth century, a fair was held annually at Lammas under the jurisdiction of the Archbishop of York. At 3 p.m. on 31 July, the bell of St Michael's, Ouse Bridge was rung for sheriffs to surrender their wands and authority in the city to the Archbishop in the Sheriff's Court on Ouse Bridge. For the duration of the fair, the sheriffs' authority to arrest citizens was suspended within the city and suburbs. Sole power of carrying out any judicial process during the fair was vested in the Archbishop's bailiff. The Archbishop of York usually held a Court of Pye Powder (dusty feet) at this fair, when a jury was chosen from the inhabitants of Wistow for settling complaints and disputes relating to the fair. Tolls were paid at the city gates for livestock coming to the fair and on those leaving after being sold. At the end of the fair at 3 p.m. on 2 August, the bell of St Michael's was rung and sheriffs were given back their wands, along with jurisdiction of the city at a celebratory dinner. (Benson, G., *An Account of the County and City of York*)

# August 1st

**1934:** A York man, Leonard Woodall, of 68 Skeldergate was fined £5 for 'exposing for sale in Sandringham Street eight gallons of milk which, when examined, was found to contain cow dung, dust and hair.' The offence had taken place on 26 April 1934, when Inspector R. Black, Assistant Sanitary Inspector for York, saw a young boy 'wheeling a filthy barrow on which was an equally filthy milk churn'. He was delivering milk in a very dirty condition and, on close examination, a sample of the milk was found to contain an average of 3,000,000 organisms per cubic centimetre (when the highest number was normally 200,000). The excuse offered by Leonard Woodall was that 'he forgot his strainer at the cattle market that day'. (*York Herald*)

———◆———

**2010:** The Yorkshire Museum reopened on Yorkshire Day 2010, following a £2 million restructuring of the interior. Three major sections were created: 'Eboracum: Face to Face with the Romans', 'York: the Power and the Glory' (Anglian, Viking and Medieval York) and 'Extinct: A Way of Life' (featuring fossils, skeletons and animal specimens.) Also on display was the Vale of York Viking hoard. Found in a field near Harrogate in 2007 and valued at £1,082,000, the tenth-century pot contained 617 silver coins and sixty-five other items. (www.historyofyork.org.uk)

# August 2nd

**1824:** The imposing buildings at 1 St Helen's Square (now known as Harkers) opened on 2 August 1824 with an inscription on its frontage reading, 'Yorkshire Insurance Company Established MDCCCXXIIII'. It compares in style and grandeur with the nearby Mansion House and was meant to reflect the power and importance of the Yorkshire Insurance Co. The first chairman was John Pemberton and his office, including the fine marble fireplace and panelled walls, remains intact on the first floor. At a much lower level, in the basement, is stonework of the Praetorian Gate, which was probably rebuilt in about AD 300. The gateway to Eboracum consisted of two arches, each one spanning a roadway measuring about 20ft in width. It guarded the approach to the Praetorium, where Julius Agricola directed the Roman legions and where, on the death of Constantius, his son, Constantine, was proclaimed Emperor. The name 'Harkers' is derived from 'Harkers Hotel', which stood in St Helen's Square until 1928, when it moved to a site close to York Racecourse. (www.nicholsonspubs.co.uk)

# August 3rd

**1759:** On this day, the trial of Eugene Aram began in York. He was accused of murdering Daniel Clark following the discovery of bones on a hillside close to Knaresborough in the summer of 1758. Aram began his working life as a gardener, and then became a book-keeper and teacher at a school in Nidderdale, before moving to Lynn in Norfolk. Enquiries by Sir John Turner led to Richard Houseman, a flax dresser who implicated Eugene Aram in Clark's disappearance, and it soon became clear that all three men were involved in large-scale fraud. Houseman spoke of their criminal activities at St Robert's Cave near Grimbald Bridge, and during the trial at York Assizes, he was acquitted before giving evidence against Aram. Eugene Aram gave conflicting evidence about his movements and strongly argued that it was impossible to determine the identity of the skull. His evidence was dismissed by the jury and following their guilty verdict, he was executed on 6 August 1759. (Naismith, J.S., *Tales from the Scaffold*)

---

**1786:** Sarah Siddons was the greatest tragic actress of her era. Her first visit to York as a star performer was in 1786, when she played eleven nights between 29 July and 28 August. On Thursday 3 August, she played Belvidera in Otway's *Venice Preserved*. (*Theatre Royal York*, York History No. 4)

# August 4th

**1824:** Robert Spence, a publisher and bookseller in York, died on this day and was buried on 22 August in St Mary's Churchyard at Bishophill Junior. Born into a humble background at Stillington, where his father was a blacksmith, Robert Spence was only sixteen months old when the family was left destitute by his father's death. As a young man, he was given a basic education and employment in Laurence Sterne's household, before working in a stables. He also became a Methodist during his teenage years, but with no prospect of more work Robert Spence took up bookbinding. He began to sell books and, after a loan of £10 allowed him to expand his business, he became an eminent publisher. (Smith, G., *History of Wesleyan Methodism: Modern Methodism*)

———— • ◆ • ————

**1914:** When war was declared against Germany on 4 August, the Lord Mayor of York set up a Citizens' Committee to dispense relief to poor members of the city during predicted periods of increased unemployment and rises in food prices. (Kightly, C. & Semlyen, R., *Lords of the City*)

# August 5th

**1781:** On this day, the Old White Swan Inn welcomed an unusual visitor. With permission from the city's Lord Mayor, the *York Chronicle* advertised an appearance by the world's tallest man at the inn. Still only twenty years of age, O'Brien, as he was known, already stood 8ft high. The inn's landlord charged his customers a shilling to observe the giant visitor. O'Brien's stay was only short, as he was travelling around Britain exhibiting his enormous stature. The Old White Swan is not only one of the city's oldest inns, but also one of the most haunted. At least nine buildings make up the premises, which date from the fifteenth century, and over the years they have served as a pigsty, barber's shop, coach house and poultry market. Four steps that can still be seen in the courtyard were originally used to board stagecoaches and are known as 'the mountings'. (www.enjoyenglandcom)

———— • ◆ • ————

**1898:** The Prince of Wales reviewed eight battalions of militia on the Knavesmire. He was attended by Lord Roberts, the Earl of Scarborough, General Thynne and others. (Knight, C.B., *City of York*)

# August 6th

**1774:** Robert Thomas was executed at Tyburn, York and afterwards hung in chains on Beacon Hill, Halifax. The *Leeds Mercury* reported, 'The gibbet whereon he is hung is strongly overlaid with iron, and what is a little remarkable, his chains are so contrived that his right hand points at the very spot where the robbery was committed.' His crime involved the murder and robbery of William Deighton, Supervisor of Taxes, in the Halifax area on the night of 9/10 November 1769, and an informer, James Broadbent, implicated Thomas and others in the violent assault. On his arrest, Thomas was found to be the owner of a pair of strong shoes with large nails that matched marks on Deighton's body, and he was soon taken from Leeds to York Castle. The trial of Robert Thomas and his co-accused took place at York Assizes on 4 August 1770 but, with conflicting evidence put forward, surprisingly they were acquitted. Officers of the Crown did not let the matter rest though and, with more evidence from their informer, charged Thomas with highway robbery. On 3 May 1774 he confessed to the murder of Deighton and was found guilty of the robbery, a crime that carried the death penalty. (*Leeds Mercury*)

# August 7th

**1411:** 'The chapel belonging to the Merchant Adventurers' Hospital in Fossgate was built in about the year 1411 for on August 7th of that year Archbishop Bowet granted a special licence to the Master of the Hospital to celebrate divine service in the new chapel and upon the new altar which had been erected there at the cost of certain citizens: also to hallow the bread and water on Sundays and the so hallowed to administer to the poor, weak and infirm people of the Hospital for ever...' (Knight, C.B., *History of the City of York*)

———•◆•———

**1864:** Lendal Bridge was opened on 8 January 1863 and until 7 August of the following year, anyone using this crossing point had to pay a toll to collectors based in toll houses at each end of the bridge. The toll houses were designed by George Page, son of the bridge designer Thomas Page, and completed by local sculptor George Walker Milburn. Decorative angels at the centre of the bridge's arch were the work of a Mr Tweedy from Newcastle, who modelled them on photographs of the Princess of Wales and Princess Alexandra of Denmark. (Murray, H., *Photographs and Photographers*)

# August 8th

**1777:** A notice appeared in the *York Chronicle* giving details of items pawned by Thomas Grimshaw of Dringhouses, 'which are supposed to have been stolen'. It read:

STOLEN GOODS
Whereas the following Articles were
found in the house of THOMAS GRIMSHAW,
at Dringhouses, (now confined in the House of Correction in York). Half a piece of 16d black ribbon – Half a piece of 14d pink ribbon, edg'd with white – One silk handkerchief – 2 3/8 yards of yard-wide book muslin – 2 3/8 yards of Scotch gauze – 7 remnants of white lace – 31 remnants of coloured ribbons – One linen handkerchief – Four small remnants of lawn – and three small lawns of Irish cloth.

Also were found, Pawnbroker's Tickets for the following goods pledged by the said Thomas Grimshaw: A silver watch, pawn'd May 27 1775 – a silver cream-jug pawn'd April 12 1776 – Two silver spoons – One plated pint, one gill, knives, forks, table cloths, and many other things too numerous to mention, all of which are supposed to have been stolen.

All persons who have missed any such goods, upon telling the marks, and describing the goods, may see them by applying to Thomas Robson, in Castlegate, York.

(*York Chronicle*, 8 August 1777)

# August 9th

**1681:** According to T.P. Cooper, in his pamphlet *The Christmas Waits and Minstrels of Bygone York*, published in 1909, a marble slab in the churchyard of St Martin's Church in Coney Street had the inscription, 'Here lyeth the body of John Edwards one of the waits of this city who dyed ye 9 Aug 1681'. This was in accordance with a statement in his will about his place of burial: '…in St Martin's Church (Coney Street) behind the south doore neare to the steeple five foot deep at least and a marble slab to be laide upon my grave'. Sadly, the marble slab seems to have been destroyed in the air raid of 29 April 1942, which badly damaged the Guildhall. (Cooper, T.P., *The Christmas Waits and Minstrels of Bygone York*)

---

**1856:** A crowd, estimated to number 15–20,000, gathered on this day to witness the public execution of William Dove. At his trial, the court heard that he had married Harriet Jenkins at the end of 1852, only to break up with her within a short time on account of his heavy drinking. He then began to administer poison to Harriet, resulting in her death on 1 March 1856. After initially denying poisoning her, Dove admitted his guilt during his trial in July. (Naismith, J.S., *Tales from the Scaffold*)

# August 10th

**1175:** A gathering of nobles at York held a council, where the King of Scotland, along with his nobles and bishops, paid homage to King Henry II and his son. During the ceremony, the King of Scotland rested his spear and shield on the high altar in York Minster. (Benson, G., *History of the City of York*)

---

**1925:** A motor lorry ran away down the steep gradient of King Street and crashed on to a pleasure steamer *River King* of Sunderland, which was moored at King's Staith. The lorry, which belonged to Messrs W.H. Thackwray & Co., wine and spirits merchants of Coppergate, rested partly on the boat and partly on the quayside. The driver stated that he left the lorry while in a public house on business. The brakes of the vehicle were on, but failed to act because of the gradient. There was considerable damage to the rails and seats of the *River King*, but the lorry, which had to be hoisted ashore again by a crane, was only slightly damaged. (*Yorkshire Evening Press*)

# August 11th

**1943:** The following letter, dated 11 August 1943, was received by the management of Betty's Ltd from the Quartering Commandant, No. 5 Area:

SUBJECT: BETTY'S CAFE, DAVYGATE, YORK
Dear Sirs,
With reference to your premises in Davygate, York, I should be glad if you would let me know what your reactions would be if the whole of your premises mentioned above were requisitioned. Would you please also inform me what you would expect in the way of compensation rental.

In his reply, dated 12 August, the Managing Director of Betty's pointed out the extent of the company's operations in York, and further correspondence from military authorities on 13 August revealed, '...it is not proposed to continue with the requisitioning of the property.' (Wild, J., *Hearts, Tarts and Rascals: The Story of Betty's*)

———— •◆• ————

**1904:** A show entitled *In Dahomey* was playing at York's Theatre Royal. It featured Don Avery and Charles Hart, with Will Marion Cook as the musical director. Reports stated, 'The cake walk (the real thing) is a feature of the play and is alone worth seeing.' (*Yorkshire Evening Press*)

# August 12th

**1825:** Business was quiet at The Clock Inn, Walmgate as Mrs Dickinson was serving behind the bar, when a well-dressed stranger walked through the door. He ordered a glass of cheap gin, known at the time as 'blue ruin' and engaged Mrs Dickinson in conversation. During their lengthy chat, he told her that he belonged to the Oldbuck School, which she assumed referred to the character, Jonathan Oldbuck, who featured in Sir Walter Scott's work *The Antiquary* (printed about nine years previously). He then indicated that he was a collector of old coins and requested to search in her till for antique items to augment his collection cabinet. She left him to his enterprise as he carefully inspected each halfpenny and silver coin, and although the volume of coins appeared to decrease she allowed him to continue the search. Concluding his forage through the till, he indicated that his search had proved fruitless but, as the stranger turned towards the door, several coins dropped from his sleeve. Mrs Dickinson challenged him and threatened to call the police, but was silenced by his affronted retort that she was disputing his honesty. When Mr Dickinson returned and checked cash in the till, a total of 7s 6d was missing and the conman had disappeared without trace. (*York Herald*)

# *August 13th*

**1814:** The programme for the Theatre Royal read:

> Preceding the Play, the Antipodean Powers of the Surprising Sieur Sanches will be exercised in the most surprising manner. He will WALK against the CEILING over the stage WITH HIS HEAD DOWNWARDS... [and] at the extremity of his walk will suspend one leg, turn on his heel, and walk back.

(Theatre Royal Programme, 13 August 1814)

———— ◆ ————

**1814:** Under the terms of her will, dated 13 August 1814, the Right Honourable Ellen Countess Dowager Conyngham handed over almost £20,000 of stock to various charitable institutions within the York area. Beneficiaries included not only her servants, but also the widows of poor deceased clergymen and ten poor clergymen who held only one living under the annual value of £100. Further awards were made to six poor widows or unmarried women aged fifty or more who lived in York and had no more than £50 per year income, as well as St Thomas' Hospital, St Catherine's, Middleton's and Mason's. In total her charitable handouts totalled almost £20,000. (Genuki, *A History of York, Yorkshire 1823, part 7*)

# August 14th

**1799:** Richard Chicken was baptised at St Michael's Church following his birth six days earlier in Low Ousegate. He was educated at Bingley Grammar School, where elocution was his favourite subject. He then joined an itinerant group of actors at a theatre in Nottingham and acquired the title Professor of Elocution and Lecturer on Defective Annunciation at York. Richard Chicken became well known around York as a courteous but eccentric character, and took up work as a clerk in the city. From about 1845, he worked alongside Alfred Dickens, brother of Charles, at a time when the author was writing *David Copperfield* and making frequent visits to York. It is likely that he met Charles Dickens, as Chicken is believed to have been the model for the character Wilkins Micawber in *David Copperfield*. He married Louisa Alexander and fathered twelve children. (Heape R.G., *Georgian York*; www.sandramidgley.com/RichardChicken)

———— • ◆ • ————

**2010:** York Minster hosted a Stone Carving Festival for masons, carvers, sculptors and apprentices from across Britain and abroad. It had been ten years since the extremely successful York Stone Festival was held and it followed the annual Stone Yard open day. (www.yorkminster.org)

# August 15th

**1119:** Thurstan, a native of Bayeux in Normandy and a royal chaplain, was appointed Archbishop of York on this day, a time when there was conflict over the link with Canterbury. He was not consecrated until 1119, at a ceremony performed by Pope Calixtus II at Rheims and his public entry into York took place during the period of Lent 1121. He is probably best remembered for his efforts to restore monastic discipline and organisation in the north of England. Five houses of Augustinian canons were set up in Yorkshire between 1120 and 1125 – notably Kirkham, Guisborough, Bridlington, Bolton and Nostell. A few years later, in 1131, the Cistercian abbey at Rievaulx was established, with Fountains at about the same time. Another Cistercian monastery was set up in 1134 at Byland, by twelve monks from Furness, on land given by Roger de Mowbray. (Knight, C.B., *History of the City of York*)

———•◆•———

**1777:** George Ireland pawned fifteen silver coat buttons, each marked 'G.I.', for 1s 0d each. His pledge, along with an earlier one by Mary Sorry, was redeemed within a month. (Blackhouse, A., *Worm-Eaten Waistcoat*)

# August 16th

**1642:** King Charles I and his court left the capital and based themselves in York for five months in the early and middle part of 1642. He entered the city on 19 March with the Prince of Wales and stayed until 16 August. During his stay, the King stayed at the residence of Sir Arthur Ingram, a stately mansion inside the city walls that was richly decorated with pictures, statues and furniture. The day after his arrival, Charles I knighted the Lord Mayor, Edward Cooper, and during his stay in York the King set up his printing press in the house of Sir Henry Jenkins at St William's College. Thirty-nine publications are credited to the Royal Press, with the last, dated 5 August 1642, itemising money, men and horses offered for His Majesty's service, along with the *Counsell of Warre*. Recent research puts the total number of publications at seventy-four. The Royal Press remained in York for about two weeks after the King's departure for Nottingham on 16 August 1642. (Sessions, W.K. & E.M., *Printing in York*)

———•◆•———

**1814:** Sieur Sanche's performance at the Theatre Royal, York, included him balancing 'six boys on the slack rope suspended by the heels, in full swing, on his hands, feet and body.' (Bebb, P., *Life in Regency York*)

# August 17th

**1525:** Henry FitzRoy, the six-year-old Duke of Richmond was received at York by the Mayor. His residence was at Sheriff Hutton Castle, where a council, termed 'The King's Council in the Northern Parts', dealt with criminal cases without a jury. (Benson, G., *City of York*)

* ◆ *

**1807:** During the early nineteenth century, the area at the Mount in York was covered by a farmhouse and open fields, but on 17 August 1807 workmen made an amazing discovery. As they excavated foundations for No. 104 The Mount, they broke into a sealed chamber that contained a glazed red urn containing human ashes. Further investigation unearthed a slate lid for the 7ft-long coffin and inside was a complete skeleton and two tear jars (glass phials to store tears of the mourners), which are now in the Yorkshire Museum. The property was offered for sale at £625,000 in 2008, and although chamber, coffin and bones were included in the sale, the tomb is an ancient monument. Future owners have a duty of care and are not allowed to sell, display or dispose of the bones. It is a criminal offence to disturb human remains and a licence would be needed to exhume them. (www.telegraph.co.uk)

# August 18th

**1874:** William Jackson is said to be the only man sentenced to death at York for the murder of his sister (known as sororicide). Following military service, he had moved back to his father's house near Kirklington, about 9 miles from Ripon, but was unable to find work. Tensions in the family home increased until he was ordered to leave. Jackson finally left the family home on a final search for work. He was accompanied on his trek by Lizzie, his sixteen-year-old sister, and, as they headed towards Ripon, William Jackson ordered his younger sibling to return home before darkness fell. She persuaded him to let her continue for a while, but then they argued fiercely and he insisted that she turn back. Initially Lizzie dropped back, but then continued some distance behind and this made William Jackson lose control of his senses. Seizing a razor, he slashed her across the throat and caused fatal injuries. He was soon arrested and tried at York Assizes, where a plea of insanity was rejected. On the morning of his execution Jackson made a full confession, before becoming the first condemned prisoner to be hanged behind locked doors in York. (Naismith, J.S., *Tales from the Scaffold*)

# August 19th

**1886:** Reverend Henry Ward Beecher, the famous American preacher, lectured in the York Festival Court Room on 'The Reign of the Common People'. The Lord Mayor presided over proceedings and many of the city clergy were present. (Knight, C.B., *History of the City of York*)

— ◆ —

**1911:** Industrial relations dominated news stories during the summer of 1911. One of the most dramatic episodes involved the General Railway Workers Union, with a newspaper headline on 19 August stating, 'MOB LAW IN YORK'. The situation stemmed from the union leaders' decision to call a general strike from 8 p.m. on 16 August. Although railway workers probably had fewer grievances than members of other unions, many in the workforce still suffered from low wages, short time and harsh management decisions. Press coverage on 19 August reported that 5,000 railwaymen were on strike in York, trains were being stoned and soldiers from the York and Lancaster Regiment patrolled some areas. Terry's factory had closed because deliveries were impossible and magistrates were prepared to read the Riot Act. Nationally, the strike ended fairly soon, but York strikers continued their campaign for two more days before leaders called an official end. (*Yorkshire Evening Press*)

# August 20th

**1583:** The question of relief for the poorer members of the community assumed importance in the Tudor period and an order dated 20 August 1583 stated that 'from henceforth no head-beggars shall be chosen; and from Christmas next John Geldart, Thomas Todd and William Curtus, now head beggars, shall not have any wages of clothing of the Common Chamber, but only their weekly allowances out of the money gathered on the assessment for relief of the poor.' (Knight, C.B., *History of York*)

———— • ◆ • ————

**1994:** The death of the top composer and former freeman of the city of York, Sydney Dale, was reported. Dale was an engineer at Rowntree's Cocoa Works in the early 1940s and played with the Bert Keech Dance Band at De Grey Rooms in the centre of York. For many years he worked on musical arrangements for band leaders such as Joe Loss, Geraldo and Ted Heath, and then penned signature tunes for a number of American television shows. Sydney Dale set up his own publishing company, Amphonic Music Ltd, which became one of the leading music libraries in the country. He died at the age of seventy. (*Yorkshire Evening Press*)

# *August 21st*

**1880:** Cases heard at the court in York Guildhall, before the Lord Mayor and Alderman James Meek, included a charge against Henry Snell for contravening the Licensing Act. According to PC Raisbeck's evidence, the defendant, who ran a provision shop in Layerthorpe and was licensed to sell beer 'off the premises', sold two pints of beer on 7 August to some men who were in charge of a wagon and horses in the street. The whole case appeared to hinge on where the beer was paid for and discussion focused on this issue, before the Lord Mayor concluded that the first pint was paid for in the street. His ruling was that the full penalty was £10, but the defendant would only be fined £1 and costs, and his licence would not be endorsed. (*York Herald*)

———◆———

**1880:** At the same court, Patrick Coulen of Charles Street was charged with assaulting his wife, Mary Ann. The defendant had been out of work for some time and had led an idle life, the court was told. He had gone home and asked for something to eat and because his wife was unable to provide food, he knocked her down, kicked her and brutally ill-treated her. Seven previous convictions were recorded against him for serious offences and magistrates sentenced him to six months' hard labour. (*York Herald*)

# August 22nd

**1572:** The seventh Earl of Northumberland was convicted of treason and executed on a large scaffold, erected outside the east-end of All Saints' Church. His body was later buried in St Crux by two of his servants and three women. An entry in the register states, 'Sir Thoms Pearsey, Erle was buried 22 of Aug. 1572'. (*All Saints' Church, Pavement,* York Guide Book)

———•◆•———

**1830:** Six members of one family, along with their friend, were drowned near Acomb landing on the River Ouse, when a pleasure boat sank. The six were all children of Mr Rigg of York and the seventh was a Miss Robinson, who was on a visit. The children of Mr Rigg were all interred together in the burial ground of St Lawrence near Walmgate Bar. (*Guide to the City of York*)

———•◆•———

**1926:** York architect Walter Brierley died on this day after practising for more than forty years, during which time he designed more than 300 buildings across northern England. He designed his own home, 'Bishopbarns', in York during 1905 and 'Goddards' on Tadcaster Road was his last work. His architectural practice still operates as Brierley Groom and is said to be the oldest architectural firm in the UK (having been established by John Carr in 1750). (www.archiseek.com)

# August 23rd

**1649:** Colonel John Morris had a chequered military career during the period of the English Civil War, before he was found guilty of treason and executed in York on this day in August. Born in South Elmsall, he trained as a soldier with his uncle, the Earl of Stafford, and won many honours during military service in Ireland. When war broke out in 1645, he was persuaded to join the parliamentary army and took part in sieges at Pontefract and Sandal castles. But when Cromwell set up the New Model Army, Morris' cavalier lifestyle did not find favour and he was not awarded a commission. This caused a change of allegiance and he played a part in re-taking Pontefract Castle for the King's forces. He then held out for some ten months against a 5,000-strong besieging Roundhead army. By March 1649, bombardment forced surrender but, before the handover, Morris and another officer made their escape. Some ten days later they were recaptured near Lancaster and brought back to York for trial and execution. (www.wakefield.gov.uk: Colonel John Morris)

# August 24th

**1789:** This Monday in August saw a visit by the Royal Highnesses the Prince of Wales and the Duke of York to York races. Arriving at the racecourse by royal carriage, they stopped some distance from the grandstand and completed their journey on horseback in front of crowds of cheering onlookers. At the end of the day's sport, they took their seats in the carriage of Earl Fitzwilliam and made their way into the city as his guests. The following day, York Corporation presented the heir to the throne with the Freedom of the City (the document enclosed in a gold box). On Thursday 27 August, the Prince of Wales attended a dinner at the Mansion House along with many members of noble families. Two days later, the Prince of Wales and the Duke of York made their way to Castle Howard, but before leaving York they arranged for Lieutenant Colonel St Leger to hand over 2,000 guineas to Walter Fawkes, High Sheriff, in support of debtors in the castle. (*Baines' Gazetteer, 1823*)

# August 25th

**1755:** The elegant classical-style grandstand at York racecourse was designed by John Carr and opened on this day. Apart from the fine room on the first floor, there were more viewing facilities on the roof. The first race to pass the new grandstand was won by 'Whistlejacket' (later featured in the painting by George Stubbs). It is now in a collection at the National Gallery. Horse racing in the York area can be traced back to Roman times and, by the early eighteenth century, it was established at Clifton. Problems with flooding caused the move to Knavesmire in 1731. Races were accompanied by sideshows, cockfights and even public executions. (www.historyofyork.org.uk)

———— • ◆ • ————

**1804:** York racecourse hosted the first known horse race to feature a female jockey against a male rider, when Alicia Meynell, riding Colonel Thornton's 'Vingarella' side saddle, took on Captain William Flint, riding 'Thornville', over a 4-mile race. 'Vingarella' failed to complete the course, but Alicia Meynell returned the following year and rode a 2-mile race on six-year-old 'Louisa', against Frank Buckle on 'Allegro', and won. (Winn, C., *I Never Knew That About Yorkshire*)

# August 26th

**1285:** William Wickwane, Archbishop of York, died at Pontigny on a journey to Rome, after a ministry which began with enthronement in 1280. His years in office were beset by disputes with ecclesiastical authorities at both Canterbury and Durham, but he is remembered as a man of simple habits and great holiness, who was most conscientious in administering business of the diocese. (Hart, A.T., *Ebor: The Archbishop of York*)

—◆—

**1685:** A large porpoise or sea hogg, 'three yards and a half in length and three thickness, having left the sea and entered the Ouse was taken from that river, in Clifton Ings, near this city; and as might be expected, the singularity of the event, excited considerable attention and surprise…' (Hargrove, W., *History and Description of the City of York*)

—◆—

**1823:** While his brother King George IV was in Scotland, H.R.H. the Duke of Sussex paid a visit to York and attended a public dinner, where he was presented with the Freedom of the City. Documents in a gold box included an address expressing admiration of the 'splendid career of useful beneficence and spirited patriotism which gave a brilliant lustre to his exalted birth'. (*Baines' Gazetteer*, 1823)

# August 27th

**1790:** A letter published in the *York Chronicle* claimed:

> If the inhabitants of this city would rouse themselves to
> some spirited exertions and the Corporation open the gates
> to all tradesmen and manufacturers inclinable to settle
> amongst us, York might again lift up its head and recover its
> ancient consequence as a principal place of commerce and
> manufacture in this mercantile county.

This anonymous letter-writer highlighted two causes of York's
problems in terms of commercial development: a lack of
manufactures and regulations against non-freemen setting up
in business. But it was several decades before these issues were
resolved. In 1827, Merchant Adventurers lost their authority
to impose regulations and the Corporation's power to fine
non-freemen for daring to trade in the city was removed by a
clause in the Municipal Reform Act of 1835. The Reform Act
of 1832 extended parliamentary franchise to non-freemen, so
there was little incentive for a citizen to become one, and soon
non-freemen of the city outnumbered freemen. (Knight, C.B.,
*History of the City of York*)

# August 28th

**1872:** A group of gentlemen in a darkened room at the York Tavern witnessed a paranormal performace by Herr Dobler. The highlight of the display involved Herr Dobler sitting in a chair with his hands tied securely behind him and a rope running down to his feet, which were firmly fastened to the chair legs. A tambourine, which had been highlighted with phosphorus, was then observed in the darkness to rise from the table and float over their heads and around the room with its bells tinkling. A few minutes later, when gas lamps were relit, the tambourine was found lying near the door. (*York Herald*)

———— • ◆ • ————

**1880:** On this day, advertisements from the front page of the *York Herald* included:

How to spend a few pleasant hours at York – Have a trip on the Ouse by the fine new steamer, *WHITE ROSE*, which leaves Lendal every afternoon at 2.30 and 7.15, circumstances permitting, for various places. Fares there and back, 6d: select 1s. Tea and refreshments on board. Can be engaged as a yacht for a short sea voyage after September 6th.

# August 29th

**1935:** The Kit Kat bar was launched on this day, under the name 'Rowntree's Chocolate Crisp' and at a cost of 2*d*. The Kit Kat brand dates back to 1911, when it was first developed by Rowntree's in York as a box of chocolates. Manufacture continued into the 1930s. Eventually 'Black Magic' and 'Dairy Box' brands were introduced and Kit Kat was discontinued. Introduction of the Kit Kat as a four-finger bar followed a recommendation from a worker at Rowntree's York factory. He placed the idea for a snack 'that a man could take to work in his pack-up' in a suggestion box. Food shortages during the Second World War brought an alteration in the recipe for the chocolate bar and a new blue wrapper, but in 1947 the original recipe and original red packaging were restored. A two-finger variation was launched in the 1930s, and in 2005 over 800 million of these were sold in the UK, with corresponding success for Kit Kat Chunky following its launch in 1999. During 1988, Nestlé took over Rowntree brands and in 2010, a new manufacturing line opened in York, producing more than one billion Kit Kat bars each year. (www.nestleprofessional. com; www.yorkpress.co.uk)

# August 30th

**1485:** 'It was determined that the gates and posterns of the city should be shut every night at nine o'clock and opened at four o'clock in the morning and that four men of every ward should watch at every gate every night for the safeguarding of the city and its inhabitants. A similar regulation had been passed in 1482 but perhaps had become more honoured in the breach than in the observance: apparently it was now judged that the present dangers called for its strict observance.' (Knight, C.B., *History of the City of York*)

———— • ◆ • ————

**1995:** The York area received a boost in the employment market as firms prepared to move into the new Monks Cross retail park. Work on the first phase of the new 100,000sq.ft shopping development, called 'The Cloisters', was due to start the following month, but there was concern that stores in the centre of York might close if they opened a branch at Monks Cross. (*Yorkshire Evening Press*)

———— • ◆ • ————

**1995:** Local Transport Minister Steven Norris strongly defended York City Council's move towards Park and Ride schemes. Rider York had been given a five-year contract to run the service for York Council and, so far, the latest Hull Road Park and Ride site has received more than £1 million of government funding. (*Yorkshire Evening Press*)

# August 31st

**1901:** The first York Hospital Sunday was held and became a regular fundraising event in the city. Along with a number of other caring institutions such as the York Dispensary, which offered free medical attention to poor patients in 1788, the hospital had been founded in the eighteenth century. (*Yorkshire Evening Press*)

———— •◆• ————

**1932:** York City FC have been based at their Bootham Crescent ground since 1932 and the official opening took place on 31 August of that year, with a Division 3 North match against Stockport County. The president of the football club carried out the traditional ceremonial cutting of a ribbon in the club's colours (chocolate brown and cream). The Bootham Crescent ground was initially rented from York CC as a replacement for the Fulfordgate premises, which had access issues, and before the first match, construction of a main stand and popular stand was completed. An amount of damage was caused during an air raid in April 1942, and in the late 1940s major ground improvements were carried out. At a shareholders' meeting in September 1948, it was announced that the club had bought the ground (which had previously been leased). (Batters, D., *York City: A Complete Record 1922–1990*)

# September 1st

**1860:** There was cause for celebration by members of the York House Painters' Association, when around forty of their number met for dinner at the Three Cranes in St Sampson's Square. During previous meetings at the inn, they had attempted to resolve a dispute with employers over a higher wage rate. Numbers of local men were leaving the area for improved rates of pay in other townships and they were requesting a weekly wage of *6d*. Most employers had agreed to the increase and, after the successful outcome, toasts were drunk to the Master Painters of York, the Guildhall, the army and navy and the landlord of the Three Cranes, William Briggs. (*York Herald*)

———— • ◆ • ————

**2010:** The University of York announced that Professor Dame Jinty Nelson had been awarded an honorary degree by the Department of History. Professor Nelson is a distinguished historian of the early Middle Ages, who specialised in ritual and politics in the Carolingian era and on the history of women and gender in the early Middle Ages. Posts that she has held include president of the Royal Historical Society (2000– 2004) and vice-president of the British Academy (1999–2001). In 2006, she was made a Dame of the British Empire. (www.york.ac.uk)

# September 2nd

**1636:** Jane Hodson, wife of Phineas Hodson, Chancellor of York, died at the age of thirty-eight. She and her husband had twenty-four children, before she died in childbirth and was buried in York Minster. (www.genuki.org.uk)

———— • ❖ • ————

**1927:** Francis Matthews was born in York on this day. He attended St Michael's Jesuit College at Leeds, before taking up an acting career with Leeds' repertory theatre. Following service in the Royal Navy, he played a number of characters for Hammer Studios during the 1950s and '60s. These included the Baron's assistant in *The Revenge of Frankenstein* (1958) and main roles in *Dracula, Prince of Darkness* and *Rasputin, the Mad Monk* (both 1965). Television work includes the role of Francis Durbridge's amateur sleuth, Paul Temple, and a variety of comedy roles in the 1960s and '70s. Many of these were with Morecambe and Wise, including *The Intelligence Men* (1965) and *That Riviera Touch* (1966). He appeared in the *Morecambe and Wise Christmas Show* in 1977. Francis Matthews is also a theatre director and, in November 2010, he directed the world premiere performance of *The Three Musketeers* at the Rose Theatre, Kingston upon Thames. (*Who's Who On Television*)

# September 3rd

**1268:** King Henry III visited York on this day, a time when incursions by Scottish forces were a constant threat. During an earlier visit in 1244, he had ordered rebuilding of the castle and this project took more than twenty years to complete. (Benson, G., *An Account of the County and City of York*)

———— • ◆ • ————

**1914:** The First World War was in its early stages during the late summer of 1914, but the grim realities of modern warfare were soon reported in York. News filtered through that the Scots Greys, who had recently been based in York, had suffered serious losses in the retreat from Mons and, on 3 September, it was reported that Major Swetenham, a well-known figure in the city as an officer in the Scots Greys, had been killed in action. (*York Herald*)

———— • ◆ • ————

**1914:** On the same day, *The Herald* included a letter from F.H. Wickenden, a local jeweller and watchmaker, in which he discounted rumours that he was of German descent or that he had any links with Germany. Among other 'aliens' to be harassed in York was the city's Labour parliamentary candidate, and a gentleman named Schloesser, who soon changed his name to Slesser. (*York Herald*)

# *September 4th*

**1841:** Albert Joseph Moore, born on this day, was the youngest of fourteen children fathered by William Moore, landscape and portrait painter. During his childhood, he was encouraged to pursue his interest in art by his father and brothers, John Collingham Moore and Henry Moore. In 1858, Albert Moore took up studies at the Royal Academy Schools, but soon gave up and concentrated on producing and exhibiting many of his pictures and drawings. His first large canvas 'Elijah's Sacrifice' was completed in 1863 during a stay in Rome and displayed at the Academy in 1865. The following year, an even bigger work, 'The Shunamite relating the Glories of King Solomon to her Maidens', was exhibited along with two smaller paintings 'Apricots' and 'Pomegranates'. Moore's approach to his painting was to avoid storytelling and to concentrate solely on decorative arrangements of lines and colour masses. He died in 1893 at his studio in Spenser Street, Westminster. (www.my-yorkshire.co.uk)

———— • ◆ • ————

**1945:** During the Second World War, York racecourse was used as a prisoner of war camp and crops such as potatoes and sugar beet were grown. Racing returned on 4 September 1945, and the following day 'Chamossaire' won the substitute St Leger. (www.greyhoundderby.com/briefyork.htm)

# September 5th

**1854:** At a court hearing on this day, it was alleged that two boys, named Watson and Murray, had been sent by Henry Varley to sweep a chimney at the Coach and Horses public house. They took with them an appliance that he had told them to use, but on arrival it was found to be too short. Instead of returning for more equipment, they decided to climb the chimney to sweep it. It was because of this risky action that Varley was summoned to appear in court on a charge of allowing two persons under twenty-one to ascend a chimney to clean it. The landlord, Joseph Giddy, also had to appear in court, but he claimed that the sweep had been ordered by his wife and that he was unaware the chimney had been swept until he received his summons. (*York Herald*)

———— • ◆ • ————

**1906:** During much of 1906, York Corporation was negotiating to take over the city's Tramways Co. The newspaper report on 5 September indicated that terms of the Tramways Act of 1870 made this possible. The chairman of the company later stated, at the half-yearly meeting, that he hoped this would be possible by agreement. (*York Evening Press*)

# September 6th

**1790:** Until the reign of Queen Victoria (1837–1901), there were two distinct governing bodies in the city of York: the Municipality, which was until 1836 self-elected, and the Dean and Chapter, who exercised sole power over the Liberty of St Peter of York. Within St Peter's Liberty, clergymen were eligible to be gamekeepers as indicated in the statement dated 6 September 1790:

> The Clerk of the Peace for the Liberty certified the Game Warrant issued by the executors of John Clough Esq. Of York, Lord of the Manor of North Newbald, appointing the Rev. Edmund Holmes of Weighton, to be our Gamekeeper of our Manor with full power, Licence and authority to kill any hare, pheasant, partridge or other game in the Manor for our own sole use and also to take and seize all such guns, bows, greyhounds, setting dogs, lurchers or other dogs to kill hares or conies, ferrets, tramels, lowbels, hays or other nets, harepipes, snares or other engines for the taking and killing of game.

(Benson, G., *An Account of the County and City of York*)

# September 7th

**1483:** One reason for constructing a new Guildhall in York was to provide a spacious area suitable for staging plays, and on Sunday, 7 September 1483, the play *Credo* was performed in front of King Richard III and his court. (Benson, G., *An Account of the County and City of York*)

——— ◆ ———

**1889:** A Lancashire and Yorkshire-terminating train ran into the buffers on platform six of York station, resulting in thirteen casualties. (Edgington, J. & Gilks, J.S., *Trains from York*)

——— ◆ ———

**1909:** One of the very last horse-drawn trams travelled along the Mount in York on 7 September 1909. York Tramways Co.'s horses were neglected in the latter period of operation and were mocked in a contemporary series of postcards, which aroused an amount of controversy. Photographs of the same period show engineers and council inspectors assessing the new electric tramlines that were being installed along Station Avenue. (www.yorkpress.co.uk)

# September 8th

**1483:** After celebrating mass at York Minster, King Richard III formally invested his son Edward, Prince of Wales, and at the same ceremony knighted the Spanish ambassador. There is some indication in contemporary records that the investiture was arranged quite hastily and it is believed that ill health may have prevented the young prince from travelling to London for his parents' coronation. His health would seem to have improved by the time that he reached the north of England. There is further uncertainty about the date of the Prince of Wales' death, as some sources suggest 31 March 1484, while others indicate 9 April 1484. He was buried in the parish church at Sheriff Hutton. (Richard III trail www.yorkwalk.co.uk)

**1835:** Small-scale music festivals were held in York on an annual basis between 1791 and 1803, but the next festival was not held until 1823. The fourth music festival in the series was attended by Princess Victoria and her mother, the Duchess of Kent. There was a performance by more than 600 vocalists and instrumentalists that made a profit of £4,000, which was shared between the Minster Restoration Fund and four hospitals. (Knight, C.B., *History of York*)

# September 9th

**1880:** The contract was approved for the building of the Holgate Carriage Works (established 1884), which covered an area of 45 acres. (Edgington, J. & Gilks, J.S., *Trains from York*)

━━━━━◆•━━━━━

**1984:** The National Trust acquired Goddards at 27 Tadcaster Road, Dringhouses, York, on a freehold basis for use as a regional office. During January 1925, Noel Terry, a member of the chocolate manufacturing company Joseph Terry & Sons, took possession of slightly more than 3 acres of land from Colonel Wilkinson of Dringhouses Manor, and an additional piece of land was added at the end of the year. Walter Brierley, the well-known York architect, was commissioned to design an Arts and Crafts style house on the site and George Dillistone worked with Brierley on designs for formal gardens. The house was completed in 1927, but the garden was not finished until later, when Dillistone described it as 'a very fine series of gardens with plenty of interest through every foot'. In 2006 the garden was first opened to visitors, during office hours in the spring and summer season. (*Goddards Garden*, The National Trust)

━━━━━◆•━━━━━

**2006:** The St Leger, oldest of Britain's five classic horse races, was run at York racecourse, as the usual course at Doncaster was being redeveloped. (www.racingbetter.co.uk)

# September 10th

**1915:** The *York Herald* reported on progress with a national register which recorded details of all individuals aged between fifteen and sixty-five years. As the First World War moved into its second year, there was much debate about issue of recruitment for the armed forces and the question of conscription. A total of 130 people acted as enumerators for the survey in York and it was reported that there were no objectors to the registration at this initial stage. Elsewhere, there were court proceedings against people who refused to cooperate. At Heywood, a schoolmaster named Harold Pugmire was imprisoned for refusing to pay a £5 fine that had been imposed when he refused to complete registration forms. At Croydon, Amelia Elizabeth Hewitt was fined £3 and costs for her non-cooperation, while a suffragette, Annie Wren Hutty, was the first person to face prosecution for refusing to supply details about herself. She was fined for several offences and, following non-payment of the fines, goods were seized by court officials. (*York Herald*)

# September 11th

**1069:** Ealdred (or Aldred), high-ranking churchman in Anglo-Saxon England, died and was buried in York Minster. He received training as a monk at Winchester and was appointed abbot of Tavistock Abbey in about 1027, before becoming Bishop of Worcester in 1046. In addition to his episcopal responsibilities, Ealdred served Edward the Confessor as a diplomat and military leader. One of his tasks was to arrange the return from Hungary of Edward the Exile so that the childless King had an heir. During 1058, he became the first English bishop to make a pilgrimage to Jerusalem and, during his time as administrator of the Diocese of Hereford, Ealdred had to negotiate a settlement of border disputes with a Welsh ruler, Gruffyd ap Llwellyn. In 1060, he was elected to the Archbishopric of York, but only received papal approval after agreeing not to hold the bishoprics of York and Worcester at the same time. During his time at York, Ealdred supervised the completion of new churches and refurbishment of others, as well as improving standards among clergy by publishing regulations for the priesthood. He crowned William of Normandy as King of England on Christmas Day 1066. (www.britannica.com)

# September 12th

**1995:** The city's Visitor and Conference Bureau were backing the campaign against closure of York's Marygate car park. Spokesman John Gallery described the proposal as 'nonsense', as it would erode trade in shops, hotels and guesthouses. He added that it was contrary to the new tourism strategy that had recently been unveiled for the city. Tourism was now York's main industry, with more than 10,000 people employed. Mr Gallery lodged the bureau's objection to the proposed closure with the council. (*York Evening Press*)

———◆———

**1995:** 'R.A.F. Linton on Ouse will exercise its freedom of the city of York on September 17th with a march to commemorate the Battle of Britain. Officers and men will march along Leeman Road and over Lendal Bridge accompanied by the pipes and drums of Royal Air Force Waddington before a service takes place in the south transept of the Minster. A highlight of the event will be a flypast at 11.15 A.M. by a formation of Tucano aircraft.' (*York Evening Press*)

# September 13th

**1819:** On this day, James Hack Tuke was born in York. He was the son of William Tuke, a tea and coffee merchant with a philanthropic outlook. James joined the family business and assisted with management of the York asylum, which had been set up by his father to provide intelligent and humane care of insane individuals. James Tuke is remembered for his work in Ireland. In 1847, and again in 1880, he provided generous support during periods of famine and published widely read accounts of his observations. (www.multitext.ucc.ie/d/James_Hack_Tuke_1819-96)

———— • ◆ • ————

**1854:** Queen Victoria and Prince Albert, with five of their children, spent half an hour at the old Station Hotel on their rail journey to Scotland. The Archbishop, Lord Mayor, Earl of Carlisle and other dignitaries had escorted the royal party from the station to the hotel, where a large crowd of local people had gathered to observe proceedings. There was some local criticism of the expense in staging this brief royal visit and it is claimed that, on hearing of this disquiet, the Queen steadfastly refused to visit the city again. (Knight, C.B., *History of the City of York*)

# September 14th

**1541:** On this day, King Henry VIII made his only visit to the city of York. He was not ceremonially greeted at Micklegate Bar, however, as would have been customary, but instead at Fulford Cross. The Mayor and members of the Corporation were dressed in penitential gowns and knelt while the Recorder spoke a pitiful address of submission. The King stayed for twelve days in York and his lodgings were in a new palace that had been constructed near the abbot's house. The churchwarden's accounts for St Michael's Church in Spurriergate record that, in readiness for Henry's visit, streets were swept, sanded and gravelled. James, King of Scotland, did not arrive for a scheduled meeting with his uncle, King Henry VIII, before the English King headed south again. His first overnight stay on this southwards journey was at Holme-on-Spalding-Moor. (Benson, G., *An Account of the County and City of York*)

---

**1914:** During the early stages of recruitment in August and September 1914, local employers gave reassurance to their workforce about families and jobs and North Eastern Railway managers made similar arrangements. On 14 September, it was announced that recruiting officers for the NER battalion (part of the Northumberland Fusiliers) would be based in York and Newcastle, with training at Hull. (*York Evening Press*)

# September 15th

**1872:** A collision of railway locomotives took place between Copmanthorpe and Chaloner's Whin Junction, when a passenger train ran into the rear of a slow-moving freight. (Edgington, J. & Gilks, J.S., *Trains from York*)

———— ◆ ————

**1901:** One of York's foremost printers, Ben Johnson, died at his home in the Holgate area of York. At his own expressed wish he was cremated in Darlington. Born in Huddersfield in 1830, he was appointed manager of the printing business and then in 1867, he took over ownership of J.W. Lancaster, Wholesale, Retail and Law Stationer, Account Book Manufacturer, Printer, Lithographer and Engraver. Richard Tesseyman was taken on as a partner, but following his death on 16 March 1873 he had to work with Tesseyman's son, Charles Edward. This partnership continued until 1880, when the company's name was changed to Ben Johnson & Company. On 28 to 29 August 1932, the Micklegate premises of Ben Johnson & Co. were totally destroyed by fire, apart from the shop and front office, but production restarted on the same site on 14 October 1932. (Sessions, W.K. & M., *Printing in York*)

# September 16th

**1909:** A significant change in York's transport system took place during September 1909, with the end of horse-drawn trams early in the month. Work on the construction of the new tramway system was carried out by Messrs Dick, Kerr & Co. but, within days of starting to lay new lines, there was industrial trouble. Press reports on 16 September claimed that the contractors were paying 5*d* an hour to the workforce, rather than the agreed rate of 6*d*, and that men sent by the city's Distress Committee to work on the scheme had been sacked and replaced by 'foreign labour'. (*York Evening Press*)

———— ◆ ————

**2011:** York Food and Drink Festival took place from 16 to 25 September at historic settings around the city. Organised by a non-profit making organisation, the festival focused on items of food and drink produced in Yorkshire and was composed of two main aspects: markets and a demonstration area were based in the Parliament Street area, where a marquee, which enclosed the fountain, was used to stage evening events, while other proceedings were staged in the Guildhall, the Mansion House and other venues across the city. (www.yorkfoodfestival.com)

# September 17th

**1764:** John Goodricke was born at Groningen in the Netherlands but spent most of his life in England, with his final years at his parents' home in York. A bout of scarlet fever at the age of five left him profoundly deaf and he was sent to Thomas Braidwood's Academy in Edinburgh and then, in 1778, to the Warrington Academy. On leaving Warrington, he came to live at his parents' home in York and, while there, formed a friendship with Edward Pigott, whose father, Nathaniel Pigott, had constructed a private observatory. John Goodricke used the observatory to pursue his interest in variable stars and is given credit for discovering the periodic variation of the namesake Cephei, of the Cepheid variable stars. Although it was already understood that several stars varied in apparent magnitude, he was the first astronomer to suggest a mechanism to explain this phenomenon. He suggested that Algol represents what is known as an eclipsing binary and presented his findings to the Royal Society in May 1783. In recognition of this work, the society awarded him the Copley Medal for this year, and on 16 April 1786, he was elected a Fellow of the Royal Society. Just four days later he died from pneumonia at the age of twenty-one. (www.goodricke.info)

# September 18th

**1913:** During the early days of aviation, the Knavesmire at York became the setting for early flights. Press reports on this day indicate that local people probably flew with the famous aviator Henri Salmet on his visit. Interest among the public had been heightened by visits to the Knavesmire from Captain C.A.H. Langcroft of the Welsh Regiment, attached to the Royal Flying Corps, and Lieutenant Herbert and Captain Waldron earlier in 1913. The *Yorkshire Evening News* added to the excitement surrounding early aviation events by offering a trophy to the winner of an air race (a 100-mile course) between the best Yorkshire and Lancashire aeroplanes. Termed the 'Wars of the Roses Air Race', it was staged on 2 October at the Yorkshire Aerodrome, close to the Leeds/Harrogate road. Aircraft had to make twenty-minute stops at York, Doncaster, Sheffield and Barnsley, where special aerial issues of the *Yorkshire Evening News* were distributed. The victory for Yorkshire was surrounded by controversy because of disputes over the timing of these stops. Plans for a repeat event in Lancashire the following year had to be abandoned because of the outbreak of the First World War. (www.earlyaviators.com)

# September 19th

**1910:** William Dalrymple Maclagan, Archbishop of York, died on this day. He was buried in the churchyard at Bishopthorpe. After training in military circles, he gained a commission in the 51st regiment Madras Native Infantry and served in India from 1847 to 1849, before returning home to take holy orders. William Maclagan soon gained a wide reputation as a preacher, for his work in setting up Sunday Schools and for improving conditions for poorer children. In 1871, he was appointed Bishop of Lichfield and some twenty years later, on 1 May 1891, he was offered the Archbishopric of York. Although he suffered from prolonged bouts of ill health, Archbishop Maclagan visited 650 parishes in his diocese between 1892 and 1895. His ministry was characterised by an insistence that newly ordained clergy must serve as assistant curates for a reasonable time before being instituted to Sunday and Church-day schools. He also worked hard, though unsuccessfully, towards unity with the Church of Rome and the Russian Orthodox Church. Back in this country, due to the incapacity of Archbishop Temple, Maclagan had the honour of crowning Queen Alexandra in 1902. In June 1908, he received an honorary DD at Oxford. (Hart, A.T., *Ebor: Archbishops of York*)

# September 20th

**1066:** Harald Hardrada and Earl Tostig sailed up the River Ouse with an estimated 10,000 Norwegian troops, ready to do battle with Earls Edwin and Morcar. An advance party peeled away from the main Norwegian force towards the city, only to be driven back towards Fulford Fields. When battle was joined, the outcome was a decisive victory for the army of Harald Hardrada and Earl Tostig, and they then moved a few miles east of the city in preparation for battle with Harold of Wessex and his English forces. (www.battleoffulfordorg.uk)

———◆———

**1995:** York City FC have a fine tradition of cup football; one of the most momentous of their matches an incredible 3–0 victory at Old Trafford in the Coca-Cola Cup. Paul Barnes opened the scoring midway through the first half and then added a second from the penalty spot, before Tony Baird completed the scoring with a header. City's defence held firm in the face of sustained attacks from United, and left the field to a standing ovation from the crowd of 29,049. The return leg was played at Bootham Crescent two weeks later and, although United triumphed 3–1, City progressed to the third round 4–3 on aggregate, after Scott Jordan scored the vital goal. (www.ycfc.net)

# September 21st

**1728:** Francis Place, artist and engraver, died in his home at King's Manor, York at the age of eighty-one. He was buried in St Olave's Church within the city. Born into a wealthy family based at Dinsdale near Darlington in 1647, he was the youngest of ten children and took up a career in law at London's Gray's Inn at the age of seventeen or eighteen. When the Great Plague broke out in 1665, he returned home. On his move back to London Place, he worked with Wenceslaus Hollar, who introduced him to print-making. It is likely that he had received much of his father's inheritance by 1681 and this allowed him to join the Virtuosi – a group of men with sufficient wealth and leisure-time to pursue their interest in art, science and philosophy. Basing himself in York, Francis Place became a member of the city's Virtuosi, which included Martin Lister, Henry Gyles, Thomas Kirke FRS and William Lodge. He travelled throughout the UK to sketch and pursue his other great interest: angling. Among many of his fine pieces of work, which include scenes of York, Amgueddfa Cymru holds fifteen views of Wales drawn by Francis Place. (www.museumwales.ac.uk)

# September 22nd

**2004:** On this day, Holgate Windmill Preservation Society was given planning permission from York City Council to restore the listed structure. Built in 1770, Holgate Windmill was operating until the early 1930s and had a number of interesting features, including five sails and double-shuttered sails. It was constructed to the Lincolnshire pattern, with a local hand-made brick tower and ogee-shaped cap. It represents the last surviving mill in a city that was, at one time, surrounded by windmills. Earliest records relating to Holgate Mill date from 1573, when the miller was William Plewman. The mill was operated by George Ward and his sons from the early 1790s to 1851 and the last known miller was Thomas Mollet. When operations stopped in 1933 the sails were removed, after becoming unsafe, but the first decade of the twenty-first century has brought steady progress on restoration of this fascinating Grade II listed structure. (www.holgatewindmill. org/history.htm)

# September 23rd

**1823:** York Musical Festival was revived on this day after a gap of twenty years and lasted four days. The Dean of York Minster, the Very Reverend William Cockburn, gave permission for the festival to be staged in the Minster, where classical works were performed to capacity audiences. (Knight, C.B. *The History of York*)

———◆———

**1927:** York City Library on Museum Street was opened on this day by the Right Honourable Earl of Elgin and Kincardine, chairman of the Carnegie United Kingdom Trust and President Elect of the Library Association. The building was designed by Walter Brierley. Until 1927, the library had been accommodated in the building that now houses York Dungeon on Clifford Street. It stands on the site of St Leonard's Hospital, which had replaced an earlier set of buildings founded by King Athelstan. Ruined sections of St Leonard's Hospital can still be seen in the adjacent library grounds. (www.vryork.com)

———◆———

**1989:** No. 91003 worked the first East Coast Mainline electric passenger train through York to Kings Cross. (Appleby, K., *Britain's Rail Super Centres: York*)

# September 24th

**1640:** The great assembly of Peers met in the Deanery at York, where the main hall was draped with tapestries and the King's chair stood at the upper end. From this position, Charles I made a speech in which he announced plans to call a parliament during the present year. He requested guidance from the Peers on how best to maintain his army in a state of readiness and how to deal with a petition from Scottish invaders which called for him to redress their grievances. The sitting of the Peers lasted from 24 September to 18 October and, during this time, commissioners held peace talks with Scottish leaders at Ripon. Hostilities were halted, but there was to be no lasting peace. (*Baines' Gazetteer*, 1823)

---

**1996:** York City's giant-killing soccer exploits continued into the 1996–7 season, when a first round Coca-Cola Cup victory brought a first ever tie against Everton. A first leg 1–1 draw at Goodison Park was followed by a 3–2 victory in front of 7,854 spectators at Bootham Crescent, to give an aggregate win by four goals to three. (www.ycfc.net)

# September 25th

**1963:** Mrs Donald Coggan, wife of the Archbishop of York, opened York's first hostel for deaf girls and spoke of her own week-long period of deafness, which had resulted from a trip to East Africa in a non-pressurised aircraft. She highlighted the isolation that could be experienced by deaf people. Four deaf girls were already living in the home, which could accommodate six people, on the top floor of the York and District Deaf and Dumb Society's headquarters in Bootham. The initial idea for a hostel had come from Miss M. Lumley, welfare officer for the society, and she would be looking after the girls. Alderman R.S. Oloman explained that the hostel covered the central area of Yorkshire and provided accommodation for girls from outlying villages. A hot breakfast would be provided in mornings before the girls left for work and they either took a packed lunch or had a midday meal at work, before returning for a hot meal in the evening. The object of the hostel, he explained, was to give the girls as full a life as possible, for, given the chance, deaf people did excellent work. (*Yorkshire Evening Press*)

# September 26th

**1905:** Difficult economic conditions were highlighted by a news item in the *York Evening Press* on this day. Under the heading 'Hard Times in York', the article reported that a total of 123 summonses for non-payment of rates had been issued in York and many of the defaulters could not pay, simply because they were unemployed. It continued, 'A defendant from the Leeman Road district said that in such times as had been experienced by workmen lately the summonses drove men to desperation. He had not had any work since a year last June, and had not done a week's regular work for five years.' (*York Evening Press*)

---

**2010:** York City Knights gained promotion to the Rugby League Championship with a 25 points to 4 victory over Oldham. York had finished the league season in third place, thirteen points behind Oldham, but they dominated the play-off from start to finish, with assistant coach Chris Thorman contributing two goals and a drop goal. The victory represented York's first promotion since moving up into National Division 1 in 2005 and came a year after narrowly losing to Halifax in the playoffs. (news.bbc.co.uk/sport2/hi/rugbyleague)

# September 27th

**1975:** The prototype High Speed Train carrying the Duke of Edinburgh arrived at York for the opening of the National Railway Museum, which houses the national collection of railway artefacts. (Previously these items had been stored at the British Transport Museum, Clapham and the York Railway Museum located on Queen Street.) The National Railway Museum's Great Hall was formerly York's North Motive Power Depot (engine shed), which housed four locomotive turntables. The largest of these turntables, measuring 21.5 metres, is still within the Great Hall area. Extensions to the museum include the Station Hall, which had been the main goods stations for York and now houses a range of exhibits including some of the world's finest royal carriages. An area known as The Works was, until 1986, York Diesel Locomotive Depot and repair shed, and when added to the museum in 1999 it tripled the size of the original site. In December 2007, a £4 million archive and research facility called Search Engine opened to the public. It provides access to artwork, documents, reports, photographs and drawings. (www.nrm.org.uk)

# September 28th

**1911:** Although it was picture palaces that drew the largest audiences in the late Edwardian era, roller-skating rinks also enjoyed a measure of short-lived popularity. On 28 September 1911, local newspapers reported the re-opening of the City Roller Skating Palace under new management. Closure in autumn of the previous year had followed valiant attempts to boost business, with appearances by acts such as 'Kardoc, the Handcuff King' and 'Jail Breaker' and, for a while after reopening the rink, hockey matches proved to be very popular. Local newspapers carried reports of preparations for matches as well as actual matches, with much attention focused on York's star player, J.W. Duxbury, 'considered… the finest player in the world'. (*York Herald*)

———◆———

**1915:** A hostilities entered a second year moves were made to set up a munitions factory in the York area and after a York Munitions Committee had investigated proposals it was announced that Armstrong, Whitworth and Co. had rented two sheds from the NER close to Queen's Street. A factory for producing shells was to be constructed immediately, with a potential workforce of around 1,000, mainly women and girls. (*York Herald*)

# September 29th

**1687:** John Moore, a native Moor, was granted the Freedom of the City of York. Sometimes referred to as 'Johannes' Moore, he is listed in the freemen's roll as John Moore – 'blacke'. Both men and women could obtain Freedom of the City of York in a number of different ways. It could be earned by serving an apprenticeship, inherited from a parent who was a freeman, granted as a reward for services given to the city, or it could be purchased. There appears to have been no defined rate for people wishing to purchase the Freedom of the City. In John Moore's case he paid two amounts: twenty nobles (13s 6d) to the Common Chamber of the city of York and £4 to the city council for this honour. It seems likely that John Moore was a fairly affluent member of the York community and, having purchased Freedom of the City, he could now bear arms, fish in the city's rivers and graze his animals on York's meadows. His situation was probably unique, as no other black man or woman is named as a freeman in the city rolls. (www.nationalarchives.gov.uk)

# September 30th

**2005:** Terry's of York closed after 250 years of production, with the loss of 316 jobs, as popular brands such as Chocolate Orange and All Gold were being moved to factories in Europe. The York-based chocolate-making operation was originally known as Bayldon and Berry's confectionery, and its original popularity in the eighteenth century stemmed from sales of saucy 'conversation lozenges' that were stamped with messages such as, 'Do you flirt?' The change of company name followed Joseph Terry's involvement in 1823. In a similar way to Rowntrees, the Terry family showed commitment to the local community. Sir Joseph Terry served four times as Lord Mayor of York and the family home in the city was bequeathed to the National Trust, for use as the Yorkshire regional headquarters. For two centuries, Terry's was run effectively, with its own cocoa plantation in Venezuela, but business suffered in the Second World War when part of the factory was taken over by an aircraft propeller firm. The catering giant Forte took over in 1963 and after several other owners it was latterly in the hands of Kraft, as a sub-division of the Swiss confectioner Suchard. The closure of Terry's meant that Nestlé-Rowntree was the last survivor from York's proud heritage of chocolate making. (www.historyofyork.org.uk)

# October 1st

**1734:** Thomas Keregan opened York's first permanent theatre in Lord Irwin's Yard on the site of a converted tennis court, with a performance of *The Wandering Patentee*. Rectangular in shape, and with a pit, boxes and gallery, it would have resembled the Georgian Theatre at Richmond in North Yorkshire. (*Theatre Royal York*: York History No. 4)

———•◆•———

**1853:** Margaret Birkbeck, a cook at the George Hotel in Coney Street, appeared in court following a violent incident on this Saturday in October. A scullery maid, Ann Scaife, was whitewashing kitchen walls at the hotel, but owing to her careless actions paint was being sprinkled over meat. At the end of her tether, Margaret seized a meat cleaver and grasped Ann by the throat. As the kitchen maid struggled, the cleaver fell and cut her arm and when she called for help from the hotel manager, Margaret Birkbeck struck the maid over her head with a rolling pin. When the court case was heard, the Lord Mayor caused 'uproarious laughter' by saying he had experience of bad-tempered female cooks. He and his fellow magistrates found the case proved and fined Margaret Birkbeck the sum of 5s. (*York Herald*)

# October 2nd

**1720:** Elizabeth Montagu was born at York into a wealthy and distinguished North Yorkshire family – the Robinsons of Rokeby. At the age of seven, her family moved to Cambridgeshire and in her formative years she was surrounded by house guests from the world of literature. In August 1742, she married Edward Montagu and combined social activities with a career as an authoress. She anonymously contributed three dialogues to Lord Lyttleton's *Dialogues of the Dead*, published in 1760 and apart from her letters, Elizabeth Montagu's main literary work was her response to Voltaire's attack on Shakespeare in *Essay on the Writings and Genius of Shakespeare*, which appeared in six editions. She died in London on 25 August 1800. (Hartley, M. & Ingilby, J., *Yorkshire Portraits*)

---

**1809:** Mary Ellen Best was baptised at St Mary's Church, Castlegate, York. By the 1840s she had become a fine watercolour painter, at a time when it was not fashionable for women to be artists. Initially she painted everyday people and domestic settings in Yorkshire. She then continued this approach during continental tours in the 1830s and after her marriage to a German in 1840. Her work is particularly noted for its accuracy and attention to detail. (Davidson C., *The World of Mary Ellen Best*)

# October 3rd

**1802:** The Lord Mayor and Commonalty rode the city boundaries of York on 2 and 3 October 1802. Every time the proclamation was made, cakes and ale were distributed. The first day was spent on the east bank of the Ouse and 30 miles were ridden before dinner was enjoyed at the Tavern. During the second day, 16 miles were covered before dinner was taken at Rose's, outside Micklegate Bar. The ceremony was next held in October 1832 with a start at 10 a.m. (Benson, G., *The City of York*)

---

**1904:** Widespread unemployment affected many areas in the early years of the twentieth century, and on 3 October 1904 a labour bureau was opened. Based at No. 16 Castlegate, it was operated by an organisation that became the York Citizen's Association for Dealing with the Unemployed. On the opening day large numbers of people gathered outside. The first applicant was a sixty-year-old man, Walter Anderson, who lived at 38 Bright Street. He was accompanied by a retired former soldier, aged sixty-six, who was attempting to live on a pension of 1s a day. (*Yorkshire Evening Press*)

# October 4th

**1893:** During October 1891, a poll of citizens showed a majority in favour of a public library and in January 1892, the city council had recommended that it should be housed in the former Institute building in Clifford Street. The library was formally opened by the Duke of York on 4 October 1893 and he was presented with a copy of Canon Raine's *History of York*, before attending a service in York Minster. (Knight, C.B., *History of the City of York*)

---

**1916:** The horrors of modern warfare were brought to the home front with Zeppelin raids and nine people were killed during an attack on York on 2 May 1916. There was another fatality on Monday 25 September and this led to a new organisation of street patrols and a debate about whether or not leaving the house should be permitted during a raid. On 4 October 1916, the chairman of the York Patrols Committee published instructions to householders, which advised the citizens of York to stay indoors during a raid. Support for this advice came from a doctor based at the Retreat in a letter about *Zeppelinophobia*. (*Yorkshire Evening Press*)

# October 5th

**1906:** A newspaper article described an 'Engine Driver's Extraordinary Experiences', which amounted to forty-five years' service on railways in France, America and Scotland as well as England. Now aged eighty-two and living with two of his daughters at No. 12 St John Street, York, Thomas Smith had been born at Naburn in 1824. His early working life was on the land, but at the age of twenty he moved to France and became a fireman and driver on routes including the Le Havre-Paris line. On his return to Scotland in 1848, he took part in the search for an express train that was almost buried in Covenshaw Bogs, but after a narrow escape when his train ran into a passenger locomotive near Slateford Station, he moved to East Anglia. After surviving 'two smashes in one night', Smith resigned his post on the following day and left Liverpool Docks for Portland, USA. He worked on the Western Line from Niagara until a serious rail crash persuaded him to return to England. On 9 March 1856, he arrived back in Rouen, where he worked for nearly twenty-five years between Rouen, Havre, Dieppe and other large towns. Caught up in the Franco-Prussian War of 1870–1, he narrowly escaped being shot as a spy, but continued to work until his return to England in October 1880. (*Yorkshire Herald*)

# October 6th

**1484:** Reference was made at the council meeting held that day to a 'great assembly' that had taken place in the city a few days previously. It was resolved that 'the most riotously disposed' who had been arrested, should be kept in custody until the King's pleasure concerning them was made known. The following day, a letter was received from the Earl of Northumberland, representative of the King's Council in the north, stating he had been informed that 'a great riot is committed' within the city of York and the franchise thereof, and demanding a full report. (Knight, C.B., *A History of the City of York*)

---

**1910:** There were conflicting fortunes for two new social activities in York at the end of the Edwardian era, as cinema-going went from strength to strength, while the skating 'craze' was in decline. The Sycamore Skating Rink had shown a net loss for the financial year July 1909 to July 1910, and on 6 October it was reported that the chairman had informed shareholders that 'the time had gone for making money out of skating rinks'. (*Yorkshire Evening Press*)

# October 7th

**1954:** Benjamin Seebohm Rowntree died after a lifetime of campaigning to improve conditions for working people. Born in York on 7 July 1871, he was educated at the York Quaker Boarding School and Owen College, Manchester before becoming a director of his father's business in York. He firmly believed that it was his duty to help poor and disadvantaged members of society and, as well as teaching at the York Adult School on Sundays, he also visited students' homes to observe living conditions. Results of his findings were published in his study *Poverty: A Study of Town Life* during 1901, and he outlined measures that were required to combat the problems of unemployment, old age and ill health. During the early 1900s, Seebohm Rowntree became a firm friend of David Lloyd George. The Old Age Pensions Act of 1908 and National Insurance Act (1911) are said to have been informed by Rowntree's findings. In 1913, Seebohm Rowntree published *The Land* and *How the Labourer Lives* and also worked closely with his father to develop social reforms in the family company. A second survey of York, *Poverty and Progress* (1941), was followed by another study, *Poverty and the Welfare State*, in which he argued that measures introduced by the Labour Government between 1945–51 were having a positive effect on poverty. (www.wardsbookofdays.com)

# October 8th

**1943:** Michael Green was born in York on this day. After an education at Wellington School in Somerset, he embarked on a career as an industrial journalist. Initial training as a reporter was with the *Somerset County Gazette*, before he moved on to posts with the *Bristol Evening Post,* the *Daily Mail* and *Daily Telegraph*. During August 1973, he joined the staff of ITN and subsequently reported on many of the major industrial issues of that era. During 1974, Michael Green fronted a large part of ITN's coverage of the miners' strike and the fall of Edward Heath's government. He also reported on a number of other dramatic episodes, including the Court Line collapse and the state rescues of Chrysler and British Leyland, as well as the Callaghan government's efforts to persuade Trade Unions to voluntarily limit pay rises. (*Who's Who on Television*, ITV Books)

# October 9th

**1482:** It was argued by the council that every warden in his ward should send for the constables and make the parishioners of every parish 'powl up the bumbylls, netylls and all oder wedys that are growing above the walls of this cite'. (Knight, C.B., *History of the City of York*)

———◆———

**1909:** Frederick Donald Coggan was born at Highgate, London. He became Archbishop of York in 1961. He was ordained a priest in 1935 and appointed Bishop of Bradford in 1956, before taking up his post at York some five years later. He spent thirteen years as Archbishop of York, before transferring to Canterbury. His ministry is remembered for his support of the ordination of women to the priesthood and a strong wish to make ecumenical progress with other churches. Dr Coggan's book *Call to the Nation* (1975) prompted 28,000 letters in response to his vision for social change through altered attitudes and less personal selfishness. During a visit to Rome in 1977, he took his hosts by surprise by calling for full intercommunion between the Anglican and Roman Catholic Church, and broke with tradition in the following year by convening the Lambeth Conference in Canterbury rather than London. Donald Coggan retired in 1980 and was created a life peer. He died on 17 May 2000. (www.archbishopofcanterbury.org)

# October 10th

**1837:** On this day, a meeting of the Yorkshire Agricultural Society at the Black Swan laid the foundations for the Great Yorkshire Show, with the stated aim '...to hold an annual meeting for the exhibition of farming stock, implements etc. and for the general promotion of agriculture.' The first Yorkshire Agricultural Society Show was held in 1838 at the Barrack Yard, Fulford, near York and, although attendance figures were not calculated, it was regarded as a success. In the following years, the show moved to Leeds, Northallerton and Hull before returning to York in 1842, when 6,044 paying customers were recorded. By the following year, it had become known as 'The Great Yorkshire Show' and, with breaks during both World Wars, the show continued to be held at different locations in Yorkshire until 1950. A site at Hook Oval, Harrogate was purchased for £16,500 and since 1951 the show has been staged there. The 2008 show was attended by Her Majesty Queen Elizabeth to celebrate its 150th anniversary, and in 2010 attendance figures reached 131,382 over the three days of events (an increase for the fourth successive year). (www.godsowncountry.co.uk)

# October 11th

**1727:** York Mansion House staged its first 'public entertainment' on the evening of King George III's coronation day, 11 October 1727, in spite of the fact it had not yet been properly roofed. Proposals to build a property as a residence for the Lord Mayors of York were probably under discussion during 1723, but it was into the early months of 1725 before work got underway. In March 1726, the building committee reported to the Corporation that almost all of the £1,000 voted to them had been spent and this proved to be one of several occasions when extra funds had to be found. Much of the building had been completed by this time and meetings were held there during 1726. In December, a custodian or porter was appointed to clean the house and light fires but in February 1727, the committee faced criticism over slow progress in completing the work. The first Lord Mayor finally took up residence in 1730, but internal decoration of the stateroom was not completely finished until 1732. (www.british-history.ac.uk)

# October 12th

**1838:** An inquest was held at the Black Horse Inn, Pavement, York into the death on the premises of a Scottish drover, William Ingles. Aged over seventy, he had journeyed south with flocks on many previous occasions and, two days earlier, he had been at the York cattle market where sheep were also being traded. On his return to his lodgings at the Black Horse, he complained of feeling unwell and a surgeon named Brown was summoned to offer support. William Ingles was also visited by his employers, who paid him three sovereigns as wages for this final journey and indicated that he should rest at the inn. Early on the morning of 12 October, he had requested a drink of tea, but by the time a servant returned with the drink 'the icy hand of death' had overtaken him. The coroner's jury returned the commonly heard verdict for death by natural causes; that he 'died suddenly by the visitation of God'. (*York Gazette*)

# October 13th

**1835:** On this day, George Hudson became chairman of the newly formed York and North Midland Railway Co. A meeting in the Guildhall at York on 10 October 1835, with the Lord Mayor, T.W. Wilson, presiding over proceedings, adopted a resolution for the immediate formation of the company. George Stephenson was appointed engineer. (Edgington, J. & Gilks, J.S., *Trains from York*)

---

**1995:** A York man, who nearly lost his own life during a city-centre attack three months before, jumped into the River Ouse to save the lives of two strangers. After a lunchtime drinking session, a Hartlepool man had leapt from Ouse Bridge and when his friend dived in to save him, an undercurrent dragged down both men. With the river in flood by about 3ft, the men were making no progress, but then twenty-seven-year-old Chris Semmens plunged in and dragged them towards the riverside, where they clutched a buoy fixed to a moored boat. (*York Evening Press*)

---

**1995:** William Britton Simpson, butler to the Lord Mayor 1934–72, was demanding that York should retain its Lord Mayor, Sheriff and Freemen when the new super council took over on 1 April the following year. (*York Evening Press*)

# October 14th

**1827:** William George Granville Venables Vernon Harcourt was born into a well-established family in York on this day. After gaining a degree in classics and mathematics, he studied law and built up a large legal practice. During the late 1860s, he became strongly involved in politics and gradually reduced his legal work. After declining several government posts, Vernon Harcourt accepted the position of Solicitor General (and a knighthood) in 1873, and when the Liberal Party regained power in April 1880, he became Home Secretary. After a short period out of power, the Liberal government returned to office in February 1886 and Harcourt became Chancellor of the Exchequer as well as close advisor to William Gladstone. When Gladstone resigned as Prime Minister in 1894, Vernon Harcourt was overlooked for this post and continued as Chancellor under Lord Roseberry. Following the Liberal defeat of June 1895, he continued as party leader until the end of the decade. He died at his family estate in Oxfordshire on 30 September 1904. Vernon Harcourt has been described as a democratic aristocrat who worked effectively for his party through thick and thin. (www.liberalhistory.org.uk)

# October 15th

**1536:** Unrest among the citizens of York over increasing levels of poverty during the summer months of 1536 was heightened by the 'Pilgrimage of Grace', which was a protest against closure of monasteries on orders from King Henry VIII. On 15 October 1536, a force numbering over 20,000 rebels assembled outside York's city walls and, although official records give few details, it seems that the Lord Mayor William Harrington felt pressured into cooperating with the mass of insurgents under their leader, Robert Aske. (Kightly, C. & Semlyen, R., *Lords of the City*)

———◆———

**1913:** A lead article in the *Yorkshire Herald* encapsulated divided opinions over class in the 'Burning Question of the Hour', as follows:

There is no antecedent objection to the appointment of a working man as Lord Mayor, although it is admitted by all sensible level-headed people that there would be an incongruity in a man going from a house rented at, say 4s or 5s per week into a building valued at £10,000 full of beautiful appointments, pictures, furnishings and silver, with a butler and staff of servants to wait upon him. Still there are working men who would do credit to the traditions of the Mansion House by native dignity, personality and character...

(Kightly, C. & Semlyen, R., *Lords of the City*)

# October 16th

**1892:** York suffered one of its most serious floods on and around 16 October 1892, when a period of heavy rain added to existing high water levels. Areas of the city adjacent to the river were submerged and keelboats were being sculled along Skeldergate. Tower Street and Walmgate were impassable and the Marygate estate, as well as many houses in the Hungate district, was under water. Beyond areas of housing, thousands of acres of ground on both banks of the river were completely submerged. The area around Clifton Ings, Middlethorpe and Fulford Ings had become huge expanses of open water and roads heading south from the city were impassable. York's sewerage system was being reconstructed and a coffer dam in the bed of the river just below Skeldergate Bridge was swept away. Closer to the city centre, the printing offices of the *Yorkshire Herald* were flooded out and publications were prepared in the premises of the *Yorkshire Gazette*. City records, which were housed in a room of the municipal buildings beside the Guildhall, were also damaged, though more valuable documents were unaffected. (Knight, C.B., *History of the City of York*)

# October 17th

**1914:** Following Britain's declaration of war against Germany on 4 August 1914, hostilities intensified on the Western Front and reports of German atrocities were soon reported in this country's press. 'Aliens' were arrested and detained, and in York the castle was full of Germans by the second week in September. An alternative place of detention was constructed on a site in Leeman Road during October, which soon attracted onlookers from the locality. Further interest was generated by the death of a detainee – August Beckert, an engineer from Selby who had been taken into custody on 26 September. The *Herald* reported, 'He was a registered alien and was detained because he was likely to become dangerous.' Following his death, Beckert was buried in York and a number of internees were given permission to attend the funeral. A photograph of them in the funeral procession was published in local newspaper reports on 17 October 1914. (*York Herald*)

# October 18th

**1844:** St Peter's School amalgamated with Clifton Proprietary School and the new educational establishment opened with Reverend William Hey as headmaster (1844–64). Founded originally in AD 627 by Paulinus of York, St Peter's is said to be one of the oldest schools in the United Kingdom and third oldest in the world. It was the original medieval school of the Minster and an early headmaster was Alcuin, who became chancellor to Emperor Charlemagne. St Peter's School was re-founded in 1557, and in 1833 it moved into new premises designed by J.P. Pritchett (1789–1868), on the site of the old deanery situated on the south side of the Minster. A successful period in the school's history during the 1830s was followed by a fall in pupil numbers, from seventy-eight in December 1837 to thirty-nine in March 1842, but the situation was retrieved through the amalgamation in 1844. (The Proprietary or Collegiate School had opened in 1838.) The school hall in the centre of the original buildings was extended as a memorial to Old Peterites, who died after involvement in the two World Wars. It was dedicated to him at a ceremony before prize giving in July 1960. (Pevsner, N. & Neave, D., *The Buildings of England*)

# October 19th

**1691:** An advertisement appeared in the *London Gazette* on this day, outlining facilities at the Northern Bagnio in Coney Street, York. Customers could sweat and bathe or be 'cupped after the German fashion for 5s. each'. Opening times were between 7 a.m. and 9 p.m., with Tuesdays and Fridays reserved for women. This northern version of a Turkish bath seems to have been short-lived, as after 1738 the Bagnio was used as a printing office by Alex Staples, Caesar Ward and Ann Ward. Though the building had a number of uses, one bath was still to be seen in 1818, and the first Annual Racing Calendar was later produced there. The Bagnio was demolished during 1924. (Benson, G., *City of York*)

———— ◆ ————

**1768:** Bridge Frodsham, an actor known as 'the York Garrick' for his performance as Hamlet, made his last appearance on the York stage on 19 October 1768. He died three days later at the age of thirty-five – a victim of 'bad hours and the brandy bottle'. (www.archive.org)

———— ◆ ————

**1914:** Mr W. Bullivant of Parliament Street, York entered the lions' den of Bostock and Wombwell's Menagerie shortly after 9 p.m. He remained in the cage for several minutes and was bold enough to stroke one of the lions before leaving to loud and prolonged applause. (*York Herald*)

# *October 20th*

**1916:** Military tribunals were set up to consider applications for exemption from military service. Most cases were brought by employers applying for exemption for an employee, individuals requesting exemption on grounds of hardship or parents arguing that their son was vitally needed at home. But the cases that aroused most discussion were those involving Conscientious Objectors to military service. For most cases the York tribunal split into two, but for 'conchies' the full bench usually heard the applications. During the later part of November 1916, a well-known York personality, James Wardropper from New Earswick, appeared before tribunals and courts as a Conscientious Objector of 'absolutist' beliefs. Wardropper had been involved in activities of both the Labour party and the Independent Labour Party whilst working for Rowntree and Co. His application for exemption had been refused and an appeal turned down before he ignored call-up papers. This resulted in a court appearance on 20 October, when he was fined the sum of £2 and handed over to army officials as an absentee. (*Evening Press*)

# October 21st

**1584:** Until their posts were abolished by an Act of Parliament in 1836, City Waites were musicians responsible to mayors for providing entertainment at civic occasions. The Lord Mayor of York and the Corporation maintained a band of City Waites for over 400 years and before 1600, their main instrument was a shawm or wayte pipe. On 21 October 1584, two waites were dismissed:

> John Clarke and Baltherston... were examined towching their evill and disorderlie behaviour, to the discredit of this cittie... for that they have gone abroad, in the contry in very evill apparell, with their hose forth at their heeles, also for that they are common drunkerdes and cannot so conynglie play on their instruments as they ought to do...

In fact, implementation of the sentence must have been delayed, as the offenders continued as waites for some time. (Merryweather, J., *York Music*)

———— ◆ ————

**1908:** Ponsonby Moore Crossthwaite chaired an enquiry into the nuisance and damage caused by traction engines on the streets of York. Newspaper reports on this day carried details of the wide-ranging discussion that ensued. While some speakers highlighted extra costs in avoiding bridges and the greater value than horses and carts, local residents spoke of being shaken in their beds, and having filaments (light bulbs) broken as traction engines rumbled past. (*Yorkshire Evening Press*)

# October 22nd

**1634:** All Saints' Church, Pavement is said to have its origins in a building constructed on the site for St Cuthbert, who was consecrated Bishop of Lindisfarne at York in AD 685. Since then, the church buildings have dominated an area used for royal proclamations for important executions and for dealing with law-breakers. Church bells were of considerable importance for both religious and secular matters and, in 1633, a plain sanctus bell was added to the two late medieval bells. On 22 October 1634 a 'bord' for a new bell frame was purchased and there was further outlay on 18 May 1678, when 7*s* and 8*d* was spent on repair of the bells. (All Saints' Church, Pavement, York)

---

**1965:** Derwent College was the first of two colleges that signalled the opening phase of development at the University of York. On this day, Queen Elizabeth II performed the official opening for the building that houses the university's politics and philosophy departments. Located on the edge of the campus close to Heslington Hall, it is near the gazebo and gardens known collectively as The Quiet Place. (www.enotes.com)

# October 23rd

**1606:** The Lady Mayoress and ladies of the aldermen travelled to Bishopthorpe to pay their respects to Mrs Matthew, wife of the Archbishop Tobias Matthew, and to welcome her at her first coming to York. They carried with them a present of two loaves of sugar which weighed, as the record meticulously states, one 28lbs and the other 27lbs. Together they cost £4 3s 6d, or 1s 6d per lb. The party travelled from York to Bishopthorpe by water and 2s was paid to the mariners and 1s 4d to the haulier for their services. The ladies were attended by the macebearer. (Knight, C.B., *History of the City of York*)

———— ◆ ————

**1919:** During the later part of 1919, educational matters came to the forefront in York, with a number of proposals for reform issued by York Education Committee. On this day, the chairman of the Education Committee, K.E.T. Wilkinson, reported that the education rate in the city of 3s 1d was providing value for money, with each child's education costing £3 10s 4d per annum. There were 14,500 children in elementary schools and 450 teachers. (*York Herald*)

# October 24th

**1983:** The sound of a sixty-year-old threshing machine echoed around the Yorkshire Museum of Farming at Murton, evoking memories of the age of steam. At the last weekend of the season, Mr Allison Raley and his son, Phillip of Hill Farm, Stillingfleet, brought their 1923 Wallis & Stevens seven-horse-powered engine to drive their threshing machine and baler. It was intended to thresh corn on the two days, but it proved impossible to obtain a supply. (*Yorkshire Evening Press*)

———◆———

**1983:** There was an unusual incident when the Archbishop of York, Dr John Hapgood, met a robot on the streets of the city, but he was delighted to join forces with his mechanical friend, 'Buddy Can', to launch a nationwide appeal to help disabled children. As vice-president of the Invalid Children's Aid Association, Dr Hapgood was celebrating the organisation's centenary by helping to raise £250,000 for special family care centres. He was assisted in his duties by willing helpers from the city's Manor School. (*Yorkshire Evening Press*)

# October 25th

**1850:** The Lord Mayor of York and other dignitaries entertained the Prince Consort and the Lord Mayor of London at a banquet held in the Guildhall. A sumptuous feast prepared by Alexis Sayer was acclaimed as his greatest culinary triumph. No expense was spared, with one dish costing a hundred guineas and consisting of turtles, capons, turkeys, pheasants, woodcocks, quails, snipes, larks and more. Trimmings included cockscombs, truffles, mushrooms and crayfish. During the evening, a concert and ball was held in the Assembly Room. (Benson, G., *The City of York*)

———◆———

**1918:** Over a period of fourteen weeks, between mid-October 1918 and early January 1919, there was a serious outbreak of influenza in York. Newspaper reports at the end of October 1918 reported twenty-eight deaths from influenza and eleven from pneumonia, giving an overall total of sixty-one deaths in York over three weeks. All entertainment venues closed and troops assisted with grave digging at York Cemetery as the number of burials increased dramatically. On 25 October, there was a report of three deaths in one family during a single week. (*York Herald*)

# October 26th

**1803:** Joseph Aloysius Hansom was born at 114 Micklegate, York (which became the Brigantes public house). He went on to build up a highly successful career as a designer and architect. Much of his work was in the Gothic style and he invented the Hansom cab, while also helping to found the architectural journal *The Builder* in 1843 (which was renamed *Building* in 1966). During a partnership with his friend Edward Welch in the late 1820s and early 1830s, Hansom designed several churches in Yorkshire and Liverpool, as well as working on the renovation of Bodelwyddan Castle in Denbighshire and King William's College on the Isle of Man. He is probably best remembered, however, for his design of a Patent Safety Cab, which was registered on 23 December 1834. With the addition of later modifications, the Hansom Cab was widely exported and became a common feature in urban streets during the nineteenth century. Between 1854 and 1879, Hansom designed and built a considerable number of important private and public properties throughout the UK, as well as in Australia and South America. He died in London on 29 June 1882. (www.1911encylclopedia.org/Joseph_Aloysius_Hansom)

# October 27th

**1906:** Mrs Elizabeth Johnson celebrated her 102nd birthday and, as licensee of the Bumper Castle Inn on Wigginton Road, York, she was also heralded as the oldest landlady in England. The old lady was reported to enjoy wonderfully good health and, although becoming feebler, she was able to move about the house and spend time in her garden during favourable weather. Unfortunately, she had recently become very deaf and this made conversation difficult, but otherwise her faculties were wonderfully intact. With particularly good eyesight, she walked with an assurance that many people thirty years younger would envy. Mrs Johnson was born at Easingwold, so she had not moved far from her birthplace. Widowed for twenty-nine years, it was sixty years since she and her husband had taken over the tenancy of the Bumper Castle Inn. On her 100th birthday she had received many gifts, including a solid silver teapot given to her by John Smith's Tadcaster Brewery Co. Ltd. [Elizabeth Johnson's death was reported on 22 July 1907. She was 103 years old.] (*York Herald*)

# October 28th

**1919:** Wartime regulations were not lifted immediately and in the post-war period, a number of safety measures were also introduced. John Dimmy's appearance in court was reported on this day, when he was fined for not having a rear light on the back of his pony and trap. Three days after this court case, local newspapers were reporting on a legal challenge that had been made to the regulation about rear lights. A DORA order, dated 30 September, confirmed a rule that vehicles had to display a rear light and the Cyclists Touring Club challenged this. Fifty bikers had been prosecuted for not showing a rear light and, although it was argued in court that reimposition 'was not in accordance with the preamble of the Act, and should have been only for the purpose of military emergency', the challenge was dismissed and each cyclist was fined 10s. (*Yorkshire Evening Press*)

———— ◆ ————

**1963:** During 1961, a temporary bridge was constructed at Clifton by the British army to handle additional traffic at the wedding of the Duke and Duchess of Kent at York Minster. On this day in 1963, a permanent bridge was officially opened. Some 4,000 tons of concrete and 50 tons of reinforced steel had been used in its construction. (www.guesthousesyork.org.uk)

# October 29th

**1603:** Sir Thomas Hesketh purchased Castle Mills, overlooking the River Foss in York, and used the annual rent to endow a hospital for eight poor men and one poor woman over fifty years of age. He began to build this hospital in the grounds of Heslington Hall. Following his death in 1606, his widow continued the building work, which was completed two years later. The Foss Navigation Co. acquired Castle Mills in 1793 and agreed to pay £50 per annum in perpetuity to the hospital. This payment is still made to the Heslington estate by York Corporation, who purchased the Navigation Co. in 1853 for £4,000. Henry Yarburgh, owner of Heslington Hall between 1789 and 1825, rebuilt the hospital on its present location in Heslington Lane during 1795. Repairs were carried out in 1968 by Richard Arthur de Yarburgh-Bateson, sixth Baron Deramore, who was a partner in the firm Cherry & Deramore Architects. (Murray, H., *Heraldry and the Buildings of York*)

# October 30th

**1995:** Princess Margaret officially opened the new headquarters of Shepherd Building Group Ltd. in Hospital Fields Road, off Fulford Road in York. The four-storey building cost £4.4 million and was to accommodate 200 staff members. In order to stop the construction jutting too far out into the Fulford skyline, Shepherd's team of designers created a special lower-ground floor which was dug into the ground. (*York Evening Press*)

---

**1995:** An ambitious scheme was announced to transform a redundant York church into a national music centre. It seemed likely to get the go-ahead from planning officers. (St Margaret's Church in Walmgate was taken over by York Civic Trust in 1975 and had been used to house scenery for the Theatre Royal.) York Early Music Foundation was hoping to receive £1 million from the National Lottery to refurbish the medieval St Margaret's building. An earlier plan had been rejected, as it had included a car park among trees, and this would have detracted from the setting of the building. (*York Evening Press*)

# October 31st

**1984:** On this day, Fairfax House was reopened by the Duchess of Kent. Fairfax House on Castlegate was designed by John Carr and built for Viscount Charles Gregory Fairfax in 1762, to provide a winter home for his family during York's winter season of events, balls and assemblies. In 1919, it was adapted to form one of the city's most popular places of entertainment, St George's Cinema and Dancehall, but some fifty years later it had fallen into disuse and disrepair. It was thanks to the efforts of York Civic Trust, with a grant from the National Heritage Memorial Fund, that this fine example of an eighteenth-century town house was saved from total ruin. A further round of funding allowed the Trust to complete refurbishment of Fairfax House. On 31 October 1984, the Duchess of Kent opened the house and praised the restoration as a model of cooperation between a local authority, grant-making organisations and an independent charitable trust – the York Civic Trust. The house is furnished with the late Noel Terry's collection of Georgian furniture and has been voted Britain's best Georgian town house. (Brown, P., *Fairfax House York*; www.artfullodger-york.co.uk/fairfax.house)

# November 1st

**866:** Halfdean and Ivar the Boneless led an attack by Danish forces on York. It seems that they chose the date deliberately because 1 November was All Saints' Day, when many of York's leaders would have been in the Cathedral, thus leaving the township vulnerable to surprise attack. (www. englandsnortheast.co.uk)

———◆———

**1266:** Walter Gifford was enthroned as Archbishop of York, after previously serving as Bishop of Bath and Wells. During his previous ministry at Bath, he had given strong support to Henry III over the excommunication of Simon de Montfort and his party, and following the Battle of Evesham he served as chancellor. Beneath his outwardly genial manner, he is said to have had a fierce temper that belied a cruel nature, and this led to a clash with the See of Durham. When he was locked out of the Cathedral on one occasion, his immediate response was to excommunicate the prior and monks. Though Walter Gifford had retired from politics when he took up the post at York, Prince Edward appointed him as tutor to his children and he assisted with the arrest of Earl Warenne for the murder of Alan de la Zouche at Westminster. He also served again as Regent during Edward's absence overseas in 1275. He was buried in York Minster following his death in 1279. (Hart, A.T., *Ebor: Archbishops of York*)

# November 2nd

**1822:** During October 1822, Philip Francis Sidney announced plans to publish a weekly newspaper under the title *Yorkshire Observer*. The first issue appeared on 2 November 1822. The printing office was on Coney Street, run by R. Johnson, and an editorial office was in Stonegate. The edition of 19 April 1823 announced that Johnson had become proprietor of the eight-page newspaper but, as a result of his attempt to avoid payment of stamp duty, the publication ended with the issue dated 14 June 1823. (www.british-history.ac.uk)

———•◆•———

**1995:** It was announced that Britain's farmers would be represented in Europe by a former pupil of Queen Anne's School, York, who had lived at New Earswick. Kate Timms, aged fifty-three, had been appointed to one of the Ministry of Agriculture's senior posts. As a deputy secretary in the ministry, she would have responsibility for agricultural commodities from February 1996. Miss Timms joined the ministry in 1970, after studying at Oxford University. Her new post involved negotiations in Brussels, on behalf of British farmers, over matters such as the future workings of the Common Agricultural Policy. (*Yorkshire Evening Press*)

# November 3rd

**1827:** During the early nineteenth century, York was a regular stopping place for drovers. On the evening of 3 November 1827, John Campbell broke his northward journey from Norwich to stay at the Black Horse in Bootham. In the early hours of the following day, he was found unconscious in bed and the landlord, Joseph Leetall, and his family members tried to take care of him, before summoning assistance from a surgeon. He promptly applied leeches to John Campbell's head, but there was no improvement in his condition and he died at around midday. Part of his head was investigated by surgeons, who found evidence of an effusion in the left ventricle of the brain. This was cited as the probable cause of his death. (*York Chronicle*)

———— ◆ ————

**1925:** David Lloyd George was made an honorary freeman of the city of York, in a ceremony that involved Arthur Frederick Wright carrying the ceremonial sword and William James 'Jack' Wilson acting as macebearer. Another main figure on this grand occasion was the Lord Mayor, Sir Robert Newbold Kaye (1869–1947), who became an attorney in 1893 and founded a firm of solicitors – Newbold Kaye in the city. He had been knighted in the New Year's Honours List of 1923 for his wartime service. (en.wikipedia.org)

# November 4th

**1910:** A hand-written order from the Lord Mayor of York to the landlord of the Lion and Lamb, dated 4 November 1910:

Dear Sir,
Kindly forward me half a dozen bottles of scotch whiskey, <u>McCullman</u> like you sent me the other day. Tonight if possible, also 3 bottles of Cognac Brandy at 5/- and oblige yours truly
James Birch
Lord Mayor

———— ◆ ————

**1988:** Queen Elizabeth II attended a service for the 'Dedication of the Restored Roof and Vault in York Minster'. During a fire in 1984, the Rose Window, which measures 6.8 metres in diameter and has seventy-three panes of stained glass, cracked into 40,000 pieces and scientific research was needed to find an adhesive that could rejoin the tiny fragments. The restored window was seen for the first time at the service and the Queen then visited the nearby Glaziers' Trust workshops in order to see how this specialist work had been carried out. (www.bbc.co.uk)

# November 5th

**1855:** On the first anniversary of the Battle of Inkerman, a large group of gentlemen gathered for a celebratory meal at the Golden Lion in St Sampson's Square, York. Newspaper reports stated that the excellent fare reflected immense credit on landlord Thomas Scott and his wife, and that the whole event was a great success. (*York Herald*)

———•✦•———

**2010:** Newspapers reported the unveiling of a stone memorial in memory of the 412 Rowntree's employees who lost their lives in the two World Wars. It replaced a number of older rolls of honour and two carved wooden memorials, which had been on display around the factory area since the last war. Some two-dozen people gathered for the ceremony and, as well as Nestlé staff and members of the Royal British Legion, the group included ninety-one-year-old Ted Griffiths. He was a veteran of service in North Africa during the Second World War and had organised York's Festival of Remembrance for the last twenty years. A spokesman for Nestlé said the changed location of the memorials would ensure the public pay their respects, while the original memorials would be preserved in the company's archive base. (www.yorkpress.co.uk)

# November 6th

**2007:** The University of York set up an Institute for Effective Education, in order to improve knowledge of the teaching and learning processes, and then to promote the most effective approaches. First proposals for a university at York were put forward in a petition to King James in 1617, and some three centuries later, F.J. Munby and a number of other interested parties, including the Yorkshire Philosophical Society, proposed establishment of a 'Victoria University of Yorkshire'. Oliver Sheldon (1894–1951), co-founder of York Civic Trust, is widely regarded as the driving force behind the founding of the university in 1963. An initial intake of 200 students were based mainly in King's Manor, in the city centre, and Heslington Hall. Work on purpose-built accommodation began a year later on the Heslington Campus. A landmark feature on this site is the Central Hall, a half-octagonal concert hall which is used for convocations and examinations, as well as theatrical and musical events. The campus lake is claimed to be the largest plastic-bottomed lake in Europe and, since completion, it has attracted a range of waterfowl. (en.wikipedia.org/wiki/University_of_york)

# November 7th

**1816:** 'An independent chapel was opened in Lendal by Rev. Dr. Raffles, Rev. Joseph Cockin and Rev. Mr Bradley when £110 13s. was collected…' (*New Guide for Strangers and Residents*)

———•◆•———

**1995:** Drought-stricken Yorkshire Water announced a radical new series of measures to stop taps running dry. These included permission to abstract 11,000 cubic metres of water a day from the River Ouse near York, to boost supplies in West Yorkshire; the go-ahead to take water from the River Wharfe; the screening of advertisements on commercial television, urging people to cut back on water consumption; and negotiations with the Ministry of Transport over the possibility of closing a lane of the M62 to allow tankers to park up and dump water taken from the River Derwent, near Selby, directly into the reservoir. (*Yorkshire Evening Press*)

———•◆•———

**1995:** The *Yorkshire Evening Press* reported that work to restore Stamford Bridge viaduct was to start the following spring. This news came from English Heritage, who had given £75,000 towards the £375,000 restoration project set up by East Yorkshire Borough Council. The Grade II listed structure took the rail line from York to Bridlington over the River Derwent, and its fate hung in the balance for twenty years while local authorities had argued over its future. (*Yorkshire Evening Press*)

# November 8th

**1777:** On this day, Mrs Addison of York Castle pawned six china cups and saucers, and two small china basins for 5s 0d. Pawnbrokers were required to take proper care of items deposited with them. Any reduction in value meant that the owner had to be compensated. The pawnbroker noted in the register, 'Not answerable to make up loss in case of accident.' (Blackhouse, A.A., *Worm-Eaten Waistcoat*)

---◆·◆·---

**1877:** The lecture hall in Goodramgate was purchased by the York Temperance Society during 1877 and, following a thorough overhaul and redecoration, it was reopened on this day as the 'Victoria Hall', with a public gathering and promenade concert. (Knight, C.B., *History of the City of York*)

---◆·◆·---

**1905:** Unemployment levels in York increased considerably during November and December 1905, and a number of charitable schemes were at the forefront of providing relief. The soup kitchen reopened, York City Mission provided Sunday breakfast for the children of poor folk and the York Emergency Kitchen supplied further help. The overall situation was highlighted by Reverend Joshua Mason in a stirring letter to *The Press* on 8 November 1905. (*Yorkshire Evening Press*)

# November 9th

**1829:** A notice was posted in York with the heading 'YORK CITY WALLS':

> Notice is hereby given:
> That a meeting of such noblemen and gentlemen connected with the County and City of York, as are desirous of the perfect restoration of the whole of the city walls, on the south side of the River Ouse will be held at the York Tavern on Thursday 26th November instant at twelve o'clock at noon for the purpose of adopting measures for carrying that object into effect.
>
> His Grace the Archbishop of York has consented to take the chair.

At the meeting on 29 November, it was unanimously resolved that the walls be repaired and that the committee should obtain estimates in order to proceed with the collection of subscriptions. (Cooper, T.P., *York*)

———— •✦• ————

**1875:** A city council meeting unanimously agreed that in the event of the proposed fine art and industrial exhibition building being erected in Bearpark's Garden, the council would pull down the Bird in Hand Hotel and devote the land on which it stood to the exhibition site. (Knight, C.B., *History of the City of York*)

# November 10th

**1711:** Robert Hay was born in London on this day. He attended Westminster School and Christ Church in Oxford, where he gained BA and MA degrees, before training to take up holy orders. In 1739, his name was legally changed to Robert Hay-Drummond, when he inherited the Cromlix and Innerpeffray estates in Perthshire. After holding office as Bishop of St Asaph (1748–61) and then of Salisbury for a few months in 1761, he became Archbishop of York in October of that year. As Archbishop-designate he preached the sermon at the Coronation of George III and Queen Charlotte on 22 September 1761. He died at Bishopthorpe on 10 December 1776. (www.thepeerage.com, Robert Hay-Drummond)

———•◆•———

**1919:** The Grand Cinema, with an entrance on Clarence Street, opened on this day. The opening programme starred Lily Elsie and Gerald Ames in *Comradeship – A Story of the GREAT WAR by LOUIS N. PARKER*. Guest of honour at the opening proceedings was a well-known local citizen, James Melrose, and the orchestra was directed by Herbert Cooper. There were a range of prices for admission: stalls, 1s 6d; reserved, 1s 3d; unreserved centre stalls, 1s 0d or 3d; and pit, 4d. (*York Herald*)

# November 11th

**1858:** Lord Brougham delivered an address dealing with the political questions of the day in the Festival Concert Rooms. He had been elected as one of four members of parliament for Yorkshire in 1830 and, soon afterwards, he was appointed Lord Chancellor. He earned a reputation as a brilliant orator and debater, as well as a great reformer of legal machinery, but fell out of favour because of unwise comments about the monarch and his political colleagues during 1834. He was not reappointed as Lord Chancellor in Melbourne's second ministry of 1835. (Knight, C.B., *History of the City of York*)

---

**1918:** When the Armistice was signed on 11 November 1918, about 10,000 people gathered for a rapidly-arranged Service of Thanksgiving at York Minster. A bugler from St Peter's School played 'The Last Post' and many workers were given a day's holiday. Parts of the city centre were decorated with bunting. Sir Edwin Lutyens, who had designed the Cenotaph in Whitehall, London, was commissioned by the North Eastern Railway to design a memorial to commemorate 2,236 men who died in the First World War. (www.historyofyork.org.uk)

# November 12th

**1971:** An object uncovered by workmen while excavating foundations for York's telephone extension provided a delicate problem for the city's museum curator, who wanted to put it on display, for all involved were unable to settle on an appropriate name. Measuring about 8ins in diameter and with a 3in-wide opening and handle, it was the first such item that Mr Allen Butterwood had seen in his career as a museum curator. He had no doubt that this was a piece of gentleman's apparatus – kept out of sight in a fifteenth-century bed chamber – and should go on show, but was unable to provide a suitable name for it. It was probably made locally, he speculated, as York produced quite a lot of pottery in those days. After the broken handle had been fixed, the 'unmentionable' object was to go on show, and Mr Butterworth was said to be welcoming sensible suggestions for its name. (*Yorkshire Evening Press*)

———— • ◆ • ————

**1971:** It was reported that the North York Moors Preservation Society was to be formally wound up at its fifth anniversary meeting in Whitby the next day and replaced by the North York Moors Historical Railway Trust. (*Yorkshire Evening Press*)

# November 13th

**1666:** Before the Municipal Corporations Act of 1835, waites were the municipal bondsmen who played music for all civic ceremonies. There is regular mention in records of their appearances from the fifteenth century through to their demise in the mid-1830s. During the mid-seventeenth century, the York music scene was dominated by the Girdler family. An era came to an end with the death of John Girdler, whose will was hastily written on his sickbed on 13 November 1666. The first mention of John Girdler appears in 1623, when he appears as a replacement for the deceased John Watson and next player of the city's saggbut (trombone). John married Jane Watson at the church of St Michael le Belfrey in 1620 and all of their four sons grew up to be professional musicians, but the civil war seriously disrupted all aspects of civic life, including waites. During this turbulent period, John Girdler continued to lead the band, but it appears that his young sons were the only assistants, and only he was paid and liveried. Waites were re-instated in 1657, but there is no mention of payment of wages. In a document of 28 November 1660, the Girdlers were required to hand over chains and badges to their successors. (Merryweather, J., *York Music*)

# November 14th

**1424:** Foss Bridge was rebuilt during the reign of Henry IV and a chapel, on the north side of the structure, was granted a licence for celebrating divine service on 14 November 1424. The chapel was dedicated to St Anne. During the late sixteenth century, the writer Camden recorded that the bridge was so covered with houses that it was impossible for a stranger to recognise the bridge's outlines. (Knight, C.B., *History of the City of York*)

———◆———

**1829:** John Dawson, a resident of Metheringham in Lincolnshire, appeared at York Guildhall to face charges of stealing a black horse near his home, before bringing it to York, where he offered it for sale at the market. A man named Lister showed interest in the horse and offered £4, although Dawson's original price was £14. It was arranged for the horse to be taken to the Red Lion in Walmgate, but Lister reported the matter to officers of the law. Dawson was detained in custody at the watch house in Walmgate and, at the subsequent court hearing, he and his partner in crime, William Peniston, were sentenced to transportation for life. (*York Herald*)

# November 15th

**1686:** It is likely that Joseph Holt was born in York, as he was baptised at Holy Trinity, Micklegate on this day in November. His father was, in all probability, the Joseph Holt who appears in the register of the Freemen of York in 1695. Joseph and his only surviving brother, Thomas, moved to Whitby, where they established a shipping business. Joseph married Ann Wilson in January 1707. Following Ann's death in June 1708, Joseph married Margaret Skelton in January 1712 and they had six children. As his business interests prospered, Joseph Holt became a master mariner and main owner of the ship *Olive Branch*, which appears to have been involved for the most part in coastal shipments of commodities such as coal, linen, timber and bricks. It seems that Joseph's father died in 1727 and as young Joseph's fortunes prospered, he formed a partnership with three others. Their Dock Company had constructed a double dry dock on the east bank of the Esk by 1734 and there is evidence that they were involved in ship repair work and shipbuilding. Joseph Holt died on 31 August 1744 and was buried in the parish churchyard at Whitby. (www.freespace. virgin.net)

# November 16th

**1631:** All Saints' Church, Pavement is probably the city's most easily-recognised parish church. Its west tower has an upper section which comprises an octagonal lantern with open stonework. Added in 1837, it is a landmark for locals and visitors alike, while the interior contains a number of interesting features. A Viking-age tomb slab, uncovered during alteration works, is on display in the north aisle and stained-glass windows date from the fourteenth and fifteenth centuries. The splendidly ornate pulpit dates from the seventeenth century and displays the date 1634. Records indicate that it was ordered on 16 November 1631 and Nicholas Hall, a joiner from Fossgate, received 1s as advanced payment for his work. The final instalment of his fee was paid seven years later; £1 paid on 22 August 1639. This tall structure has detail carved on its sides with a tester or sounding board above. John Wesley is said to have preached here on several occasions and, during the 1640s, Presbyterian ministers or 'lecturers' preached from the pulpit. One of the best known was Edward Bowles, who is said to have petitioned parliament in 1647 to establish a university at York. (All Saints' Church, Pavement, York)

# November 17th

**1971:** The name of the sculptor of the lead bust of Thomas Fairfax, now on exhibition at the City Art Gallery, still remains a mystery. A report on this day revealed that reader Miss Anne Hattersley of Heworth Green, York, thought she had the answer with the sculptor Roubiliac, because the late Miss I.P. Pressley, a local scholar connected with York Georgian Society, attributed the bust to him. But Mr John Ingamells, curator of the City Art Gallery, says that Roubiliac was an eighteenth-century sculptor and the bust of Fairfax is believed to have been made between 1645 and 1650. He believed that it was a contemporary bust and that the artist would have been Le Seur, who was one of the leading sculptors of that period. But, although the bust had the quality of his work, Le Seur was generally on the Royalist side, so the identity of the artist remains unknown. (*Yorkshire Evening Press*)

——— ◆ ———

**1971:** An exhibition of work by the sculptor Arthur Dooley opened at Heslington Hall, York University. Working from a disused pub, he was described as an artist capable of doing and saying something different. (*Yorkshire Evening Press*)

# November 18th

**1482:** An order was issued that the gates and posterns of York be closed every night at nine o'clock and opened again at five o'clock in the morning. This directive should be seen in the context of Edward IV's reign (1461–70 and 1471–83), when there was a general restoration of law and order, after the general lawlessness that characterised the reign of Henry VI. (Knight, C.B., *History of the City of York*)

———— • ◆ • ————

**1935:** A chapter in York's transport history came to an end when the city saw the last day of service by an electric tram. They had been in use since 20 January 1910 and were replaced by motor buses. The first electric tramway in Britain, the Blackpool Tramway, opened on 29 September 1885 and operated along Blackpool promenade. After 1960, it remained the only first-generation operational tramway in the UK. It is still in use today. (en.wikipedia.org/wiki/TramsinEurope)

# November 19th

**1951:** At the opening of a Clean Food Exhibition in York Public Library, Alderman F. Wright paid tribute to York's food traders. His comments followed visits to about 1,300 premises by members of the city's sanitary department. It was reported that about 13,000 people, or one eighth of York's population, were engaged in the food industry. Such figures stressed the necessity for ensuring that food was clean. The city's Lord Mayor, Alderman J.H. Kaye, said the campaign had the goodwill of three main groups of people – food handlers in shops, food handlers in catering establishments and housewives (he and the Lady Mayoress commended the exhibition to all housewives). Display stands and working exhibits included the latest glass-washing machines, bathroom equipment with hot running water, and film shows. One of two models of a shop showed how to keep food clean and the other showed how it became contaminated. York's Sheriff, Mr Scruton, as chairman of the Education Committee, said he was very interested in clean food as they were catering for 16,000 school children. A total of 170 members of catering staff prepared and served more than 6,000 meals every day. (*Local Government in York 1951–53*, Vol. 23)

# November 20th

**1917:** Among early prosecutions brought by the York Food Control Committee was a case against Emma Knewshaw, a market trader, who was fined for selling an amount of butter above the permitted price of 2s 5d (she charged 2s 5½d). York Food Committee had been re-established under a new set of regulations some two months earlier, but there were difficulties from the start, with the York Cooperative Society particularly resentful because it did not have representation on the committee. Concerns about food supplies became more acute in the later weeks of 1917 and amounts of margarine, in particular, were hard to find. In response to these increasing difficulties, new restrictions were introduced on a daily basis. One example was a requirement that breakfasts consumed in public eating places should be meatless with no glasses of milk sold with them. As shortages became more pronounced, a rationing scheme was introduced and, although complaints and criticisms were still directed towards the Food Control Committee, it is generally accepted that the agency performed valuable work in the final months of the First World War. (*Yorkshire Herald*)

# November 21st

**1916:** As hostilities continued through 1916, so the effects on domestic life in Britain intensified. This included a significant increase in the cost of living. During November, there was an overall price rise of 3 per cent on foodstuffs and prices generally were 84 per cent higher than when war began in August 1914. Two new food orders had been issued by November in order to regulate the price of milk. The Milling Order (1916) specified percentages of flour to be obtained from different qualities of wheat. Newspaper reports on 21 November outlined the changes which would result in a 'national' or 'standard' loaf with defined percentages of flour from English and other wheat. In December, the Regulation of Meals Order (1916) was issued by the Board of Trade, and this restricted restaurant and hotel meals to either three courses for evening meals or two at other times of day. (*Yorkshire Evening Press*)

# *November 22nd*

**1922:** The *Yorkshire Herald* reported on the inaugural lecture of the winter series, arranged by the Yorkshire Architectural and York Archaeological Society, which was given in the Tempest Anderson Hall. A huge audience had listened with great appreciation to a lecture by Mr Ian B. Stoughton Holborn MA on Art and Citizenship. In the course of his lecture, Mr Holborn emphasised that the beauty of York was an inspiration possessed by very few cities in the world, and said the people of York were the guardians of a sacred and spiritual treasure, every bit of which was precious. Mr Holborn said that it was about the sixty-fifth time he had lectured in York and referred to it as one of the most artistic cities, not only in Britain but in the world. He said, 'If it was desired to build a modern city let them go somewhere else but not destroy what they had.' At the end of his lecture he showed lantern slides of historic places of York. Mr Percy Spalding, in moving a vote of thanks to Mr Holborn, said they were at the end of the lecture prouder than ever of York. (*Yorkshire Herald*)

# November 23rd

**1912:** New Earswick Primary School was opened on this day as an element of the garden suburb development on the outskirts of York, under the Joseph Rowntree Village Trust. Brick built and with Georgian aspects of design, the large, one-storey school was completed with all classrooms on the south side. Although work began at New Earswick in 1902, the Joseph Rowntree Village Trust was only established in 1904. Planned from the outset as a garden village rather than a garden suburb, it was preceded by similar schemes at Port Sunlight, near Liverpool, for the Lever family, and near Birmingham for the Cadbury's Bournville project. In fact, it differed from these developments as it was constructed by the Joseph Rowntree Trust rather than the firm of Rowntree's, and it was not only for Rowntree's employees. From the beginning, the architect at New Earswick was Raymond Unwin. Another early feature of the scheme was the Folk Hall, opened in 1907. (*The Joseph Rowntree Inheritance 1904-2004*, 2004)

---

**1915:** The Liquor Control Board introduced a new set of opening hours for York, with six hours drinking on week days and five on Sundays. The *Yorkshire Herald* of 23 November 1915 reviewed the new arrangements and reported 'a mixed reception' among customers, as some were 'treating the matter with a certain amount of levity and others looked on them with great seriousness and concern.' (*Yorkshire Herald*)

# November 24th

**1906:** The headquarters building of the North Eastern Railway (NER), referred to in some sources as 'a huge palace business', opened on this day. Horace Field was a surprising choice as architect, as he was based in London and had not established a reputation. However, working with NER's company architect, William Bell, a fine building took shape. To make a link with company history, the walls display shields and badges of early companies which amalgamated in 1854 to form the NER, as well as York's coat of arms. Since April 2010, the headquarters building has accommodated the city's first five star hotel – 'The Cedar Court Grand Hotel. (www.cedarcourtgrandco.uk/aboutus-history.asp)

———— • ◆ • ————

**1917:** During November 1917, a play entitled *Damaged Goods* was performed at York Theatre Royal. Written by Eugene Brieux, it was advertised as 'The Great Play on the Social Evil' and had 'been approved by the highest Ecclesiastical and Medical Authorities'. A press announcement indicated that the play had been specially licensed 'by the Lord Chamberlain for propaganda purposes with all profits going to the institutions engaged in combating the ravages' of VD. (*Yorkshire Herald*)

# November 25th

**1896:** A report of the Ancient Society of York Florists' Chrysanthemum Show, held at the Exhibition Building, stated, 'The orchestra was tastefully adorned with palms and shrubs and presented a picturesque appearance.' This was at a time when the society was widely regarded as one of the prestigious societies in the north of England. It is claimed to be the oldest existing horticultural society, with records dating back to 1768, and it is unique in retaining the word 'florists' in its title. In the early days of the society, only six florists' flowers were accepted, but during the nineteenth century, other societies were established and more flowers were introduced into the shows. As a result of the First World War, there was a marked decline in support by the nobility towards horticultural shows, but members of the working class boosted membership of the York society, and chrysanthemum growing became a central feature of the city's allotments. (www.ancientsocietyofyorkflorists.co.uk)

# November 26th

**1736:** Francis Drake presented to the York Guildhall a copy of his book, *Eboracum or The History and Antiquities of the City of York*. Around 800 pages in length, it is still widely regarded as the first and most influential history of the city. Born at Pontefract in 1696, he was apprenticed at an early age to the York surgeon Christopher Birbeck and took over the practice on Birbeck's death. Drake was awarded the title of City Surgeon and, as well as becoming Grandmaster of the York lodge, he was a leading personality in the Gentleman's Spalding Club. During 1720, Francis Drake married Mary Woodyeare, but tragically the next eight years saw the death of three of their five sons and then Mary, his wife, died too. Immersing himself in medical work, he was awarded the title of honorary surgeon to the York County Hospital. His contribution to historical research was rewarded with membership of the Royal Society. Drake's work *Eboracum* was dedicated to the Earl of Burlington, designer of York Assembly Rooms and Mansion House, and it later transpired that the earl had not only contributed £50 towards preparation of *Eboracum*, but had also paid Francis Drake's debts, in order to secure his release from a debtors' prison in London. Francis Drake died in 1771. (Biggins, J.M., *Historian of York*)

# November 27th

**1819:** On this Saturday in November, Barnard Smith and Cooke Taylor, who were referred to in the *Yorkshire Gazette* as 'our present spirited Sheriffs', revived the ceremony of 'The Sheriffs Riding' after a gap of seventeen years. Along with their friends, they gathered at Mr Whisker's in Spurriergate, where they enjoyed 'a cold collation and burnt wine' before visiting seven stations to deliver their traditional proclamation. (*Yorkshire Gazette*)

---

**1963:** The Beatles appeared at the Rialto Theatre York on this Wednesday evening, for their fourth and final concert at that venue. Previous visits were all during 1963; on 27 February, 13 March and 29 May. This performance in November was the twenty-second date of the group's 1963 autumn tour. As with all the other tour dates, The Beatles performed a standard set of ten songs: 'I Saw Her Standing There', 'From Me to You', 'All My Loving', 'You Really Got a Hold on Me', 'Roll Over Beethoven', 'Boys', 'Till There Was You', 'She Loves You', 'Money (That's What I Want)' and 'Twist and Shout'. (www.beatlesbible.com)

# November 28th

**1850:** On this Wednesday, a waterman, John Taylor, appeared at the Guildhall on a charge of trying to drown himself by leaping into the River Ouse at King's Staith, while in a state of intoxication. He had been thrown out of The Fortunate Tar on King's Staith when the river was in full flood, almost to the level of the footpath. As the landlord turned to go back inside, he heard a loud cry and saw that his unwanted customer was in the water. In court he described the cry as drunken nonsense, calculated to disturb other people, and went on to inform magistrates that Taylor had no intention of drowning himself. He said it was merely a dodge to obtain a glass of hot water and brandy, but instead he got a good dousing of cold water and mud. The magistrates agreed and ordered Taylor to pay 5s and costs or go to the House of Correction for seven days, where instead of brandy and water he would only receive the latter in its purity. (*York Herald*)

# November 29th

**1539:** St Mary's Abbey was dissolved by the King's commissioners when there were fifty-one monks on site, and its annual value was estimated by one source as £1,550, while another gave a total of £2,085. Abbot William Thornton received a pension of 400 marks for life, while the prior, sub-prior and monks were granted lesser amounts. In 1566, stone was removed to rebuild the centre of Ouse Bridge. More was taken to repair damage caused to St Olave's Church during the Civil War, and in 1717 stone from the abbey was used to repair Beverley Minster, but during the early nineteenth century restoration work got underway. Samuel Sharp was awarded the Sloane medal for his part in this work in 1838. (Knight, C.B., *A History of the City of York*)

---

**1615:** Clifford's Tower, which is now in the care of English Heritage, was in a sad state of repair by the early seventeenth century. Partly ruined, it was granted by King James I, along with about 3 acres of land, to Edmund Duffield and John Babington, for an annual rental of fourpence. However, on 29 November 1615, they transferred ownership to Francis Darley, who was apparently Crown bailiff for the lands of St Mary's Abbey. (Knight, C.B., *A History of the City of York*)

# November 30th

**2005:** The enthronement of Right Reverend John Sentamu saw him become the first black Archbishop in the Church of England. Before the service, which began at 11.30 a.m., the Lord Mayor of York led a civic procession through the city and, on his arrival at York Minster, Dr Sentamu banged on the door with a staff that symbolised the pastoral care of the diocese and province. (The staff is known as the Braganza Crozier and it has been used almost continuously since 1688 by Archbishops at functions in York Minster.) A congregation of 3,000 witnessed the ceremony, which included ancient ritual and African dancers. Dr Sentamu, aged fifty-six, wore a brightly-coloured cope and mitre with a design based on a picture called 'The Tree of Life'. He took his oath on a 1,000-year-old manuscript. Archbishop Sentamu, who holds the second highest post in the Church of England, was educated in Uganda, where he practised as a barrister before moving to the UK in 1974. (www.news.bbc.co.uk)

# December 1st

**1539:** On this day, the deed of surrender of St Leonard's Hospital was signed by Thomas Magnus, Master of St Leonard's Hospital, 'with the unanimous consent of all the brethren'. It had been founded soon after the Norman Conquest and is believed to have been the largest medieval hospital in the north of England. Annual revenue at the time of closure is said to have been £362 11*s* 1½*d*, and from this time York had no hospital until 1740. Remains of the hospital can be reached from Museum Street and the high ceilings and large windows of St Leonard's serve as a reminder that sickness during the medieval period was believed to result from 'bad air'. High ceilings and windows were considered important in order to circulate fresh air. (Benson, G., *An Account of the County and City of York*; www.historyofyork.org.uk)

———◆———

**1762:** A violent hurricane raged in York. It began at nine o'clock at night and continued unabated until eight o'clock the following morning. The weathercock and part of the battlement of the west-end of the Minster were blown down and many houses in the city suffered considerable damage. (Knight, C.B., *History of the City of York*)

# December 2nd

**1914:** Following the dramatic announcement in York newspapers on 5 August 1914, 'WAR DECLARED ON GERMANY', large numbers of men volunteered for military service, but by the end of the year there was a dramatic decline in enlistments and measures were taken to boost recruitment. One development was the setting up of 'Bantam' battalions for men who were too small in stature for normal entry to the army. When 'Bantam' recruitment began in York during 1914, measurements required were 5ft to 5ft 3ins in height and a chest size of 33 to 34. On 2 December, York newspapers reported on the country's first Bantam, R.S. Parker (who actually joined at Birkenhead) but was from York. Proud mention was also made in local papers of two other York men, J. Howard and T. Middleton, who joined the Hull Bantams. The Earl of Feversham was given permission to raise a battalion from the York area, which became known as the Yeoman Rifles. In the city itself, an unsuccessful attempt was made to raise a second Heavy Battery. (*Yorkshire Herald*)

# December 3rd

**1848:** At about 11 p.m. on this Wednesday in December, Mary Kitchen, a maidservant at the King's Head in Fossgate, heard her mistress' young child scream. When she went upstairs to calm the child and bring it downstairs, she noticed someone hiding under the bed but calmly continued back down before alerting others. When the bedroom was searched, a man was found and, the following day, Isaac Thompson appeared at the Guildhall on a charge of being concealed in the house. His defence was that he had arrived late in York from Preston and, without cash or accommodation, he crept into the public house and made his way upstairs to sleep. It was pointed out that during the previous week, he had been detained in similar circumstances at the Admiral Hawke in Walmgate. He was sent to the House of Correction for three months. (*York Herald*)

———◆———

**1915:** Wartime regulations included 'black out' conditions from one hour after sunset until one hour before sunrise, but many people objected to the potential dangers posed by the intense darkness. A writer to the *York Herald* asked if a cage lamp, similar to an earlier one on Scarborough Bridge, could be positioned near Lendal Bridge, where steps caused a real hazard. (*Yorkshire Herald*)

# December 4th

**1641:** John Williams, the sixty-fourth Archbishop of York, was translated (transferred) from Lincoln to York on this day. His enthronement, on 27 June 1642, took place at a time when King Charles II was holding his court at York. Williams was critical of Sir John Hotham's actions at Hull and this resulted in Sir John's son making a threat on his life. Archbishop Williams promptly fled to Wales. He never returned to his diocese and died at Golthaeth in Carnarvonshire on 25 March 1860. (Knight, C.B., *History of the City of York*)

---

**1936:** An article appeared in the *Yorkshire Gazette* on this day, stating that Mrs Lumley, wife of York's MP Roger Lumley, had opened the city's first nursery school in St Paul's Square. Mr and Mrs Arnold Rowntree had provided the building and the Joseph Rowntree Trust gave a sizeable donation towards its refurbishment. The nursery was opened initially for children of unemployed fathers and many of the pupils were found to have rickets, but after appropriate food and care they left at the age of five, fit and well. In 1947, the Education Authority took over running of St Paul's Nursery and in July 2010, the overall effectiveness of the school was found to be 'outstanding'. (*St Paul's Nursery School York: A Brief History*)

# December 5th

**1974:** The Great Pram Spectacular was advertised on this day:

The Great Pram Race to be run through the centre of York on December 15th will raise money to send more than a hundred underprivileged children in the area to the *Aladdin* pantomime at the Theatre Royal.

There will be prizes for the best pram, the best baby and the best pusher. Judges will include Mr. Bob Strachan, Chairman of York City F.C. and skipper of the team Barry Swallow. Judging will start at 11 A.M. and the race at 12.30 from the Cross Keys, Dringhouses via the Windmill, Blossom Street, Walker's Bar, Tavern in the Town, Painted Wagon, Three Cranes, the Old Starre Inn and the Half Moon. These pubs have each entered three prams which are now being decorated.

Mr Paul Barton, landlord of the Cross Keys and one of the main organisers said the search was on for more prams but anyone prompted to make an offer should not expect their pram back in one piece.

(*Yorkshire Evening Press*)

———•◆•———

**1974:** Members of York Musical Society were rolling up their sleeves to build a do-it-yourself concert platform for the traditional performance of Handel's *Messiah* in York Minster. The society could not afford the hire charge after paying heating costs and music fees. (*Yorkshire Evening Press*)

# December 6th

1907: Newspaper reports on 6 December gave details of the next day's wedding, of Captain Adrian Rose and Miss Nancy Lycett Green, at York Minster:

> The wedding which will be carried out on a scale of great magnificence with a military setting and fashionable company will rank as one of the most brilliant seen in the north in recent years.
>
> Many York people will see for the first time the famous Blues [Troop of Horse Guards] or a portion at any rate. A troop of the B Squadron will attend the wedding and form a guard of honour in the choir where the bridal party will pass through lines of troops and after the ceremony will pass through an archway of crossed swords.
>
> …The service will be fully choral, conducted by the Dean of York and Rev. E. Evans, Vicar of Dringhouses…
>
> A feature of the service will be that bridesmaids will distribute favours – some five hundred in number, each appropriately tied with green and rose ribbons to guests during the signing of the nuptial contract.
>
> Four hundred and fifty seats in the choir are reserved for relatives and personal friends of the bride and bridegroom's families… In the nave will be servants, tenantry and clerical staff.
>
> The bride will enter by the west door which is only used on occasions of importance.

(*Yorkshire Herald*)

# December 7th

**1822:** William Salmond, Anthony Thorpe and James Atkinson had all recently taken ownership of collections of fossil bones discovered in a cave at Kirkdale, near Kirbymoorside, in July 1821. They met in York on this 7 December 1822. Their main topic of discussion was the formation of a scientific and antiquarian society, to promote the study of botany, zoology, geology and archaeology in the county of Yorkshire. The proposed premises would also include a library and a museum and the organisation would be known as the Yorkshire Philosophical Society. On 5 March 1823, the society moved into premises close to Ouse Bridge and, in November of that year, William Venables-Vernon was elected first president of the Yorkshire Philosophical Society. The need for larger buildings was soon clear and a building fund was set up in 1825, but it was 2 February 1830 before the new building was officially opened on a site adjacent to the ruins of St Mary's Abbey. (Murray, H., *Heraldry and the Buildings of York*)

# December 8th

**1922:** Miss Doris Grisdale gave a dramatic recital in the Assembly Rooms, York and her powers of elocution won her much admiration from the large audience. The artiste opened with Henley's 'England, My England', in which she manifested a pleasing dramatic action. This was followed by a scene from Shakespeare's *The Two Gentlemen of Verona*. Miss Grisdale evinced a realism of the production in the true sense of the word. A series of lighter items were greatly appreciated and in *The Gentle Art of Shopping* (Ernest Denny) the artiste was fully alive to the humour of the piece. In the second part of the programme, Miss Grisdale presented *The Sundial* (Austin Dobson) with charm. A scene from Shakespeare's *Twelfth Night* was cleverly portrayed, this probably being her greatest success, though the whole programme was an achievement on her part, fully meriting the applause accorded her. The concluding items were also ably presented. During the interval, a collection was taken for the funds of the York County Hospital and the sum of £20 10s 7d was raised. (*Yorkshire Herald*)

# December 9th

**1934:** Judith Olivia Dench was born in Heworth, York, on 9 December 1934. She was brought up as a Methodist until she began to attend the Mount School and became a Quaker. Her parents' links with York Theatre, where her father was doctor and her mother wardrobe mistress, brought regular contact with members of the theatrical world. During the 1950s, Judi was involved in the first three productions of the modern revival of the York Mystery Plays. In 1957, she played the role of the Virgin Mary on a fixed stage in the Museum Gardens. She graduated from the Central School of Speech and Drama with a first-class degree and four acting prizes, including the Outstanding Student gold medal. In September 1957, she made her professional stage debut with the Old Vic Company at Liverpool's Royal Court Theatre, before transferring to the Old Vic in London. Since then, her career in television, film and theatre has gone from strength to strength, with roles ranging from 'M' in James Bond films to light-hearted characters in television shows such as *A Fine Romance* and *As Time Goes By*. Her honours include an OBE in 1970 and Dame Commander of the Order in 1988, while in February 2008 she was named first official patron of the York Youth Mysteries 2008. (www.tmaw.co.uk.Judid)

# December 10th

**2010:** This date marked the thirtieth anniversary of Berwick Kaler's performances as the dame in York Theatre Royal's pantomime productions. Born in 1947 in an industrial area of Sunderland, he was one of several children brought up by their widowed mother, with very little income. After leaving school at the age of fifteen, he decided to pursue a stage career, in spite of the fact that most southerners could not follow his north-east 'twang'. Whilst painting a stage set, he is said to have asked Laurence Harvey about the importance of going to stage school and was told to buy a copy of *The Stage* and attend auditions. This approach saw him taken on at 'Dreamland' in Margate, as the straight man feeding lines to music-hall comedians. Since then, Berwick Kaler has played many roles on television and in theatrical productions, but he is best known for the York pantomimes which he has written, produced, directed and performed in. Critics have referred to him as 'the panto's biggest asset and its biggest liability', but the pantomime's popularity is amazing, with well over 30,000 tickets sold. In 2002, he received a honourary degree from York University. Berwick Kaler has also been awarded the Freedom of the City. (www.independent.co.uk)

# December 11th

**1777:** During the eighteenth century, an assortment of items, including books, were offered as pledges with pawnbrokers. Many members of the working class were illiterate, so a book may have been less useful to them than the money, which usually amounted to around 2s. A typical example, on 11 December 1777, was when Jane Newcombe of Fossgate pawned 'one old book, history of Scotland…' (Backhouse, A., *The Worm-Eaten Waistcoat*)

———◆———

**1976:** The *Yorkshire Evening News* printed an article under the title, 'Army asks schoolboy to inspect the troops':

When little Wayne Whiteside went soldier hunting after school last week he didn't think he would end up inspecting the troops with a general, but yesterday eleven year old Wayne of the Ainsty Hotel, Boroughbridge Road, York spent the afternoon casting a careful eye over the forty-two men of Imphal Platoon at their passing-out parade.

After spending all his pocket money to get to Strensall Barracks on a previous occasion all he had seen from the roadside was a guard on the gate but an army 'spy' had tipped off the camp about his fruitless visit and he was traced to Knavesmire Secondary School.

# December 12th

**1796:** Mildred Bourchier died on 12 December 1796 at York, aged eighty, and was buried at Newton-on-Ouse with her husband, John, who had died in 1749. They had married in 1738 at York Minster and featured prominently in York society of the mid-eighteenth century. John Bourchier had inherited Beningbrough Hall in 1736 and Mildred (neé Roundell) was co-heiress of a rich landowner, Richard Roundell of Hutton Walmsley. He became High Sheriff of Yorkshire in 1749 and, in addition to their rural residence at Beningbrough, they had Micklegate House built for their stays in York. It is said to have been designed by John Carr and, on completion in 1752, it represented one of the finest town houses in the city. Along with other members of the gentry and aristocracy, the Bourchiers would visit York for entertainment in the form of horse racing, a theatre visit or even a day in the law courts, which often culminated in a public hanging. On the death of John Bourchier, Beningbrough was claimed by Dr Ralph Bourchier, while his widow, Mildred, lived at Micklegate House. (www.acehotelyork.co.uk/ace-hotel-york; *Beningbrough Hall Guide Book*)

# December 13th

**1756:** An agreement relating to the Enclosure Act of 1757 was signed by John Taylor, the Lord of the Manor of Gate Fulford; Francis Meek of Beverley, the tithe owner; the Lord Mayor and Commonalty of York; the trustees of Fremington School in Swaledale (to whom had been bequeathed lands in Fulford); and for the fifth part, a considerable number of interested parties. Three Enclosure Commissioners were appointed to carry out the award: Robert Bowlay and Richard Mason, both from York, and Samuel Milbourn of Kirby Grindalyth. The Act (occupying fifteen printed pages) also provided for the abolition of tithes and laid down the most detailed instructions of the exact sum, down to the last penny that each landowner had to pay Francis Meek. Ecclesiastical dues, surplice fees and Easter offerings were excepted, being offerings to the church or its incumbent, as distinct from payments to a lay tithe holder. The amount awarded to Francis Meek was £4,118 0s 6d, and sixty-two people shared this cost between them. (*A History of Fulford*)

# December 14th

**1903:** Leisure activities for the working classes were severely limited in the early twentieth century. Local soccer and rugby clubs offered weekend entertainment and, from 1903, York Opera House began to stage 'varieties', while local Temperance groups also provided educational and sporting events. Several adult schools were established in York and, on 14 December 1903, it was reported that a redoubtable lady by the name of Miss Knocker had begun a series of Saturday night penny-concerts at the Exhibition Hall, with an offering of good music and entertainment of an improving kind. (*Yorkshire Evening Press*)

———•◆•———

**1917:** As the First World War entered its later stages, a number of women's associations became active in the York area. In April 1917, the Workers' Suffrage Federation had been set up, and during the summer the National Union of Women Workers petitioned, without success, for the appointment of women police officers. Another women's group, the National Union of Uncertificated Teachers, made public its affiliation to the local Trades' Council and York Labour Party in the local press on 14 December 1917. (*Yorkshire Evening Press*)

# December 15th

**1679:** Council minutes from this day state that a committee, including the Lord Mayor and others, should negotiate 'with Mr Gyles about ye glasse window to be sett upp in the Guildhall according to the modell now presented to this court and make the best bargaine they can.' In 1684, the minutes show that Mr Gyles was paid £20 for the completion of his window. A description of the window appears in the York historian Francis Drake's book of 1736, *History and Antiquities of York*: 'The window over the lord mayor's court... is adorned with the city's arms, sword, mace and cap of maintenance in fine painted glass...' The view of the window is shown in the 1807 engraving of the interior of the Guildhall by Joseph Halfpenny. In 1863, the window was replaced by a memorial window to the late Alderman Meek. There was opposition to this move, but the change took place and Gyles' window was probably re-set in Acomb Priory, before transfer to its present position in the Victoria and Albert Museum. (Notes on The Guildhall Window)

# December 16th

**1784:** A significant number of private schools were operating in York during the second half of the eighteenth century. These included a 'Commercial Academy' set up by a Mr Randall in the Thursday Market Hall in 1756. Subjects on the curriculum were, 'Latin, Greek, French, the Best English Authors, Writing, Arithmetic, the Italian Method of Book-keeping, the Terrestrial Globe Considered as a Map of the World, with the Astronomical Parts of Geography'. Mr Randall was assisted by Mr George Brown and Mr Cross, and after retiring in December 1776 he continued to give private lessons at his home in Bedern. On 16 December 1784, the York Corporation ordered Thursday Market Cross to be altered and the upper level removed. It seems clear that the 'Academy', which probably had a maximum of fifty students on roll, closed at about this time. (Knight, C.B., *A History of the City of York*)

---

**1919:** York's Grand Cinema had opened on 10 November 1919 and some five weeks later, on 16 December, it showed *Exploits of a German Submarine*, a film based on the wartime exploits of U.35, which sank a total of 224 ships. (*Yorkshire Evening Press*)

# December 17th

**1846:** A celebratory dinner for George Hudson, during his term of office as Lord Mayor, was held at York Guildhall on this day, and a most impressive and varied menu was on offer for guests. The fish course offered a choice of nine dishes, from turbot with lobster sauce, cod with oyster sauce, whiting, haddock, smelt, sole, salmon or dorey; while the choice of game was from woodcock, black game, pheasant, partridge, hare, wild duck or snipe. Born in Howsham in 1800, on leaving school he joined a firm of drapers in York and in 1821 married Elizabeth Nicholson, daughter of one of the partners in the firm. Using a legacy of £30,000 to join the York establishment, Hudson became a Tory party member and was elected to York City Council in 1835. In 1837–8, he held office as Lord Mayor and was re-appointed for 1838–9. During the 1830s, he had also built an interest in railway projects and by 1846, when he became MP for Sunderland, his organisations controlled over a quarter of England's railway companies. His career was at its peak, but his subsequent demise, when sharp business practices were exposed, was rapid and spectacular. (www.historyofyork.org.uk)

# *December 18th*

**2009:** The Archbishop of York, Dr John Sentamu, had a double reason for celebration on this day in 2009, because he watched his daughter marry as well as conducting the wedding ceremony. Wearing the full Archbishop regalia, the Most Reverend Dr Sentamu married his daughter Grace to Tim Baverstock at York, in front of more than 200 guests. Some invited guests were not present because of the snowy weather around the region. The bride herself arrived at church wearing a pair of green wellington boots, as did the bridesmaids. Margaret Sentamu, the Archbishop's wife, stood in for her husband by giving their daughter away. After the ceremony, the newlyweds and guests moved on to a reception at Bishopthorpe Palace, the Archbishop's official residence at York. Dr Sentamu was appointed the UK's first black Archbishop. Born in Uganda, the Archbishop married Margaret in 1973 and they fled to Britain from Idi Amin's regime during the following year. A number of Grace and Tim Baverstock's wedding photographs, with serious expressions and formal poses, were taken to match those of Dr John and Margaret's wedding in Uganda. (www.dailymail.co.uk)

# December 19th

**1904:** Newspaper reports on this day state that Arnold Rowntree had informed a conference held at the Homestead, residence of B.S. Rowntree, that 1,258 people were registered with the York Citizens' Association for Dealing with the Unemployed. In fact, the actual total was considerably higher, as many Trade Unionists had not registered, and the work of the bureau was criticised. There was some success resulting from an appeal to companies and individuals to bring forward work which they planned for the following spring or summer. Rowntree and Co. agreed to employ workers from the bureau's lists and they brought forward a number of maintenance projects. This was followed by the laying of a cricket pitch at a cost of around £600 on land covering some 7 acres of ground. Planned work on York Minster was also re-scheduled for an earlier date, but unemployment continued to cause serious social problems. Christmas 1904 was particularly difficult for many families and over 1,200 invitations were issued by organisers of the Aged and Poor People's Christmas Dinner Fund. (*Yorkshire Evening Press*)

# December 20th

**1951:** Kate Atkinson was born in York. After graduating from Dundee University with a degree in English Literature in 1974, she researched a postgraduate doctorate in English Literature. While teaching in Dundee, she started to write short stories for women's magazines and won the *Women's Own* short story competition. Her first novel, *Behind the Scenes at the Museum*, won the 1995 Whitbread Book of the Year Award, beating Salman Rushdie and Roy Jenkins. The book is set in Yorkshire and narrated by Ruby Lennox, who guides the reader through the complex history of her family by covering events during the twentieth century and reaching back into the past to uncover the lives of distant ancestors. *One Good Turn* (2006) was shortlisted for the British Books Award Crime Thriller of the Year and in 2009, *When Will There Be Good News?* was awarded British Book Award's Richard and Judy Best Read of the Year. One feature of Atkinson's fiction is the ambiguous atmospheres established, with settings switching from the present to 1950s York, 1970s Dundee or Shakespeare's Forest of Arden, and between dreams and nightmares. (www.contemporarywriters.com)

# December 21st

**1871:** The funeral cortege of George Hudson, 'the Railway King', passed through York on the way to Scrayingham for burial in St Peter's Churchyard. He had become ill whilst in York earlier in December and returned to London, where he died at his home. It was appropriate that Hudson's coffin was brought by train from the capital to York, as he had been a leading character in the 'railway mania' of the mid-1800s. By 1844, he controlled more than 1,000 miles of railway and his accumulated wealth enabled him to purchase several Yorkshire estates, including the 12,000 acre Londesborough estate and Newby Park. George Hudson's fall from grace began in 1848 and at the time of his death, the former millionaire had assets valued at less than £200. His gravestone – to the west of the porch at St Peter's, Scrayingham – is set among other Hudson family burials and an inscription states, 'The graves were renovated in 1935 by members of the Hudson family and a few admirers of George Hudson, known as the Railway King.' (www.historyofyork.org.uk)

# December 22nd

**1896:** August Carlsen was the last person to be executed at York when he went to the scaffold on this day, after being found guilty of the murder of Julia Wood. During 1891, Carlsen had met Julia Wood in the docklands area of Hull and, while the Swedish seaman was away at sea, they exchanged letters. On completion of his travels, he crossed the North Sea from Rotterdam to meet up again with his lover at Hull, where they booked into Mrs McCann's Rooming House. Drink flowed freely as the couple appeared to enjoy each other's company, but events took a sinister turn when Julia Wood appeared at the breakfast table with facial injuries. Carlsen admitted to another resident that he had assaulted her and made threats to kill her. Throughout the next day, the pair drank considerable amounts of beer and brandy, and in the early evening Carlsen alerted the landlady that he had murdered Julia Wood. During his trial at York Assizes, Carlsen's lawyer argued that he should be found guilty of manslaughter, but after less than an hour of deliberations the jury found him guilty (though with a strong recommendation for mercy). The Home Secretary rejected a possible reprieve and at 9.00 a.m., Billington, the official executioner, carried out the sentence. (www.york-united-kingdom.co.uk/gallows)

# December 23rd

**1848:** An inquest was held into the death of George Berry, who was a prominent figure in the establishment of Terry's of York. In 1767, William Bayldon and Robert Berry had opened a shop near Bootham Bar selling a range of sweets. In 1823, an apothecary named Joseph Terry joined the business. William Bayldon soon left the business and Robert Berry died, leaving Terry to run the firm – now renamed Terry's – along with Berry's son George, from premises in St Helen's Square. During 1827, Terry decided to extend the firm's range of products to include more confectionery, and the partnership with George Berry dissolved. New products included marmalade, mushroom ketchup and Love Hearts, stamped with messages such as 'Can you polka?' After leaving the business, Berry's health deteriorated and, one day, when he failed to attend parish church, a neighbour found him dead at his home in Mason's buildings. The inquest returned a finding that he 'died by a visitation from God'. Expansion of Britain's railway network saw Terry's business prosper and by 1840, the company's products were being sold in seventy-five towns all over the north of England. (*The Story of Terry's* by Van Wilson)

# December 24th

**1696:** A tombstone in St Mary's Churchyard at York has an inscription in memory of a young maid who accidentally drowned on this day. It is believed to have been arranged by her lover and reads:

Nigh to the River Ouse, in York's fair city
Unto this pretty maid Death show'd no pity;
As soon as she'd her pail with water fill'd
Came sudden death, and Life like water spill'd

(en.wikisource.org/wiki/Epitaphs for Country Churchyards)

———•◆•———

**1967:** York's Theatre Royal reopened after extensive refurbishment, which included new front-of-house facilities and a staircase to all levels within the award-winning concrete and glass foyer extension. Dressing rooms were improved and a counterweight flying system installed backstage, while the auditorium, with a green colour scheme, now seated 899. (www.yorktheatreroyal.co.uk)

# December 25th

**Annually:** York Minster is the only cathedral in the UK that places mistletoe, as well as holly, on its high altar at Christmas. This ancient use of mistletoe links to Britain's Druidic past and also to York and the north of England generally. Druids believed that it had the power to ward off evil spirits and in the north of England it grows on lime, poplar, apple and hawthorn trees. It was used as a sign of friendship – leading to the custom of kissing under the mistletoe, but because of its connection with Druids the early church associated it with sinners and evil and banned its use or display in church. However, mistletoe remained popular at York, where it was incorporated into a service of repentance and pardon. York Minster held a winter mistletoe service, where the city's miscreants and wrongdoers were invited to seek forgiveness. Holding a branch of mistletoe, the priest declared 'public and universal liberty, pardon and freedom of all sorts of inferior and wicked people at the Minster gates and the gates of the city, towards the four quarters of heaven.' Nowadays, the mistletoe service is no longer celebrated in such a way, but a sprig of mistletoe still decorates the high altar during the holiday season, as a reminder of ancient customs and the spirit of forgiveness. (gouk.about. com/yorkminstfacts)

# December 26th

**1251:** York Minster was the setting for the marriage of Margaret, second daughter of King Henry III and Queen Eleanor of Provence, to Alexander III, King of the Scots, who had succeeded his father to the throne in 1249. Both Margaret and Alexander were under the age of eleven, but festivities were on a grand scale with many members of both English and Scottish courts present at the wedding. The period 1266 to the death of Margaret on 26 February 1275 is often cited as a 'golden age' in Scottish history. After defeating King Hakon IV of Norway at Largs in 1263, and signing the Treaty of Perth in 1266, Alexander's authority was mainly undisputed and his kingdom enjoyed a favourable period of trade. Margaret died at Cupar Castle, aged thirty-four, and was buried at Dunfermline Abbey. Alexander married Yolande de Dreux at Jedburgh Abbey on 1 November 1285, but on his death at Kinghorn, Fife in March 1286, there was no immediate heir. His three children from the marriage to Margaret had already died and a period of conflict followed as the English interfered in Scottish matters. (www.btinternet.com)

# December 27th

**1725:** A lodge was held at Philomen March's in Petergate, where three gentlemen were admitted into the ancient Society of Free Masons. As it was the festival of St John the Evangelist, the society went in procession to the Merchants' Hall where, after the Grand Feast, the Worshipful Chas. Bathurst Esquire was chosen as Grand Master. A year later, the Worshipful and Ancient Society of Free and Accepted Masons held a grand lodge at the Merchants' Hall. The junior Grand Warden was Francis Drake, the York historian, who commented in his speech, 'If the study of Geometry and Architecture might likewise be admitted, how pleasant and beneficial they would be.' The honourable Society of Free Masons took up this interest in geometry and architecture and adopted, as symbols, the tools and marks of the working mason. (Benson, G., *An Account of the County and City of York*)

———•◆•———

**1894:** Between 7 December 1894 and the beginning of March 1895, there were only three days without ground frost and the river froze over to give a 'grand surface' on the three-quarter mile stretch between Linton Lock and Aldwark Bridge. Skating was possible, except for a few slight breaks, as far as Ripon and when the ice on the Foss near the gasworks was first broken by barges in March, it was found to be 6ins thick. (*Yorkshire Herald*)

# December 28th

**1813:** The lunatic asylum close to York's Bootham Bar was built 'by general subscription in 1774 from a plan proposed by Mr Alderman Carr.' The original intention of the institution was to provide an asylum for poorer members of the community, but the arrangement was later changed to admit 'opulent patients', so that payments by the rich would contribute to support for the poorer inmates. Following this change of approach, there were failings over a long period and it took the 'benevolent interference' of Mr S. Tuke and Geoffrey Higgins Esquire 'to restore the institution to its original benevolent purpose'. Work was underway during the latter part of 1813, but a wing of the asylum was discovered to be on fire on 28 December. Damage to property and the building itself amounted to £2,392, and four patients died in the blaze. Evidence of maladministration was destroyed in the blaze, but investigations continued and the outcome was that 'all the servants of the house' were dismissed and Dr Best, the physician, resigned. Consequently, 'From this time the whole system underwent a complete renovation.' (www.genuki.org.uk)

# December 29th

**2008:** Fire broke out at the Minster Stoneyard and spread to consume two offices, before posing a threat to the 311 panes that make up the lower half of York Minster's Great East Window. When the alarm was raised, more than thirty-fire fighters, six fire engines and an aerial platform converged on the scene from stations around York. Although the fire was confined to an upstairs office and a store room, the window was removed because of the risk of water damage. The Great East Window was completed in 1408 and contains the largest area of medieval stained glass in a single window, covering 194 square metres, which is roughly the size of a tennis court. It illustrates the beginning and end of the world, using scenes from the Book of Genesis and the Book of Revelation, the first and last books in the Bible. The window had been removed from its position at the east end of the Minster in 2008, with restoration work expected to take ten years to complete. As well as the window, other items were also saved from the fire, including stonemason's templates and irreplaceable wooden carvings from the Minster. (*Northern Echo*)

# December 30th

**1922:** On this day, a letter was printed in the *Yorkshire Herald*. [How attitudes change!]

Letters to the Editor
Public Smoking for Public Libraries
Sir, I have just returned from spending Christmas at York where almost everyone I met (and of both sexes) approved most heartily of the suggestion which you were good enough to publish from me some twelve months ago that York should follow America's lead and allow men and women to smoke while they are reading the daily and weekly papers in the public library.

...Any objection that there may be to this altogether innocent proposal is founded on a similar refusal to face facts. There are those who think that smoking is a "filthy" habit. It is true that nicotine from the cheaper cigarettes does produce an unpleasant stain on the fingers but that is not the case with Turkish and Egyptian cigarettes smoked by people of taste and among those are the majority of women.

...The question is whether York proposes to keep on being more puritanical than the United States...

Yours...
A LONDON YORKSHIREMAN

(*Yorkshire Herald*)

# December 31st

**1662:** On this day, the Olde Starre Inn, Stonegate was sold to William Wyvill, in trust for Henry Thompson, Lord Mayor. In 1683, it was inherited by Edward Thompson, grandfather of General Wolfe, who also owned the house that is now the Old Black Swan, Peasholme Green. The Olde Starre Inn dates back to at least 1644 and is York's oldest continuously licensed premises. Its name may be a reference to the Star of Bethlehem, guiding travellers to the Minster (and the inn), or to the crest of the innkeepers' company, which is a sixteen-pointed star. In 1773 the landlord, Thomas Bulman, erected a sign from one side of the road to the other and paid John Moore, a shoemaker, and George Ambler, a saddler, 5s each at Candlemas for fixing the sign to the premises, on condition that they spent the payment in his pub. (www.visityork.org, Historic Inns and Pubs in York)

---

**1885:** Application was made for a provisional order to allow the Corporation to acquire properties in Skeldergate, Gillygate and Holgate Road areas, in order to carry out improvements. A government inquiry was held in February 1886 and the order was granted, but work was not carried out until 1888. (Knight, C.B., *History of the City of York*)